THE
NATIONAL PARKS
OF
AMERICA

THE NATIONAL PARKS OF AMERICA

JAMES MURFIN

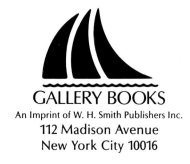

GALLERY BOOKS

An Imprint of W. H. Smith Publishers Inc.
112 Madison Avenue
New York City 10016

End paper *Thor's Hammer, one of the fantastic rock formations in Arches National Park, Utah*

Half title *A cow moose, a common sight at Yellowstone Glacier and Isle Royale and to be found in many more of the national parks*

Title *The National Parks Service is the proud custodian of Mount Rushmore*

Contents *The National Park System are not only the vast open spaces of America: Vanderbilt Mansion in New York is one of its national historic sites*

This book was devised and produced by Multimedia Books Ltd.

Editor: Valerie Passmore
Production: Karen Bromley
Design: Terry Allen
Picture Research: Tessa Paul and Mike Black

First published in the United States of America 1989 by Gallery Books, an imprint of W. H. Smith Publishers Inc., 112 Madison Avenue, New York, NY 10016.

ISBN 0 8317 6328 0

Typeset by Text Filmsetters Limited
Printed in Italy by Imago Publishing

CONTENTS

*The natural and manmade sites which are the heritage
of the American nation are grouped state by state,
and also listed in the index at the back of the book.*

THIS BOOK IS DEDICATED TO THE RANGERS AND INTERPRETERS
OF THE NATIONAL PARK SERVICE

INTRODUCTION

The magic of our national parks has been expressed by artists, photographers and writers for more than a century now, and, in fact, was the subject of military reports and canvases long before Yellowstone was set aside as the first national park in 1872. This was at a time when the populated East was highly skeptical of the stories coming out of the West. Magazines editors rejected the tales of early explorers, telling the authors that they did not publish fiction. All of this was just too unbelievable. It was the stuff of make-believe and the stories of geysers and giant trees, some of them turned to stone, and great canyons a mile deep were pure fraud.

There is still something mystical about these places, and one tends to stare in disbelief at the canyons and petrified trees and the great granite monoliths. In fact, there is something mystical about the National Park Service itself, that in a world seemingly bent on greed, corruption and self destruction, we are still able to pause long enough to protect some of our resources, much less visit and admire what we have protected.

The National Park Service is unique among government agencies. It enjoys the highest profile and commands the greatest respect. When asked what area of government spending or the use of their tax dollars to which they least object, the American public invariably ranks national park programs as something that must be carried on. Yet, in the crunch, it is the national parks that feel the budget cuts.

As this book goes to press, the National Park Service enters a new era. On one hand it has probably the most energetic director since the very earliest days, a man so keenly devoted to keeping the parks going that he astounds even the most hardened rangers; on the other hand, the Gramm-Rudman Act dictates that for the first time in recent memory, parks will close early, visiting seasons will be shortened, and park staffs will be dramatically reduced. It is a situation that will tax the strengths of this organization and Director William Penn Mott with his boundless enthusiasm.

There is no doubt the National Park Service will survive. It has survived continual crises since its beginnings and its resiliency is a marvel. The public will not allow it to founder.

This, then, is a guide to one of America's greatest achievements, the establishment of national parks, the preservation of natural and historical resources, the protection and maintenance of a nation's most precious possessions. Here listed are more than 300 sites, from the Virgin Islands in the Atlantic to the island of Guam in the Pacific, and from the rocky coast of Maine to Point Loma at San Diego. The descriptions are brief; they include the park name, address, phone number, directions, and activities. They also include something unusual.

Almost every national park visitor center has a bookstore selling literature of all kinds pertaining to any given park and to the National Park System as a whole. These small stores are managed by non-profit, educational organizations that donate their profits back to the parks. In 1985, collectively, the 64 "cooperating associations" presented to the National Park Service more than five million dollars to help maintain the campfire programs, nature walks, museum exhibits, living history demonstrations, and hundreds of other everyday activities that visitors enjoy.

While five million dollars is but a drop in the bucket according to annual park budgets, it may well be these and related organizations that keep the parks open from here on. The natural history and historical associations, eg, Grand Canyon Natural History Association, have one primary purpose – to publish and distribute interpretive literature fostering a better understanding of our national parks. Each entry in this guide, therefore, has listed the association responsible for booksales in that park. Catalogs of publications can be obtained in advance of your visit by writing to the association in care of the park address. And, once at the park, you will be surprised at the large selection of applicable literature, from trail guides and post cards, to park histories and scientific studies. There are no other bookstores quite like these in the United States.

So, enjoy America's national parks and monuments and historic sites and... there are 17 or so different terms for these grand places. It might be a national lakeshore or a national seashore or a national battlefield or a battlefield site. These are administrative titles that are really important to no one but bureaucrats whose job it is to measure acreage and political status. The only truly essential thing visitors need to know is that there are 48 *national parks*, that is sites that carry the specific title of *national park*, the Yellowstones, Yosemites, Grand Canyons, etc. All of the 337 (last total) sites that are a part of the National Park Service are identified by the ageless arrowhead symbol, brown signing system along the highways, and the familiar gray-green uniforms of the park ranger.

These are your parks. Respect them. Protect them. Love them. They are our national treasures. We have none greater. They will reward you many times over for all of your life.

Subalpine flowered meadows give way to forested slopes, above which rises the snow-covered peak of Mount Rainier

ALABAMA

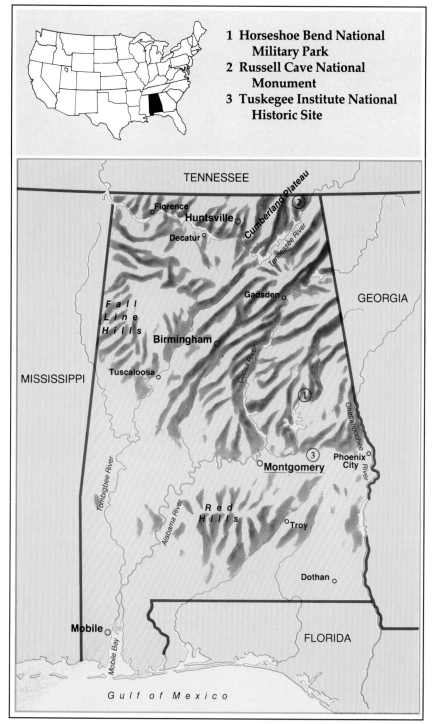

1 Horseshoe Bend National Military Park
2 Russell Cave National Monument
3 Tuskegee Institute National Historic Site

Horseshoe Bend National Military Park

Route 1, Box 103, Daviston, AL 36256
205/234-7111

On AL 49, 12 miles north of Dadeville, 18 miles northeast of Alexander City. Visitor center, exhibits, guided tours, self-guiding tours, picnicking, hiking; bookstore by Eastern National Park and Monument Association. Accommodations in Dadeville and Alexander City; campground in nearby Talledega National Forest, Wind Creek and Mount Cheaha state parks.

At this bend in the Tallapoosa River, a bend "which resembles in its curvature that of a horse-shoe," on March 27, 1814, General Andrew Jackson and his soldiers from Tennessee defeated the Creek Indian Confederacy under the leadership of Chief Menawa. The battle ended the Creek Indian War and opened the Old Southeast to settlers. For Andrew Jackson the victory at Horseshoe Bend was the first step on the road to national fame and the White House.

Russell Cave National Monument

Route 1, Box 175, Bridgeport, AL 35740
205/495-2672

8 miles west of Bridgeport; from US 72 at Bridgeport, follow Jackson County Routes 91 and 75. Visitor center, exhibits, self-guiding trail, hiking, horseback riding; bookstore by Eastern National Park and Monument Association. Accommodations in South Pittsburg, TN, and Stevenson, AL.

Excavated as late as 1953, Russell Cave has revealed evidence of human life dating from about 6000 BC to about AD 1650, encompassing the archaic, woodland and Mississippian periods.

Tuskegee Institute National Historic Site

503 Old Montgomery Road, Tuskegee Institute, AL 36083
205/727-6390

On Old Montgomery Road (AL 126) adjacent to the city of Tuskegee. Visitor center, museum, exhibits, guided tours, self-guiding nature trail; bookstore by Eastern National Park and Monument Association. Accommodations on Tuskegee Institute's campus during regular academic periods, and within city of Tuskegee; US Forest Service camping facilities within 15 miles of site.

Booker T. Washington founded this college for black Americans in 1881 and in 1896 invited George Washington Carver to head the Institute's Department of Agriculture. Washington died in 1915; Carver lived and worked at Tuskegee until his death in 1943. Preserved here in a 50-acre historic district are student-made brick buildings: The Oaks, the Washington family home; Carver's laboratory, now a museum; and an antebellum mansion, Grey Columns, which is the visitor center. The Institute, still in operation, now includes more than 150 buildings.

The George Washington Carver Museum at Tuskegee Institute

The skunk is a forest dweller, though it may venture out of the forest in places where plenty of rocks or crevices offer hiding places

ALASKA

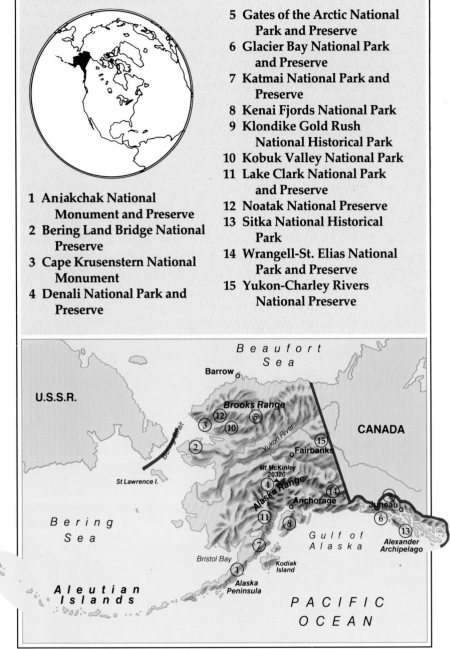

5 Gates of the Arctic National Park and Preserve
6 Glacier Bay National Park and Preserve
7 Katmai National Park and Preserve
8 Kenai Fjords National Park
9 Klondike Gold Rush National Historical Park
10 Kobuk Valley National Park
11 Lake Clark National Park and Preserve
12 Noatak National Preserve
13 Sitka National Historical Park
14 Wrangell-St. Elias National Park and Preserve
15 Yukon-Charley Rivers National Preserve

1 Aniakchak National Monument and Preserve
2 Bering Land Bridge National Preserve
3 Cape Krusenstern National Monument
4 Denali National Park and Preserve

Aniakchak National Monument and Preserve

PO Box 7, King Salmon, AK 99613
907/246-3305

400 miles from Anchorage; access by scheduled, then chartered, aircraft or floatplane from King Salmon or Port Heiden.

The central feature of the Aniakchak National Monument and Preserve is the Aniakchak Caldera created by the collapse of the central part of a volcano sometime after the last glaciation. The caldera covers 30 square miles and is 6 miles wide. Later activity built a cone, Vent Mountain, inside the caldera. Aniakchak last erupted in 1931.

The caldera's Surprise Lake, heated by hot springs, cascades through a 1,500-foot rift in the crater wall. Such volcanic features as lava flows, cinder cones, and explosion pits can be seen here, along with hardy pioneer plant communities inching life into a silent moonscape.

Bering Land Bridge National Preserve

PO Box 220, Nome, AK 99762
907/443-2522

Access by scheduled, then chartered, aircraft out of Nome and Kotzebue.

Bering Land Bridge National Preserve is a remnant of the land bridge that connected Asia with North America more than 13,000 years ago. The land bridge itself now lies beneath the Chukchi and the Bering seas. During the glacial epoch this was part of a migration route for people, animals, and plants whenever ocean levels fell enough to expose it. Scientists find it one of the most likely regions where prehistoric Asian hunters entered the New World.

Cape Krusenstern National Monument

PO Box 287, Kotzebue, AK 99752
907/442-3890

Access by scheduled aircraft from Anchorage and Fairbanks to Kotzebue, then chartered aircraft and boats. Visitor center; bookstore by Alaska Natural History Association.

The gravel beachscape of Cape Krusenstern National Monument chronologically records 5,000 years of marine mammal hunting by Eskimo peoples. These unrivaled archeological records are locked in 114 lateral beach ridges that describe the land's growth into the Chukchi Sea. The beach ridges were formed by changing sea levels and the action of wind and waves. Artifacts from nearby creek bluffs date back 6,000 years and act as a benchmark for predating the cape's beach ridges.

Eskimos still hunt seals along the cape's outermost beach. With rifles instead of traditional harpoons they hazard the dangerous spring ice floes to take the oogruk, or bearded seal. At shoreline campsites the women trim and render the catch for the hides, meat, and seal oil still vital to their diet. As old sites became landbound by the shoreline's seaward advance, the people abandoned their tents and sod houses to establish new camps nearer the sea. This process has continued ever since Eskimos of arctic Alaska first turned to the sea.

Sunset over Cape Krusenstern National Monument, above the Arctic Circle in America's northernmost state

Denali National Park and Preserve

PO Box 9, Denali National Park, AK 99755
907/683-2294

240 miles north of Anchorage and 193 miles south of Fairbanks on AK3 .
Visitor center, exhibits, guided tours, self-guiding trails, camping, backcountry permits, hiking, mountain climbing, horseback riding, fishing, handicap access to campgrounds/restrooms/visitor center; bookstore by Alaska Natural History Association. Accommodations available in park.

Mount McKinley, at 20,320 feet, is North America's highest mountain; measured from its base to the summit, it is the highest mountain in the world. If that were all that could be said about this magnificent place it would be quite enough, for of all the Alaskan scenery this is the most majestic. But there is much more to this significant link to the great glacial age that sculpted much of the northern hemisphere.

The 600-mile Alaska range, of which McKinley stands tallest, is the interface of the largest crustal break of North America, the Denali fault system, where millions of years ago two great land masses met and folded together, one pushed deep into the earth, the other raised to great heights. Here, this juxtaposing of crustal plates created the highest and most vertical rise of any mountain on earth.

Captain George Vancouver, the man who first saw and named Mount Rainier, was the first European to record these "distant stupendous mountains" in 1794. Beyond these few words in Vancouver's log, the early human history of McKinley is virtually non existent. Long before the white man arrived, the Athabascan Indians called the mountain Denali, "the high one." This is about all we know.

Its modern name comes, quite obviously, from President William McKinley, but not before a series of other names. When Secretary of State William H. Seward bought Alaska from Russia for $7.2 million in 1867, he was the laughing stock of the nation and not a little chastised by the tax payers for such an extravagant waste of money. "Seward's Folly," it was called, and then, not surprisingly, forgotten for the next twenty years. At that point, Denali was only a dot on the map with few Americans knowing or, for that matter, caring about it. It was called "Tenada", christened by Baron Ferdinand P. von Wrangell, governor of the Russian-American Company.

Frank Densmore was one of those legendary Alaskan characters who not only prospected for gold near Denali in 1889 but also wrote a great deal about the mountain and the territory. His contemporaries named Denali Densmore's Mountain, probably without knowing anything about Tenada. Then in 1896, when William McKinley was a candidate for the presidency, William Dickey, another gold prospector and writer, christened Denali Mount McKinley in an article for the *New York Sun*, because he and McKinley agreed on the "gold standard," the hottest political issue of the day. McKinley stuck. In 1917 President Woodrow Wilson signed legislation authorizing Mount McKinley National Park. In 1980 the park's name was changed to Denali.

Under Mount McKinley's shadow are barren-ground caribou, grizzly bears, wolves, moose, Dall sheep, and other wildlife; meandering, glacier-born rivers laden with silt create natural dams and periodically change course across wide, flat valleys. The scenery is spectacular.

Gates of the Arctic National Park and Preserve

Box 74680, Fairbanks, AK 99707
907/456-0281

Access by scheduled, then chartered, aircraft. Visitor center; bookstore by Alaska Natural History Association.

Lying entirely north of the Arctic Circle, this park and preserve includes a portion of the Central Brooks Range, the northernmost extension of the Rocky mountains. Often referred to as the greatest remaining wilderness in North America, this second largest unit of the National Park System is characterized by jagged peaks, gentle arctic valleys, wild rivers and numerous lakes. The forested southern slopes contrast with the barren northern reaches of the site at the edge of Alaska's "north slope." The park and preserve contains the Alatna, John, Kobuk, part of the Noatak, the North Fork of the Koyukuk and the Tinayguk Wild rivers.

Left *The Great Johns Hopkins Glacier, which began its current advance 50 years ago, in Glacier Bay National Park and Preserve*

Far left *Caribou, North America's version of the reindeer, roam the tundra of Denali National Park in summer*

All 7,952,000 acres of Gates of the Arctic National Park on Alaska's "north edge" are above the Arctic Circle

The trumpeter swan, threatened in the lower 48 states, can be found in the Alaska parks

Glacier Bay National Park and Preserve

Bartlett Cove, Gustavus, AK 99826
907/697-3341

Access by commercial cruiseship, charter boat or aircraft, or by scheduled air and boat service from Juneau and other southeastern Alaska communities. Exhibits, guided tours, camping, hiking, mountain climbing, fishing; bookstore by Alaska Natural History Association. Accommodations in park.

Explorer George Vancouver found Icy Strait choked with ice in 1794, and Glacier Bay was a barely indented glacier. That glacier was more than 4,000 feet thick, up to 20 miles or more wide, and extended more than 100 miles to the St. Elias range of mountains. But by 1879 naturalist John Muir found that the ice had retreated 48 miles up the bay and by 1916 the Grand Pacific Glacier headed Tarr Inlet 65 miles from Glacier Bay's mouth. Such rapid retreat is known nowhere else.

Glacier Bay National Park and Preserve contains some of the world's most impressive examples of tidewater glaciers. The bay has experienced at least four major advances and retreats of glaciers and serves as an outdoor laboratory for contemporary research. Mountains rise here almost three miles from tidewater. The dramatic variety of plant communities ranges from terrain just recovering from glacier retreat to lush temperate rain forest. Nowhere is the story of plant succession more richly told than here at Glacier Bay.

Right *Hoouah Glacier at Johns Hopkins Inlet, one of many great tidewater glaciers in Glacier Bay National Park*

Below *The comings and goings of glaciers have left their unmistakable legacy in the St Elias Mountains of Glacier Bay*

Left *Nebesna Glacier in the northern reaches of Wrangell-St. Elias National Park and Preserve, which encompasses the greatest extent of glaciers in America*

Below *The grizzly bear is aggressive, extremely strong, and probably the most dangerous of all mammals found in National Parks. It is rarely seen, but can be found in Denali, Yellowstone, and Wrangell-St. Elias, among others*

Katmai National Park and Preserve

PO Box 7, King Salmon, AK 99613
907/246-3305

Scheduled flights from Anchorage serve King Salmon on the park's west side; from June through Labor Day, daily commercial flights operate between King Salmon and Brooks Lodge; air charters from King Salmon or Iliamna are available from May through October. Visitor center, guided tours, self-guiding trails, picnicking, camping, hiking, mountain climbing, boating, fishing, hunting, handicap access to visitor center; bookstore by Alaska Natural History Association. Accommodations in park.

In 1912 a tremendous volcano erupted in the unexplored wilderness that today is Katmai National Park and Preserve. The blast in which Mount Katmai collapsed was one of the most violent ever recorded. Afterwards, in what would become known as the Valley of Ten Thousand Smokes, fumaroles by the thousands issued steam hot enough to melt zinc. Only a few active vents remain and the crater holds a lake.

Katmai's scenery boasts lakes, rivers, glaciers, waterfalls, and a coastline of plunging cliffs and islets. This is the home of the huge brown bear – the world's largest terrestrial carnivore – which in summer fishes the park and preserve's streams to feast on migrating salmon. Scientists regard this area as critical for the brown bear's survival on the Alaska peninsula. The park also boasts some of southwestern Alaska's best trophy sportfishing.

Kenai Fjords National Park

PO Box 1727, Seward, AK 99664
907/224-3874

10 miles from Seward; access by air or highway, charter boat or aircraft. Visitor center; bookstore by Alaska Natural History Association.

Kenai Fjords National Park features the seaward interface for the Harding Icefield, one of four major ice caps in the United States. This may be a remnant of Pleistocene ice masses once covering half of Alaska. Along the coastline are the scenic Kenai fjords, whose shoreline was carved by glaciers. Sea stacks, islets and jagged shoreline are remnants of mountains that today inch imperceptibly into the sea under the geological force of the North Pacific tectonic plate. Exit Glacier, the most accessible area of the park, can be reached by car and a short walk.

Klondike Gold Rush National Historical Park

PO Box 517, Skagway, AK 99840
907/983-2921

Access by automobile, air taxi, commuter airline, ferry, cruiseship. Visitor center at 2nd and Broadway; bookstore by Alaska Natural History Association. See also Klondike Gold Rush National Historical Park, Seattle, WA.

An 1897 *Seattle Post-Intelligencer* report of a steamer from Alaska putting in at Seattle with a ton of gold aboard set off the last of the great gold rushes. At the height of the rush John Muir called Skagway "a nest of ants taken into a strange country and stirred up by a stick." Klondike Gold Rush National Historical Park preserves historic buildings from this period in Skagway, and portions of the Chilkoot and White Pass trails into the Klondike.

The park offers a variety of experiences, from small town to wilderness. A lively nightlife thrives in Skagway, a regular port of call for cruiseships. The Trail of '98 Museum is housed in Alaska's first granite building.

Kobuk Valley National Park

PO Box 287, Kotzebue, AK 99752
907/442-3890

Access by scheduled, then chartered, aircraft or boats. Visitor center; bookstore by Alaska Natural History Association.

The dry, cold climate of the Kobuk Valley still approximates that of late Pleistocene times, supporting a remnant flora once marking the vast arctic steppe tundra bridging Alaska and Asia. Great herds of caribou still cross the Kobuk river at Onion Portage, and are hunted by today's Eskimo people. These herds once fed the Woodland Eskimo people of the thirteenth century. Human occupation at the portage dates back 12,500 years, forming a benchmark by which all other arctic sites are measured. The valley remains an important area for traditional subsistence harvest of moose, bears, caribou, fish, waterfowl and many edible and medicinal plants.

The Great Kobuk Sand Dunes – 25 square miles of shifting dunes where summer temperatures can exceed 100° Fahrenheit – is the largest active dune field in arctic latitudes. Both the Kobuk and Salmon rivers offer easy canoeing and kayaking.

Far left *Salmon, here leaping Brooks Falls in Katmai National Park, are prey to both the Alaska brown bear and fishermen*

Left *Brilliantly-colored flowers flourish in the brief northern summer of Glacier Bay National Park*

Lake Clark National Park and Preserve

701 "C" Street, Box 61, Anchorage, AK 99513
907/271-3751

Access by chartered aircraft from Anchorage and Kenai.
Accommodations, from primitive to modern, available from private
operators within the park and preserve.

Lake Clark National Park and Preserve has been described as the
Alaskan Alps, for here the Alaska and Aleutian ranges meet. Set in the
heart of the Chigmit mountains along Cook Inlet's western shore, the
park boasts great geologic diversity. Its jagged peaks, granite spires,
glaciers, two active volcanoes, and 50-mile-long Lake Clark provide a
dazzling array of scenery. The lake, fed by hundreds of waterfalls
throughout its rimming mountains, is part of an important red salmon
spawning ground. All these features combine to create a maze of
natural river running and hiking routes providing spectacular wilderness experiences.

Noatak National Preserve

PO Box 287, Kotzebue, AK 99752
907/442-3890

Access by scheduled, then chartered, aircraft. No public facilities within
the preserve, but arrangements can be made in Kotzebue to float
and fish the Noatak river. Visitor center; bookstore by Alaska
Natural History Association.

Noatak National Preserve protects the largest untouched river basin
in the United States. Above the Arctic Circle the Noatak river runs
from glacial melt atop Mount Igikpak in the Brooks range out to
Kotzebue sound. Along its 425-mile course it has carved out the Grand
Canyon of the Noatak. This striking, scenic canyon serves as a
migration route for plants and animals between subarctic and arctic
environment. In recognition of this fine and vast wilderness
UNESCO has made the Noatak river basin an International
Biosphere Reserve.

Sitka National Historical Park

PO Box 738, Sitka, AK 99835
907/747-6281

*In Alaska's southeastern panhandle; access by commercial airline direct
from Seattle, Juneau, and Anchorage.* Visitor center, exhibits, guided
tours, self-guiding tours, picnicking, hiking, fishing; handicap
access to visitor center; bookstore by Alaska Natural History
Association. Accommodations in Sitka.

Sitka National Historical Park preserves the site of the 1804 fort and
battle that marked the last major resistance of the Tlingit Indians to
Russian colonization. This was Alaska's economic and cultural capital
for half a century, serving as the center of the Russian-American
Company's fur and other trading operations. The park displays a
collection of totems and its visitor center explains Pacific northwest
coast Indian art.

Wrangell-St. Elias National Park and Preserve

PO Box 29, Glennallen, AK 99588
907/822-5234

Access by highway, then 4-wheel-drive vehicle or chartered aircraft.

The Wrangell-St. Elias National Park and Preserve abuts Canada's Kluane National Park just across the border in Yukon Territory. This is North America's "mountain kingdom." Here the Wrangell, St. Elias and Chugach mountain ranges converge. The park and preserve contains the North American continent's most extensive glaciers and its greatest collection of peaks over 16,000 feet. One glacier, the Malaspina, is larger than the state of Rhode Island. Mount St. Elias, at 18,008 feet, is the second highest peak in the United States.

The park and preserve is characterized by rugged mountains, remote valleys, wild rivers, and exemplary populations of wildlife. It also embraces coastal beaches on the Gulf of Alaska. The area abounds in opportunities for wilderness backpacking, lake fishing, car camping, river running, cross-country skiing and mountain climbing. In both stature and numbers, Dall sheep populations of the Wrangells are considered the world's finest. This is our largest national park.

Yukon-Charley Rivers National Preserve

PO Box 64, Eagle, AK 99738
907/547-2233

Access by Taylor Highway to Eagle or Steese Highway from Fairbanks to Circle; scheduled flights serve both towns from Fairbanks. Visitor center; bookstore by Alaska Natural History Association.

The Yukon-Charley Rivers National Preserve contains 115 miles of the Yukon river and the entire 88-mile Charley river basin. Old cabins and relics recall the Yukon's importance in the gold rush era. Archeological and paleontological sites in the preserve provide evidence of various forms of life millions of years in the past. The two rivers are quite different: the broad and swift Yukon flows with glacial silt while the smaller Charley flows crystal clear. The Charley is considered one of Alaska's finest recreational streams. The rivers merge between the early-day boom towns of Eagle and Circle. Cliffs and bluffs along the two rivers provide nesting habitat for peregrine and gyrfalcons. Beyond the riverbanks grizzly bears, Dall sheep, and moose may be seen. Floating the Yukon, whether by raft, canoe, or powerboat, is a popular way to see wildlife and scenic resources. The Charley river demands more advanced river skills.

Left Blockade Glacier at Lake Clark Pass in the new and magnificent Lake Clark National Park and Preserve

Below Threemile Lake to Dan Creek area in Wrangell-St. Elias National Park and Preserve, the largest in the system

ARIZONA

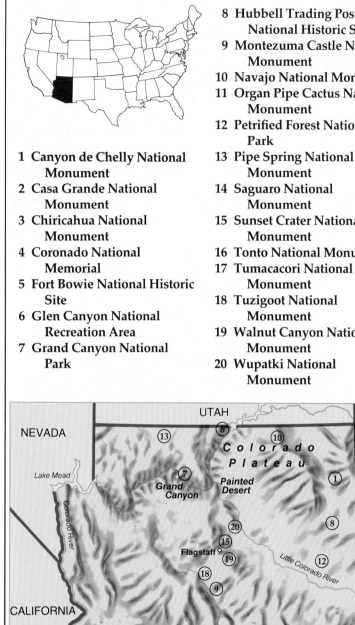

8 **Hubbell Trading Post National Historic Site**
9 **Montezuma Castle National Monument**
10 **Navajo National Monument**
11 **Organ Pipe Cactus National Monument**
12 **Petrified Forest National Park**
13 **Pipe Spring National Monument**
14 **Saguaro National Monument**
15 **Sunset Crater National Monument**
16 **Tonto National Monument**
17 **Tumacacori National Monument**
18 **Tuzigoot National Monument**
19 **Walnut Canyon National Monument**
20 **Wupatki National Monument**

1 **Canyon de Chelly National Monument**
2 **Casa Grande National Monument**
3 **Chiricahua National Monument**
4 **Coronado National Memorial**
5 **Fort Bowie National Historic Site**
6 **Glen Canyon National Recreation Area**
7 **Grand Canyon National Park**

Canyon de Chelly National Monument

PO Box 588, Chinle, AZ 86503
602/674-5436

From Gallup, NM, northwest on US 666 to NM 264 to US 191 to Chinle; visitor center 3 miles from AZ 191 in Chinle. Visitor center, exhibits, guided tours, self-guiding trails, picnicking, camping, backcountry permits, hiking, horseback riding, handicap access to campgrounds/restrooms; tribal permits are necessary for fishing; bookstore by Southwest Parks and Monuments Association. Accommodations in park and in Chinle.

Canyon de Chelly (pronounced de shay) is one of the loveliest of all our national park sites, encompassing a vast geological and human history. Some 300 Navajos live and farm in the summer on the floor of the canyon, pasturing their cattle beneath red sandstone walls rising from 40 feet at the mouth to 1,000 feet some 30 miles back into the far reaches. Most striking for visitors are the many mysterious cliff-dweller ruins that were occupied between 350 and 1300.

Casa Grande National Monument

PO Box 518, Coolidge, AZ 85228
602/723-3172

Within town of Coolidge, on AZ 87, halfway between Phoenix and Tucson. Day use area only. Entrance fee; visitor center, guided tours, self-guiding trail, picnicking, handicap access to restrooms; bookstore by Southwest Parks and Monuments Association. Accommodations in Coolidge and town of Casa Grande; private campground nearby.

Here are the ruins of a massive four-story building constructed of high-lime desert soil by Indians who farmed the Gila valley 600 years ago. The ruins were discovered by the Spanish missionary Father Kino in 1694.

Chiricahua National Monument

Dos Cabezas Route, Box 6500, Willcox, AZ 85643
602/824-3560

36 miles southeast of Willcox, off AZ 186. Entrance fee; visitor center, exhibits, guided tours, self-guiding trail, picnicking, camping, hiking, handicap access to restrooms; bookstore by Southwest Parks and Monuments Association. Accommodations and commercial campground in Willcox; small camping area in monument's Bonita Canyon.

Nearly 30 million years of the earth's geological history can be seen in this wonderland of rocks first formed by volcanic activity and then eroded by wind and water. The park nestles high in the Chiricahua mountains, near the former lands of the Apache leader Cochise and his band of warriors.

Above *The gigantic monoliths of Chiricahua National Monument were once the stronghold of Apache chief Cochise and his braves. Now, bird watchers consider this a choice place for spotting a wide variety of southwestern species.*

Left *Ruined cliff dwellings which were inhabited for over a thousand years by native Indians. Navajo Indians farm in the Canyon de Chelly National Monument to this day*

Coronado National Memorial

Rural Route 1, PO Box 126, Hereford, AZ 85615
602/366-5515

22 miles south of Sierra Vista, and 30 miles southwest of Bisbee, off AZ 92.
Visitor center, exhibits, self-guiding trail, picnicking, hiking;
bookstore by Southwest Parks and Monuments Association.
Accommodations at Sierra and Bisbee; camping 18 miles west at US
Forest Service campgrounds at Parker Lake.

This small park on the boundary with Mexico commemorates the first
European exploration of the southwest by Francisco Vasquez de
Coronado in 1540-42. A well-marked hiking trail leading from the
parking area at Montezuma pass to Coronado peak presents a
magnificent view of the desolate country of northern Mexico through
which the expedition passed.

Fort Bowie National Historic Site

PO Box 158, Bowie, AZ 85605
602/847-2500

*From Willcox on I-10, 12 miles south on AZ 186 to graded road leading
east to Apache pass; or from Bowie on I-10, 12 miles south on graded dirt
road and bear west into Apache pass.* Walk-in and day use area only;
rugged 1½-mile sand and gravel trail from parking lot to site. Ruins
of fort, exhibits, self-guiding trail, picnicking, hiking; bookstore by
Southwest Parks and Monuments Association. Accommodations at
Bowie or Willcox; National Park Service campground 25 miles
southwest at Chiricahua National Monument.

Here are the ruins of Fort Bowie, a military post built in 1862 as the
center of operations against Cochise and Geronimo, the famed
Chiricahua Apache leaders. Some of the walls of the old fort still stand.

Glen Canyon National Recreation Area

(Arizona and Utah)
PO Box 1507, Page, AZ 86040
602/645-2471

Visitor center 1 mile from Page, AZ, on US 89. Visitor center, exhibits,
guided tours, self-guiding tours, picnicking, camping, hiking,
swimming, boating, fishing, hunting, handicap access to
restrooms/visitor center; bookstore by Grand Canyon Natural
History Association. Accommodations in park and in Page.

Glen Canyon Dam, set high between tall cliffs of red sandstone, was
built by the Bureau of Reclamation to harness the turbulent waters of
the Colorado river. Behind this white concrete monolith Lake Powell
stretches more than 180 miles to the northeast, a sparkling surface of
blue, twisted and branched into the ancient shape of Glen Canyon,
one of the most beautiful of the Colorado river canyons before it was
flooded in the 1960s. Irretrievable, Glen Canyon and all its splendor
lives now only in memories.

Lake Powell covers 1,875 square miles with 1,900 miles of shoreline,
and with this comes some of the most spectacular recreational
activities within the National Park Service – activities the same as in
other recreation areas, but special here for the unusual landscape – the
brilliant colors, nature's incredible architecture, albeit altered to
satisfy man's needs for water and power. Most people who use Lake
Powell are totally unaware of what lies beneath them; a handful will
care enough to ask, to read, to see the photographs.

Grand Canyon National Park

PO Box 129, Grand Canyon, AZ 86023
602/638-7888

*South Rim visitor center 3½ miles north of the South Entrance, in Grand
Canyon Village, 60 miles north of Williams and 57 miles west of Cameron,
both on AZ 64; North Rim information station on AZ 67, 45 miles south of
Jacob Lake.* Entrance fee; visitor centers, exhibits, guided tours, self-
guiding trails, picnicking, camping, backcountry permits, hiking,
horseback riding, handicap access to campgrounds/restrooms/
visitor centers; bookstores by Grand Canyon Natural History
Association. Accommodations in park.

After more than 100 years of study, significant parts of the geological
story of the Grand Canyon of the Colorado are still obscure. We do
know that the Grand Canyon is a product of the conflict between two
great earth forces – mountain-building and gravity. This portion of the
earth's crust has been elevated 1½ miles above sea level, and water,
powered by gravity, is slowly but surely wearing a great cleft in it. The
vehicle is the mighty Colorado river.

Today the Grand Canyon is about a mile deep; it ranges in width
from about 600 feet to 18 miles; and the river, with all its twists and
turns, is 277 miles long. From the rims of the canyon we look down on
the tops of mountains that measure 2,000 feet or more from their bases
within the canyon.

Left *Mountain lions, one of the secretive animals found in the Grand
Canyon*

Right *The Colorado continues to carve its way through the Grand Canyon*

Perhaps nowhere else on earth has such a geological record been so clearly exposed and defined. Within the walls of the Grand Canyon we have a view of geological time – a view that stretches back as far as 2,000 million years.

Besides providing insights into geologic history, the Grand Canyon is a vast biological museum. The "grand" canyon and its innumerable side canyons are bounded by high plateaus that have cool north-facing slopes and hot south-facing slopes, year-round and intermittent streams, and seasonal climatic variations. These various environments support life in abundance – from desert life forms at the lower elevations near the river and on the canyon walls to the conifer forest communities on the rims.

In the Grand Canyon geological and biological processes are combined in one awesome spectacle. An appreciation and an understanding of this spectacle come with a recognition that creation of the canyon is a continuing process that is happening today and every day.

Someone who understood this was the man who led the first expedition down the Colorado river in 1869: geologist John Wesley Powell, a one-armed veteran of the Civil War. Riding the river seated in a chair strapped to a wooden boat, Powell charted and described the canyon's every turn in a brilliantly written guide still used by canyon hikers and river runners. The last paragraphs of Powell's journal are perhaps the most eloquent of any descriptions:

The Grand Canyon of the Colorado is a canyon composed of many canyons. It is a composite of thousands, of tens of thousands, of gorges. In like manner, each wall of the canyon is a composite structure, a wall composed of many walls, but never a repetition. Every one of these almost innumerable gorges is a world of beauty in itself. In the Grand Canyon there are thousands of gorges like that below Niagara Falls, and there are a thousand Yosemites. Yet all these canyons unite to form one grand canyon, the most sublime spectacles on the earth. Pluck up Mt. Washington by the roots to the level of the sea and drop it headfirst into the Grand Canyon, and the dam will not force its waters over the walls. Pluck up the Blue Ridge and hurl it into the Grand Canyon, and it will not fill it.

The glories and the beauties of form, color, and sound

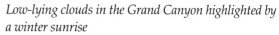

Low-lying clouds in the Grand Canyon highlighted by a winter sunrise

unite in the Grand Canyon – forms unrivaled even by the mountains, colors that vie with sunsets, and sounds that span the diapason from tempest to tinkling raindrop, from cataract to bubbling fountain. But more: it is a vast district of country. Were it a valley plain it would make a state. It can be seen only in parts from hour to hour and from day to day and from week to week and from month to month. A year scarcely suffices to see it all. It has infinite variety, and no part is ever duplicated. Its colors, though many and complex at any instant, change with the ascending and declining sun; lights and shadows appear and vanish with the passing clouds, and the changing seasons mark their passage in changing colors. You cannot see the Grand Canyon in one view, as if it were a changeless spectacle from which a curtain might be lifted, but to see it you have to toil from month to month through its labyrinths. It is a region more difficult to traverse than the Alps or the Himalayas, but if strength and courage are sufficient for the task, by a year's toil a concept of sublimity can be obtained never again to be equaled on the hither side of Paradise.

Above *The bald eagle is America's national bird. The adult, over 5 years old, has a snow-white head, neck, and tail; the rest of the body is brownish-black*

Left *The constantly changing colors of the mighty Grand Canyon stilled by the camera*

A summer storm over the Grand Canyon

Left *Navajo women weave their intricate designs in demonstrations at the Hubbell Trading Post visitor center*

Right *The organ pipe cactus which gave the national monument its name rears above other cacti and wild flowers*

Hubbell Trading Post National Historic Site

PO Box 150, Ganado, AZ 86505
602/755-3475

On Navajo Indian Reservation, 1 mile west of Ganado, and 55 miles from Gallup, NM. Visitor center, weaving demonstrations, self-guiding trail, tours through Hubbell house; Indian crafts (jewelry, rugs, baskets) and interpretive literature for sale by Southwest Parks and Monuments Association. Accommodations at Window Rock, 30 miles from Hubbell, off AZ 264; also at College of Ganado (limited motel units) and Three Mission Restaurant, operated by students.

John Lorenzo Hubbell, friend of the Navajo and admirer of their culture, established his trading post here in 1878. His adobe house, with its magnificent Navajo rugs and other crafts scattered about, appears as it did when "Don Lorenzo" was trading white man's supplies for the natives' handiwork. Hubbell used the Indians' handiwork and thus one walks through the house on guided tours, stepping back in time on priceless rugs. The trading post continues to market rugs, baskets, jewelry, and other items made on the Navajo reservation and the grocery store next door still serves the Indians' basic needs. Some of the finest Navajo crafts in the southwest, carefully selected by a latter-day Lorenzo Hubbell, can be bought here.

Montezuma Castle National Monument

PO Box 219, Camp Verde, AZ 86322
602/567-3322

2½ miles off I-17; 5 miles north of Camp Verde. Entrance fee; visitor center, exhibits, self-guiding trail, picnicking, handicap access to restrooms; bookstore by Southwest Parks and Monuments Association. Accommodations at Camp Verde.

One of the best-preserved cliff dwellings in the United States, this 5-story, 20-room castle is 90 percent intact. Thought by many to have been constructed by Aztecs (hence the name), Montezuma Castle was built in a limestone cliff 100 feet above the valley floor during the twelfth and thirteenth centuries.

Montezuma Well, a separate section of the monument, is 10½ miles north of Montezuma Castle. This natural sinkhole is fed continuously by spring water at the rate of 1½ million gallons a day.

Navajo National Monument

Tonalea, AZ 86044
602/672-2366

20 miles northwest from Kayenta on AZ 160; turn north on AZ 564 for 10 miles. Daily guided tours into the canyon prehistoric sites late spring through early fall; limited to 20 people per tour. Entrance fee; visitor center, exhibits, self-guiding trail, picnicking, camping, Navajo art and craft shops; bookstore by Southwest Parks and Monuments Association. Accommodations in Kayenta.

Here are two of the most elaborate and best preserved cliff dwellings in the southwest: Betatakin with 135 rooms and Keet Seel with 157 rooms. Both were occupied during the late thirteenth century by Pueblo peoples.

Organ Pipe Cactus National Monument

Route 1, Box 100, Ajo, AZ 85321
602/387-6849

On the border with Mexico; access by US 80 and AZ 85, 140 miles south of Phoenix; headquarters is 40 miles south of town of Ajo. Visitor center, exhibits, guided tours, self-guiding trail, picnicking, camping, backcountry permits, hiking; bookstore by Southwest Parks and Monuments Association. Campground 1½ miles south of visitor center. Accommodations in Lukeville, AZ, Sonoita, Mexico, and Ajo, 40 miles north.

This monument preserves a segment of the Sonoran desert, which stretches from northwestern Mexico to southeastern California. It is named for one of the many cactus species found in the park, the rare Organ Pipe, the country's second largest cactus, which produces a cluster of stems, some reaching 20 feet in height. The park contains traces of the historic Camino del Diablo Trail.

Petrified Forest National Park

PO Box 217, Petrified Forest National Park, AZ 86028
602/524-6228

Painted Desert Visitor Center 26 miles east of Holbrook on I-40; Rainbow Forest entrance station 19 miles east of Holbrook on US 180. Entrance fee; visitor centers, exhibits, self-guiding tours, picnicking, backcountry permits, hiking, handicap access to restrooms/visitor centers; bookstore by Petrified Forest Museum Association. Food available in park; accommodations in Holbrook.

This high dry tableland was once a vast floodplain crossed by many streams. To the south tall stately pine-like trees grew along the headwaters. Crocodile-like reptiles, giant fish-eating amphibians, and small dinosaurs lived among a variety of ferns, cycads and other plants and animals that are known only as fossils today. The tall trees – Araucarioxylon, Woodworthia, and Schilderia – fell and were washed by swollen streams into the floodplain. There they were covered by silt, mud and volcanic ash, and this blanket of deposits cut off oxygen and slowed the logs' decay. Gradually, silica-bearing ground waters seeped through the logs, and, bit by bit, replaced the original wood tissues with silica deposits. Slowly the process continued, the silica hardened, and the logs were preserved as petrified wood.

That was about 200 million years ago in the late Triassic. After that time the area sank, was flooded and covered with freshwater sediments. Later it was lifted far above sea level and this uplift created stresses that cracked the giant logs. Still later, in recent geological time, wind and water wore away the gradually accumulated layers of hardened sediments. Now the petrified logs and fossilized animal and plant remains are exposed on the land's surface and the Painted Desert has its present sculpted form.

Today the ever present forces of wind and water continue to erode the giant logs and reach for the logs and other remaining fossils still buried below the surface. In some places up to 300 feet of fossil-bearing material remains. The petrified logs, the other fossils of plants and creatures that lived in the area, and the rocks locking them in place all testify to changes in the environment through millions of years.

But there are other stories here; that of man is readily seen on the landscape. Sites throughout the park tell of human history in the area for more than 2,000 years. We don't know the entire story, but there were separate occupations, a cultural transition from wandering families to settled agricultural villages – pueblos – and trading ties with neighboring villages. Then this story of early people, told by pot-sherds, rubble and pictures on the rocks, fades in the early fifteenth century.

In the mid-1800s US Army mappers and surveyors came into this area and carried back east stories of the remarkable "Painted Desert and its trees turned to stone." Next came farmers, ranchers and sightseers. After a period of using the wood for souvenirs and numerous commercial ventures, territorial residents recognized that the supply of petrified wood was not endless. In 1906 selected "forests" were set aside as Petrified Forest National Monument.

In 1932 some 2,500 acres more of the Painted Desert were purchased and added to the monument; in 1962 the area became a national park and 50,000 additional acres were set aside as wilderness in 1970. In 1985 the oldest known dinosaur bone was found here.

Left *The trees of Petrified Forest, turned to stone millions of years ago, now scattered about the desert like so much rubble*

Right *The Blue Mesa area of the Painted Desert in Petrified Forest National Park*

Below *The uncanny combination of a recognizable tree form in a hard and brilliant material*

Pipe Spring National Monument

Moccasin, AZ 86022
602/643-7105

15 miles south of Fredonia, AZ; reached from US 89 via AZ 398; from US 91, UT 15 and 17 connect with UT 59 at Hurricane, UT; paved road leads to the monument from there. Entrance fee; exhibits, guided tours of fort and grounds, self-guiding trail, handicap access to restrooms. Food available in park; accommodations in Fredonia and Hurricane.

The fort and other structures built by Mormon pioneers commemorate the struggle for explorations and settlement of the southwest.

Saguaro National Monument

Route 8, Box 695, Tucson, AZ 85730
602/298-2036

Rincon Mountain Visitor Center on Old Spanish Trail at Freeman Road, 2 miles east of Tucson; Tucson Mountain Visitor Center on Kinney Road, 2 miles west of Arizona-Sonora Desert Museum. Entrance fee; visitor centers, exhibits, self-guiding trails, handicap access to restrooms/ visitor centers; bookstores by Southwest Parks and Monuments Association. Food available in park; accommodations in Tucson.

Embracing the southeastern corner of California, southwestern Arizona, most of the Mexican state of Sonora and most of Baja California is the vast, lonely Sonoran Desert. Two small, picturesque sections of this desert near Tucson, Arizona, have been set aside as Saguaro (pronounced sa-**war**-oh) National Monument. The park was established to protect the superb stand of the giant saguaro cactus; but its altitude range of almost 6,550 feet provides a diversity of habitats.

At the lower elevations there are plants and animals similar to those of northwestern Mexico and in the higher elevations of the eastern (Rincon mountain) section plant communities similar in character to forests of southern Canada and with a number of animal species in common with those forests.

Sunset Crater National Monument

Route 3, Box 149, Flagstaff, AZ 86001
602/527-7042

16 miles north of Flagstaff on US 89. Visitor center, exhibits, guided tours, self-guiding trail, hiking, camping; bookstore by Southwest Parks and Monuments Association. Accommodations in Flagstaff.

This 1,000-foot volcanic cinder cone was formed in 1064-65. Its lava flows and related igneous features give the illusion of perpetual sunset, hence the name.

Tonto National Monument

PO Box 707, Roosevelt, AZ 85545
602/467-2241

From Phoenix US 60-70 to Apache Junction, then AZ 88 northeast to Roosevelt; monument turnoff is 2 miles southeast of Roosevelt. Day use area only. Visitor center, exhibits, self-guiding trail, picnicking; bookstore by Southwest Parks and Monuments Association. Food in Roosevelt; accommodations 25 miles southeast at Globe; camping nearby in Tonto National Forest.

These well-preserved thirteenth and fourteenth century cliff dwellings were occupied by Solado Indians farming the Salt river valley.

Tumacacori National Monument

PO Box 67, Tumacacori, AZ 85640
602/398-2341

Exit 29 on I-19, 19 miles north of Nogales and 45 miles south of Tucson. Day use area only. Entrance fee; visitor center, exhibits, guided tours, self-guiding trail, picnicking, weekend craft demonstrations; bookstore by Southwest Parks and Monuments Association. Food available near park; accommodations at Nogales, Rio Rico and Tucson; US Forest Service campground at Pena Blanca Lake, 21 miles south and west of monument.

San Jose de Tucumcori was the northernmost mission of a chain built in the Sonoran desert in 1822; the church was abandoned in 1848 but preserved as an example of Spanish influence in the southwest.

Tuzigoot National Monument

PO Box 68, Clarkdale, AZ 86324
602/634-5564

48 miles southwest of Flagstaff, off US 89A. Day use area only. Entrance fee; visitor center, exhibits, self-guiding trail, handicap access to campgrounds/restrooms; bookstore by Southwest Parks and Monuments Association. Accommodations at Clarkdale and Cottonwood, 2 miles from monument.

These excavated ruins of a large Indian pueblo may have housed up to 400 people when a Pueblo Indian community flourished in the Verde Valley between 1000 and 1400. It disappeared about 1450, but for what reasons no one is really certain.

Left *The distinctive colored landscape of the Painted Desert*

Right *The stately remains of the church built in 1822 and abandoned in 1848 by the Spanish at Tumacacori National Monument*

Walnut Canyon National Monument

Walnut Canyon Road, Flagstaff, AZ 86001
602/526-3367

Off US 66, I-40, 12 miles east of Flagstaff. Day use area only. Entrance fee; visitor center, exhibits, self-guiding trail, picnicking, handicap access to restrooms; bookstore by Southwest Parks and Monuments Association. Accommodations in Flagstaff.

These cliff dwellings in shallow caves under limestone ledges were built and inhabited by Sinagua Indians some 800 years ago. Access to the cliff dwellings is a steep set of rugged steps; a hardy walk.

Wupatki National Monument

HC 33, Box 444A, Flagstaff, AZ 86001
602/527-7040

Off US 89, 30 miles north of Flagstaff; connected to Sunset Crater National Monument by paved road from Coconino National Forest. Visitor center, exhibits, guided tours, self-guiding trails, picnicking, hiking; bookstore by Southwest Parks and Monuments Association. Accommodations in Flagstaff; Forest Service campground 18 miles south, across from Sunset Crater visitor center.

Here are the ruins of masonry pueblos built by Sinagua and Anasazi Indian farmers between 1100 and 1225. Eruptions from the volcano that is now Sunset Crater made the land quite productive and the area became one of the most densely populated in the southwest. Some 800 ruins dot the landscape; among the outstanding are the Tall House and the Citadel.

ARKANSAS

1 **Arkansas Post National Memorial**
2 **Buffalo National River**
3 **Fort Smith National Historic Site**
4 **Hot Springs National Park**
5 **Pea Ridge National Military Park**

Arkansas Post National Memorial

Route 1, Box 16, Gillett, AR 72055
501/548-2432

On AR 169, 7 miles south of Gillett via US 165, and about 20 miles northeast of Dumas via US 165. Visitor center, exhibits, guided tour, self-guiding tours, wildlife sanctuary, picnicking, handicap access to restrooms; bookstore by Eastern National Park and Monument Association. Accommodations in Gillett and Dumas.

This tranquil place was once a strategic military and commercial center on the frontier. Much of the early history of Arkansas focuses on this all-but-forgotten outpost. Often called the birthplace of Arkansas, the post was the site of French and Spanish forts and trading stations, the scene of a skirmish in the wake of the Revolutionary War, a territorial capital, a thriving river port and a battleground of the Civil War. Arkansas Post was the focal point of numerous encounters between Indian and European cultures, and its colorful history spanned the reigns of several nations.

Buffalo National River

PO Box 1173, Harrison, AR 72601
501/741-5443

Buffalo Point off AR 14, 17 miles south of Yellville; information centers at Buffalo Point, Silver Hill and Pruitt district ranger stations; headquarters at the Federal Building, Walnut and Erie Streets, Harrison. Exhibits, guided tour, self-guiding trail, picnicking, camping, hiking, swimming, boating, fishing, hunting, cabin rentals; bookstore by Eastern National Park and Monument Association. Food available in park; accommodations in Yellville, Harrison, Jasper, Marshall, and Mountain Home.

The Buffalo is one of the few remaining unpolluted, free-flowing rivers in the coterminous United States, running 132 miles through the Ozarks of northwest Arkansas to Buffalo City on the White river. The Buffalo has countless side canyons, cliffs, caves and waterfalls, including one of the largest free-leaping waterfalls in the country.

Fort Smith National Historic Site

PO Box 1406, Fort Smith, AR 72902
501/783-3961

Downtown Fort Smith, on Rogers Avenue, between Second and Third Streets. Visitor center, exhibits, self-guiding tours, picnicking; bookstore by Eastern National Park and Monument Association. Accommodations in town of Fort Smith.

Fort Smith was one of the first US military posts in the Louisiana Territory, from 1817 to 1896 a center of authority for the untamed region to the west. During this time it housed the famed court of Isaac C. Parker, the "Hanging Judge," who sentenced 160 men to the gallows while spreading law through the wild frontier. The site preserves the remains of two forts and Parker's court.

Hot Springs National Park

PO Box 1860, Hot Springs, AR 71901
501/624-3383

Access via US 70, 270, and AR 7; visitor center on corner of Central and Reserve Avenues. Visitor center, exhibits, self-guiding tours, picnicking, camping, hiking, handicap access to campgrounds/restrooms/visitor center; bookstore by Eastern National Park and Monument Association. Accommodations in the immediate area.

People have been coming here for some 10,000 years. Stone artifacts found near the springs offer firm evidence that Indians used the waters extensively. For them the area became a neutral ground where different tribes came to hunt, trade and bathe in peace. Since its beginning, then, Hot Springs has been a unique place; certainly it is a national park different from any other.

Tradition has it that the first European to see the springs was the Spanish explorer Hernando de Soto in 1541. Be that as it may, it is certain that French trappers, hunters, and traders became familiar with the area in the late seventeenth century.

The United States acquired the area with the Louisiana Territory in 1803. The next year President Thomas Jefferson dispatched an expedition led by William Dunbar and George Hunter to explore the newly acquired springs. Their report was widely publicized and created interest in the "Hot Springs of the Washita." In the years that followed more and more people came here to bathe in the hot waters. Soon the idea that the springs should be reserved for the nation was put before the Congress. In 1832 the federal government took the unprecedented step of setting aside four sections of land around the springs as a reservation, the first in the country. By 1921 this was a national park.

To the northeast of the springs outcroppings of Bigfork Chert and Arkansas Novaculite absorb rainfall and conduct the water deep into the earth through the pores and fractures in the rock. The water comes in contact with highly heated rock and begins its journey to the surface again in the faults and joints of Hot Springs Sandstone. Carbon dating has shown that the water's journey through the rocks takes an average of 4,000 years. The combined flow of all the springs averages 850,000 gallons a day; the average temperature is 143°F.

Bathhouses provide traditional tub baths and other methods of enjoying the waters, but there is much more to enjoy. The park ranges in altitude from 600 to 1,400 feet on the hillsides, where there is a 24-mile network of trails through dense forests.

Pea Ridge National Military Park

Pea Ridge, AR 72751
501/451-8122

10 miles north of Rogers, off US 62. Visitor center, exhibits, guided tours, handicap access to visitor center; bookstore by Eastern National Park and Monument Association. Accommodations at Rogers.

This is the scene of one of the major Civil War battles west of the Mississippi, fought on March 7-8, 1862 when a Confederate army of 16,000 under Major General Earl Van Dorn clashed with 10,500 Union troops under Brigadier General Samuel Curtis, just south of the Missouri border. The Union victory secured Missouri for the North.

Below *Civil War cannon stand as silent sentinels at the scene of the Battle of Pea Ridge*

Bottom *Elkhorn Tavern, the focal point of the Battle of Pea Ridge, March 7-8, 1862*

CALIFORNIA

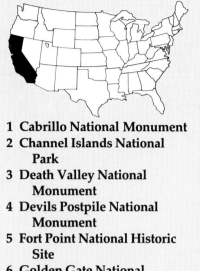

1 Cabrillo National Monument
2 Channel Islands National Park
3 Death Valley National Monument
4 Devils Postpile National Monument
5 Fort Point National Historic Site
6 Golden Gate National Recreation Area
7 Joshua Tree National Monument

8 Lassen Volcanic National Park
9 Lava Beds National Monument
10 John Muir National Historic Site
11 Muir Woods National Monument
12 Pinnacles National Monument
13 Point Reyes National Seashore
14 Redwood National Park
15 Santa Monica Mountains National Recreation Area
16 Sequoia/Kings Canyon National Parks
17 Whiskeytown-Shasta-Trinity National Recreation Area
18 Yosemite National Park

Cabrillo National Monument

PO Box 6670, San Diego, CA 92106
619/293-5450

At the end of Catalina Boulevard, through the gates of the Naval Oceans Systems Center; follow Rosecrans Street to Canon Street (CA 209), merge into Catalina Boulevard. Visitor center, exhibits, self-guiding tours, handicap access to visitor center; bookstore by Cabrillo Historical Association. Accommodations in San Diego.

This lovely park commemorates the discovery of California by Juan Rodriguez Cabrillo, whose landfall in his Pacific coast explorations was here at Point Loma. Fifty years after Columbus landed in the New World Cabrillo set out on his epic voyage of discovery. Commanding two small sailing ships, he braved "great storms of rain, heavy clouds, great darkness, and heavy air" as he ranged into unknown waters, into "no more beyond." He explored the entire length of the California coast, taking possession in the name of the King of Spain and the Viceroy of Mexico. On September 28, 1542, he stepped ashore at a harbor "closed and very good." He named it San Miguel, the site of modern San Diego. A statue of Cabrillo faces the actual landing site; a visitor center nearby interprets the story of his discovery.

But Cabrillo National Monument is much more than just the commemoration of a historical event. It is probably more popular as a place for watching gray whales offshore, and the National Park Service finds no fault with this; in fact, officials have made every effort to accommodate the visitors.

If you visit the park in late December to February you can see one of nature's great spectacles: the annual migration of the California gray whale. Every year the whales pass Point Loma on their way from the Arctic Ocean to the lagoons of Baja California. They leave their summer feeding grounds in the Bering and Chukchi seas in late September, when the surface begins to freeze. Their 5,000-mile journey takes them to the sheltered waters of Scammons Lagoon and Magdalene Bay, where the pregnant females bear their calves.

Cabrillo National Monument is still more: the old Point Loma lighthouse on the very tip of the point is a reminder of simpler times – of sailing ships and oil lamps and the men and women who day after day faithfully tended the coastal lights that guided mariners.

Far left The gray whale, seen diving here, is something of an attraction at Cabrillo National Monument, when it migrates to and from its breeding grounds by Point Loma in view of thousands of visitors

Left The lighthouse at Point Loma, Cabrillo National Monument, San Diego, which has been restored to its condition in the 1880s, its busiest period

Channel Islands National Park

1901 Spinnaker Drive, Ventura, CA 93001
805/644-8262

Visitor center on Spinnaker Drive, off US 101. Visitor center, museum, exhibits, self-guiding trails, picnic area, camping, hiking, swimming, fishing, handicap access to restrooms/visitor center; bookstore by Southwest Parks and Monuments Association. Food and accommodations on mainland.

Channel Islands, an island chain lying just off California's southern coast, appear quite close on clear days. Five of the eight islands and their surrounding six nautical miles of ocean, with its kelp forests, comprise Channel Islands National Park and National Marine Sanctuary. In 1980 Congress designated Anacapa, Santa Cruz, Santa Rosa, San Miguel and Santa Barbara islands and 125,000 acres of submerged lands as a national park in recognition of their outstanding and unique natural and cultural resources. The National Marine Sanctuary was established later that year. The park and the sanctuary provide habitat for marine life ranging from microscopic plankton to the largest creature on earth: the blue whale.

Seafaring Indians plied the Santa Barbara channel in swift, seaworthy canoes called tomols. The Chumash, or "island people," had villages on the larger islands and traded with the mainland Indians. In 1542 explorer Juan Rodriguez Cabrillo entered the Santa Barbara channel. Cabrillo was the first European to land on the islands. While on his northbound odyssey of discovery Cabrillo wintered on an island he called San Lucas (San Miguel or possibly Santa Rosa island). He died on the island as a result of a fall and is believed to have been buried on one of the Channel Islands, but his grave has never been found. Subsequent explorers included Sebastian Vizcaino, Gaspar de Portola and English Captain George Vancouver, who in 1793 fixed the present names of the islands on nautical charts. Beginning in the late 1700s, and on into the 1800s, Russian, British and American fur traders searched the islands' coves and shorelines for sea otter. Because its fur was highly valued, the otter was hunted almost to extinction. Hunters then concentrated on taking seals and sea lions for their fur and oil. Several of these species faced extinction as well. In the early 1800s the Chumash Indians were removed to the mainland missions.

Hunters, settlers and ranchers soon came to the islands. By the mid-1800s, except for the fishermen who operated from cove camps, ranching was the economic mainstay. The Santa Cruz island ranch produced sheep, cattle, honey, olives and some of the finest early California wines. In the late 1800s the ranch on Santa Rosa island was a major supplier of sheep to Santa Barbara and Los Angeles County markets. Anacapa, San Miguel and Santa Barbara islands also were heavily grazed or cultivated. In the early 1900s the US Lighthouse Service (later the US Coast Guard) began its stay on Anacapa island. The US Navy assumed control of San Miguel island just before World War II. The islands played an important role in southern California's coastal defenses. The military's presence on San Miguel, Santa Rosa and the other Channel Islands is evident even today.

A series of Federal and landowner initiatives have helped preserve these nationally significant island treasures. Federal efforts began in 1938, when President Franklin D. Roosevelt proclaimed Santa Barbara and Anacapa islands as Channel Islands National Monument. In 1976 a US Navy and National Park Service agreement allowed supervised visiting to San Miguel island. In 1978 a conservation partnership between the Nature Conservancy, a national non-profit conservation organization, and the Santa Cruz Island Company provided for continued protection, research and educational use of most of privately owned Santa Cruz. Finally, in 1980, Congress designated the four northern islands and Santa Barbara island and the waters for one nautical mile around each as the fortieth national park. Today Channel Islands National Park is part of the International Man and the Biosphere program to conserve genetic diversity and an environmental baseline for research and monitoring.

Far left *Elephant seals, one of the many marine life species which find a haven in the Channel Islands National Park, bask in the California sunshine*

Left *Anacapa Island, one of the islands of the Channel Islands National Park*

California

Death Valley National Monument

Death Valley, CA 92328
619/786-2331

US 395 passes west of Death Valley and connects with CA 178 and 190 to park; US 95 passes east and connects with NV 267, 374 and 373 to park; I-15 passes southeast and connects with CA 127, which in turn connects with CA 178 and 190 to park. Visitor centers, exhibits, guided tours, self-guiding trails, picnicking, camping, backcountry permits, hiking, horseback riding, bicycling, cabin rental, handicap access to campgrounds/restrooms/visitor centers; bookstore by Death Valley Natural History Association. Accommodations in park.

The name Death Valley conjures up forbidding images of desert and heat, and indeed there are those, but this is also one of the colorful parks in the system. In the valley, much of it below sea level, or in its surrounding mountains, you can find spectacular wildflower displays, snow-covered peaks, beautiful sand dunes, abandoned mines and industrial structures, and the hottest spot in North America.

G.K. Gilbert, a geologist who worked in the area in the 1870s, noted that the rock formations were "beautifully delineated on the slopes of the distant mountains, revealing at a glance relations that in a fertile country would appear only as the results of extended and laborious investigation." The rock layers that Gilbert noticed comprise a nearly complete record of the earth's past, but jumbled out of sequence. The reason is that the rock layers that form the mountains are very ancient, but only in recent geologic time have they risen.

Even as mountains rose, erosion began to wear them down. An example of this is the formation of the alluvial fans. Intermittent streams, resulting mostly from the bursts of infrequent rains, rush down the steep canyons scouring boulders, soil and other debris and pushing and carrying the whole mass with it and then depositing it on the valley floor at the canyon's mouth.

On any given day this valley floor shimmers silently in the heat. The air is clear – so much so that distances are telescoped – and the sky, except perhaps for a wisp of cloud, is a deep blue. For six months of the year the heat is unmerciful. Rain rarely gets past the guardian mountains. The little that falls, however, is the life force of the wildflowers that transform this desert into a vast garden.

Despite the harshness and severity of the environment, more than 900 kinds of plants live within the park. Those on the valley floor have adapted to a desert life by a variety of means: some have roots that go down 50 feet or more, some have a root system just below the surface but extending far in all directions and others have skins that allow very little evaporation. Different forms of wildlife, too, have learned to deal with this heat. The animals that live in the desert are mainly nocturnal, for once the sun sets the temperature falls quickly because of the dry air. Night, the time of seeming vast emptiness, is the time of innumerable comings and goings by little animals. Larger animals, such as the desert bighorn, live in the cooler, higher elevations. With height moisture increases too, until on the high peaks there are forests with juniper, mountain-mahogany, pinyon and other pines. And often the peaks surrounding the valley are snow covered. This then is an active world of exciting contrasts and wonders – quite the opposite of its name.

The desolate dunes of Death Valley National Monument, rippled by the wind

Devils Postpile National Monument

Three Rivers, CA 93271
619/934-2289 (summer only)

16 miles from US 395; shuttle bus from Minaret Summit to monument in summer for nominal fee. Visitor center, exhibits, self-guiding trail, picnicking, hiking, fishing, camping, horseback riding; bookstore by Sequoia Natural History Association. Accommodations in Mammoth Lakes and Red Meadows.

Hot lava cooled and cracked here 900,000 years ago to form basalt columns 40 to 60 feet high, resembling a giant pipe organ. The monument is crossed by the John Muir Trail.

Fort Point National Historic Site

PO Box 29333, Presidio of San Francisco, CA 94129
415/556-1693

Signed from CA 101 at the south end of Golden Gate Bridge. Visitor center, exhibits, guided tour, handicap access to restrooms/visitor center; bookstore by Golden Gate National Park Association. Accommodations in greater San Franciso Bay area.

Fort Point was built in the mid-1800s to protect San Francisco Bay. At the water-level beneath the San Francisco end of the Golden Gate Bridge, Fort Point's history ranges from the Civil War to the Spanish American War. It is the largest of the west coast fortifications.

Golden Gate National Recreation Area

Fort Mason, Building 201, San Francisco, CA 94123
415/556-0560

A complete guide to the entire GGNRA is available by writing to the National Park Service at the address listed above. Visitor centers, museums, exhibits, guided tours, self-guiding tours and trails, picnicking, camping, hiking, horseback riding, swimming, fishing, bicycling, handicap access to campgrounds/restrooms/visitor centers; bookstores by Golden Gate National Park Association. Food available at some sites; accommodations in greater San Francisco Bay area.

Two "gateway" recreation areas were created at the same time in 1972, one in the San Francisco Bay area, the other around the New York City harbor, both efforts to bring parks to people in urban areas. GGNRA offers a wide variety of recreational, scenic, natural, and historic areas virtually on San Francisco's doorstep, a park that encompasses some 25,000 acres of open space on both sides of the Golden Gate.

The park includes on the south side of the Golden Gate Bridge the National Maritime Museum, including six historic ships, Aquatic Park, Fort Mason, Marina Green, Crissy Field and the Golden Gate Promenade, Fort Point National Historic Site, Baker Beach, China Beach, Land's End, Cliff House, Ocean Beach and Fort Funston; on the north side Marine Headlines, Tennessee Valley, Muir Woods National Monument, Muir Beach, Stinson Beach, and Olema Valley and in the Bay itself Alcatraz Island.

On both sides of the Golden Gate Bridge the 25,000 acres of the National Recreation Area provide a haven for the city dwellers of San Francisco

Joshua Tree National Monument

74485 National Monument Drive, Twentynine Palms, CA 92277
619/367-7511

Access by I-10 (US 60) and Twentynine Palms Highway. (CA 62) to north entrances at Joshua Tree and Twentynine Palms; south entrance 25 miles east of Indio, CA, via I-10 (US 60). Visitor center, exhibits, guided tours, self-guiding trails, picnicking, camping, backcountry permits, hiking, mountain climbing, horseback riding, handicap access to campgrounds/restrooms/visitor center; bookstore by Joshua Tree Natural History Association. Accommodations at Twentynine Palms, Yucca Valley and Joshua Tree.

Two deserts, two large ecosystems primarily determined by elevation, come together at Joshua Tree National Monument. Few areas more vividly illustrate the contrast between high and low desert. Below 3,000 feet the Colorado Desert, occupying the eastern half of the monument, is dominated by the abundant creosote bush. Adding interest to this arid land are small stands of spidery ocotillo and jumping cholla cactus. The higher, slightly cooler, and wetter Mohave Desert is the special habitat of the undisciplined Joshua tree, extensive stands of which occur throughout the western half of the monument.

The Joshua tree is found only in the arid lands of California, western Arizona, Nevada and southern Utah. It varies in height from 10 to 40 feet and has densely clustered, sharp-pointed leaves and long greenish-white blossoms. This fine monument preserves a spectacular piece of the steadily diminishing Southern California desert.

Kings Canyon National Park

(see Sequoia/Kings Canyon National Parks)

Lassen Volcanic National Park

Mineral, CA 96063
916/595-4444

Access from north and south via CA 89; from east and west via CA 36 and 44. Entrance fee; visitor center, exhibits, guided tours, self-guiding trails, picnicking, camping, backcountry permits, hiking, horseback riding, swimming, boating, fishing, cross-country skiing, cabin rental, handicap access to campgrounds/restrooms/visitor center; bookstore by Loomis Museum Association. Accommodations in park and in Mineral.

This 106,000-acre expanse of coniferous forest, with 50 wilderness lakes and almost as many mountains, is dominated by Lassen Peak, a 10,457-foot plug-dome volcano at the southern tip of the Cascades. The great mass of Lassen Peak began as stiff, pasty lava forced from a vent on the north slope of a larger extinct volcano known as Tehama.

Right *Sunset softens the desert harshness of Joshua Tree National Monument*

Inset *Round textured rocks in the desert landscape of Joshua Tree National Monument*

The lava formed a rough, dome-shaped mass, plugging the vent from which it came, after which Lassen Peak was calm for a long period. Beginning on May 30, 1914, however, eruptions occurred intermittently for more than seven years. Other evidence of volcanic activity here are the beautiful symmetrical Cinder Cone and the active hot springs, steaming fumaroles and sulfurous vents.

Lassen Park Road winds around three sides of Lassen Peak with many beautiful views of the volcano, examples of its destructive action and vistas of woodlands and meadows, clear brooks and lakes.

Some 150 miles of foot trails lead you through this sweet-smelling and sparkling land. In the course of a hike, you may see a variety of conifers – pines, firs and cedars. Stands of broadleaf trees – aspens and cottonwoods – add color to the autumn landscape. Willows and alders border Lassen's many streams and lakes. Wildflowers are usually abundant from mid-June through September.

Because this national park is so well watered and has such a variety of habitats, it is rich in animal life – some 50 kinds of mammal, 150 species of bird, about 12 different kinds of amphibian and reptile and a wealth of insects.

Lava Beds National Monument

PO Box 867, Tulelake, CA 96134
916/667-2282

30 miles south of Tulelake and 60 miles south of Klamath Falls, OR, off CA 139. Visitor center, exhibits, guided tours, self-guiding trails, picnicking, backcountry permits, hiking, handicap access to campgrounds/restrooms/visitor center; bookstore operated by Lava Beds Natural History Association. Accommodations in Tulelake.

Centuries ago a group of volcanoes erupted great masses of molten basaltic lava, which spread over the surrounding level land as rivers of liquid rock. The lava cooled and hardened, forming a rugged landscape, part of which is now preserved in Lava Beds National Monument. The monument, lying on the flank of the Medicine Lake Highlands, ranges in elevation from about 4,000 to 5,700 feet. Its grassland, chaparral and pine-forest communities are habitat for a variety of wildlife. Tulelake National Wildlife Refuge adjoining the monument on the north is a haven for millions of birds, especially during the spring and fall migrations.

A major Indian war, the only one on Californian territory, was fought in these rugged laval flows. In 1872, after several years of disputes with settlers, "Captain Jack" and his band of Modoc Indians took refuge in the lava beds immediately south of Tulelake. In the area now known as Captain Jack's Stronghold the small Modoc band held out against Federal and volunteer troops for nearly six months. This and four other sites prominent in the Modoc War are included in the monument.

John Muir National Historic Site

4202 Alhambra Avenue, Martinez, CA 94553
415/228-8860

At foot of-off ramp of Alhambra Avenue exit of CA 4, 10 miles east of I-80. Day use area only. Entrance fee; visitor center, guided tours, self-guiding tours, picnicking, handicap access to restrooms/visitor center; bookstore by Golden Gate National Park Association. Accommodations in Martinez.

The John Muir House, where he lived from 1890 to 1914, and the adjacent Martinez Adobe, the home of his eldest daughter and her husband, commemorate Muir's contribution to conservation and literature. It was during this period that Muir founded the Sierra Club, the conservation organization that carries on his work.

Muir Woods National Monument

Mill Valley, CA 94941
415/388-2595

17 miles north of San Francisco; access via US 101 and CA 1. Visitor center, exhibits, self-guiding trail, hiking, handicap access to restrooms/visitor center; bookstore by Golden Gate National Park Association. Food available in park; accommodations nearby.

Here in the one-square-mile, V-shaped valley of Muir Woods near San Francisco the nearby ocean produces abundant fog, the damp climate needed for the redwood tree. Some specimens exceed 240 feet in height. Redwood is the only important lumber tree in the Bay Area. During the gold rush the ancient redwood forests were cut to build the growing city of San Francisco. Muir Woods was spared mainly because it stands in an isolated box canyon and is now a part of Golden Gate National Recreation Area.

Pinnacles National Monument

Paicines, CA 95043
408/389-4578

East entrance 35 miles south of Hollister on CA/[A] 146; west entrance 11 miles east of Soledad on 146. Entrance fee; visitor center, exhibits, self-guiding trails, interpretive talks, campground, handicap access to campgrounds/restrooms/visitor center; caves may be closed periodically; bookstore by Southwest Parks and Monuments Association. Accommodations in Hollister on the east and King City, 30 miles southwest; commercial campground on east side.

Spire-like rock formations 500 to 1,200 feet high, the last remnants of an ancient volcano, contrast with the rolling hills of the surrounding California countryside. The dense, brushy plant mantle covering these rugged slopes is an exemplary Coast Range chaparral. A blanket of wildflowers makes the hiking trails popular in the spring.

Point Reyes National Seashore

Point Reyes, CA 94956
415/663-1092

40 miles north of San Francisco via US 101 and Sir Francis Drake Boulevard; also via US 1 near Mill Valley. Visitor center, museum, exhibits, guided tours, self-guiding trails, picnicking, camping, backcountry permits, hiking, horseback riding, swimming, fishing, bicycling, handicap access to restrooms/visitor center; bookstore by Coastal Parks Association. Accommodations at Point Reyes Station, Olema and Inverness.

Just 35 miles north of San Francisco lies an oasis of California nature that has escaped development, primarily because the land was for many years cattle and dairy ranch land, but also because here on this beautiful peninsula wind and fog are more prevalent than in any other part of California. The fact that this is also a "land in motion" has probably deterred any major housing projects: the San Andreas Fault runs through Point Reyes National Seashore.

For centuries before Europeans arrived the Coast Miwok Indians inhabited these shores. Their lives were shaped by a pattern of changing seasons and the uneven temper of the weather along the coast. As peaceful hunters and gatherers they moved about in this plentiful land only to harvest acorns and berries, to catch salmon and shellfish and to hunt deer and elk. In the summer of 1579 these friendly Indians greeted Francis Drake, an adventurer in the service of Queen Elizabeth I of England, as he beached his ship *Golden Hinde* to make repairs. Although it is not definitely known, Drake's anchorage is believed to have been in the protected curve of Point Reyes near what is now called Drake's Beach.

The new Bear Valley Interpretive Center exhibits the story of this wonderful land of long beaches, sand dunes, lagoons, grasslands, forest ridges and tall cliffs.

The odd spirelike rock formations which gave Pinnacles National Monument its name

Redwood National Park

1111 2nd Street, Crescent City, CA 95531
707/464-6101

Access on US 101 south from Oregon coast; north from Eureka and Arcata, and from east via US 199 from Grants Pass and Medford. Visitor centers, exhibits, guided tours, self-guiding trails, picnicking, camping, hiking, horseback riding, swimming, fishing, handicap access to restrooms/visitor centers; bookstore by Redwood Natural History Association. Accommodations along US 101.

The coast redwood (*Sequoia sempervirens*) towers over all other trees in the world. At 367.8 feet the coast redwood discovered on the banks of Redwood Creek by the National Geographic Society in 1963 is the tallest known tree. Redwoods develop the greatest reported volume of living matter per unit of land surface. The giant sequoias, cousins to the coast redwoods, grow larger in diameter and bulk, but not as tall. Coast redwoods can survive to be about 2,000 years old – perhaps half the age of giant sequoias – and average probably 500-700 years. The living tree has no known killing diseases, and the insects associated with it cause no significant damage. Fire is the worst hazard, but usually only to young trees, which lack the protection of thick bark. As with most conifers, redwoods lack a taproot, and their broad, shallow root system sometimes provides inadequate support for the massive trunk. Wind topples many mature trees.

Coast redwoods grow only along the Pacific coast from Curry County in southern Oregon to south of Monterey, California. They grow within 30 miles of the coast and at elevations below 3,000 feet. They grow tallest on flood plains of streams and rivers, and are best developed on cool, moist sites.

The first written record of the redwood was by Fray Juan Crespiu in 1769. Its botanical discoverer was Archibald Menzies, whose collections are dated 1794. The name "redwood" comes from the first (Spanish) description of the huge trees, *palo colorado*, red trees.

Almost from their discovery coast redwoods inspired people to seek their preservation. Success first came in 1902 with the creation of Big Basin Redwoods State Park in a campaign led by the Sempervirens Club. National protection for redwoods was won in 1908, when

President Theodore Roosevelt set aside Muir Woods National Monument under the Antiquities Act of 1906. Those lands were bought by Congressman William Kent for donation to the Federal Government for their preservation.

The Save-the-Redwoods League was organized in 1918. Deeply concerned by the rapidly diminishing old growth redwoods, the group pressed the preservation cause. Within two years it bought four pieces of redwoods land and then sought and won formation of the California State Park System and its State Parks Commission. Equally important, it secured a state system of matching private parkland acquisition funds with state bond issues. The league and countless concerned citizens helped establish more than 280 memorial groves, a public-spirited practice which continues to the present.

Nearly 90 years of spirited advocacy finally bore fruit in 1968 when Congress created Redwood National Park. Its boundaries include three state parks: Jedediah Smith, Del Norte Coast and Prairie Creek. The national park was enlarged in 1978 to its present 106,000 acres, about 70 percent Federal land.

Santa Monica Mountains National Recreation Area

22900 Ventura Blvd, Suite 140, Woodland Hills, CA 91364
2113/888-3770

Some areas are close to Los Angeles, others remote. Maps and information available through park. Visitor centers, exhibits, guided tours, self-guiding trails, picnicking, camping, hiking, horseback riding, swimming, fishing, handicap access to campgrounds/restrooms; bookstore by Southwest Parks and Monuments Association. Food and supplies in park; accommodations in greater Los Angeles.

The Santa Monica Mountains stretch from Griffith Park in downtown Los Angeles to Point Mugu on the Pacific Coast, some 50 miles and 150,000 acres. The park was formed in 1978 after 15 years of effort to preserve and protect these mountains and seashores used first by ancient tribes of Indians and later by the motion picture industry as settings for thousands of films representing places all over the world.

Native to north America, the magnificently antlered elk now lives mainly along the Pacific Coast and in the Rockies

Sequoia/Kings Canyon National Parks

Three Rivers, CA 93271
209/565-3341

South entrance to Sequoia via CA 198 from CA 99; Kings Canyon via CA 180 from CA 99. Entrance fee; visitor centers, exhibits, guided tours, self-guiding trails, picnicking, camping, backcountry permits, hiking, mountain climbing, horseback riding, fishing, cross-country skiing, cabin rental, handicap access to campgrounds/restrooms/visitor centers; bookstores by Sequoia Natural History Association. Accommodations in parks.

The first record of the giant sequoia was published in Pennsylvania in 1839, but before the papers were distributed the printing company burned down. A June 1852 article received wider circulation and 1852 is considered the species' discovery date. Devastating logging followed immediately; many large trees were cut for national and international exhibitions. Public-spirited efforts to preserve the Big Trees began almost with their discovery. Yosemite came under state protection in 1864, but John Muir and many legislators still feared for the trees' future. In September 1890, after a sawmill was built just nine miles from the Giant Forest, Sequoia and General Grant National Parks were created. Sequoia became the nation's second national park, after Yellowstone; Yosemite was made a national park only days later. Concern remained, however, and when Theodore Roosevelt became President in 1901 a petition of 1,437,260 signatures was sent to him to save additional sequoia lands in California. Other lands were subsequently protected, and in 1940 Kings Canyon National Park was created. It included the General Grant National Park lands previously set aside.

The giant sequoia's early ancestors ranged over the entire northern hemisphere, but as the climate changed the giants retreated and their natural range is now restricted to the western slope of California's Sierra Nevada, a strip about 360 miles long and 60 to 80 miles wide.

In volume of total wood, the giant sequoia (*Sequoiadendron giganteum*) is the largest living thing on earth: one tree lives longer, another has a greater diameter, three others grow taller but none is larger.

The age of the General Sherman tree, the largest of the sequoias, is estimated at 2,200 years and the estimated weight of its trunk is 1,385 tons, height above base is 274.9 feet, circumference at ground 102.6 feet and the diameter of the largest branch 6.8 feet. Few records show mature sequoias ever having died from disease or insect attack. They usually die of toppling.

It is difficult to appreciate the size of the General Sherman tree at Giant Forest and the General Grant tree at Grant Grove because neighboring trees are so large. The diameters of these trees at their bases exceed the width of many city streets.

In Sequoia and Kings Canyon National Parks you might well miss the forest for the trees. Here stand not only the largest living thing in the world, but also the highest mountain in the United States outside Alaska. Mount Whitney, at 14,495 feet, caps the Sierra Nevada, which John Muir called "the Range of Light."

The superlatives do not stop with trees and mountains: there are also spectacular valleys. Muir found the Valley of the Kings even "grander" than Yosemite Valley. In fact these parks contain two such spectacular valleys, and Mount Whitney does not stand alone. The parks are unique in that their comparatively small area embraces many peaks more than 14,000 feet above sea level. The two parks encompass a vast stretch of the Sierra crest and the only slightly less high intermediate crest known as the Great Western Divide. Here is a hiker's world of unbounded superlatives. More so than any other, this corner of the earth nearly rendered the effusive John Muir speechless.

Right The giant trees of Sequoia National Park dwarf a visitor

Below There is more to Sequoia/Kings Canyon National Parks than just the mighty trees: a visitor contemplates the mountains across a peaceful stretch of water

Whiskeytown-Shasta-Trinity National Recreation Area

PO Box 188, Whiskeytown, CA 96095
916/241-6584

Visitor center is Overlook Information Station, at intersection of CA 299 and Kennedy Memorial Drive. Visitor center, exhibits, guided tours, self-guiding trails, picnicking, camping, backcountry use permits, hiking, horseback riding, swimming, boating, fishing, hunting, handicap access to campgrounds/restrooms/visitor center; bookstore by Southwest Parks and Monuments Association. Supplies in park; accommodations at Redding.

The National Park Service administers the Whiskeytown Unit of this three-unit national recreation area. Whiskeytown is the smallest of the recreation area's three impounded lakes, but its constant level in the summer makes it ideal for recreation. Popular water sports here include sailing, canoeing, power boating, jet skiing, swimming, sunbathing and fishing from boat and shoreline on the lake and streams.

Some of the most beautiful scenery in northern California is in the area surrounding Whiskeytown. Approaching from either the east or the west, you see the lake's blue waters dotted with wooded isles blending into green hills. Conifers predominate, especially digger pines, ponderosa and Douglas-firs. Undergrowth consists of low-growing shrubs, mostly manzanita with its distinctive deep-red bark. Temperatures on and around the lake and in bordering woodlands are moderate – ideal for outdoor recreation.

Right *The black bear's range extends from Acadia in the east to Glacier Bay in Alaska. Yosemite is one of the six national parks in which it is most plentiful and likely to be seen*

Below *A typical sailing day at Whiskeytown National Recreation Area*

Yosemite National Park

PO Box 577, Yosemite National Park, CA 95389
209/372-4605

Access via CA 140 and 120 eastbound from Merced and Manteca; CA 41 northbound from Fresno; CA 120 westbound from Lee Vining (closed in winter). Entrance fee; visitor center, museum, exhibits, guided tours, self-guiding trails, picnicking, camping, backcountry permits, hiking, swimming, boating, fishing, bicycling, cross-country skiing, cabin rental, handicap access to campgrounds/restrooms/visitor center; bookstore by Yosemite Association. Accommodations in park and at Lee Vining, Groveland, El Portal, Wawona, Oakhurst, Fish Camp and Mariposa.

Yosemite National Park embraces a vast tract of scenic wildlands set aside in 1890 to preserve a portion of the Sierra Nevada mountains that stretches along California's eastern flank. The park ranges from 2,000 to more than 13,000 feet above sea level and offers three major features: alpine wilderness, groves of giant sequoias and Yosemite Valley. The 200 miles of roads give access to all these features either by car or by free shuttlebus in some areas. To get to know the real Yosemite, however, you must leave your car and take a few steps on a trail. You don't have to walk far to discover the grandeur that can be found here and the values this special place offers.

The story of Yosemite began about 500 million years ago when the Sierra Nevada region lay beneath an ancient sea. Thick layers of sediment lay on the sea bed, which was eventually folded and twisted and thrust above sea level. Simultaneously molten rock welled up from deep within the earth and cooled slowly beneath the layers of sediment to form granite. Erosion gradually wore away almost all the overlying rock and exposed the granite. Even as uplifts continued to form the Sierra, water and then glaciers went to work to carve the face of Yosemite. Weathering and erosion continue to shape it today.

"The Incomparable Valley," as it has been called, is probably the

best known glacier-carved canyon. Its leaping waterfalls, towering cliffs, rounded domes and massive monoliths make it a preeminent natural marvel. These attributes have inspired poets, painters, photographers and millions of visitors, beginning with John Muir, for more than a hundred years.

Nowhere in Yosemite is the sense of scale so dramatic. Yosemite Valley is characterized by sheer walls and a flat floor. Its evolution began when alpine glaciers lumbered through the canyon of the Merced River. The ice carved through weaker sections of granite, plucking and scouring rock but leaving harder, more solid portions – such as El Capitan and Cathedral Rocks – intact and greatly enlarging the canyon that the Merced River had carved through successive uplifts of the Sierra. Finally the glacier began to melt and the terminal moraine left by the last glacier advance into the valley dammed the melting water to form ancient Lake Yosemite, which sat in the newly-carved U-shaped valley. Sediment eventually filled in the lake, forming the flat valley floor you see today. This same process is now filling Mirror Lake at the base of Half Dome.

In contrast to the valley's sheer walls, the Merced Canyon along California 140 outside the park is a typical river-cut, V-shaped canyon, for the glaciers did not extend this far. Back from the rim of the valley itself, forested slopes show some glacier polish, but for the most part these areas were not glaciated.

The valley is a mosaic of open meadows sprinkled with wildflowers and flowering shrubs, oak woodlands and mixed-conifer forests of ponderosa pine, incense-cedar and Douglas-fir. Wildlife from monarch butterflies to mule deer and black bears flourishes in these communities. Around the valley's perimeter waterfalls, which reach their maximum flow in May and June, crash to the floor. Yosemite, Bridalveil, Vernal, Nevada and Illilouette are the best-known of these falls, some of which have little or no water from mid-August through early fall.

The Indian Cultural Museum and the Indian Village behind the Valley Visitor Center commemorate the native Americans who inhabited this region long before it was "discovered." The Ahwahneechee Indians lived in the valley for several thousand years. Acorns were a food staple, as were the animals they hunted and fished.

Left *The wintry silhouette of Cathedral Rock in Yosemite*

Right *Half Dome, one of Yosemite's most distinctive features, looms high over Yosemite Park*

Inset *The sheer and forbidding surface of Half Dome*

Below *A ranger of the National Parks Service lectures to an entranced audience of visitors in Yosemite*

Right *The Merced River runs quietly through the splendor of Yosemite Valley*

Below *Winter beauty in Yosemite: El Capitan in the snow*

Left *Yosemite Falls, one of the leaping waterfalls to be found in Yosemite National Park*

Right *A visitor is dwarfed by the mighty landscape of Yosemite*

COLORADO

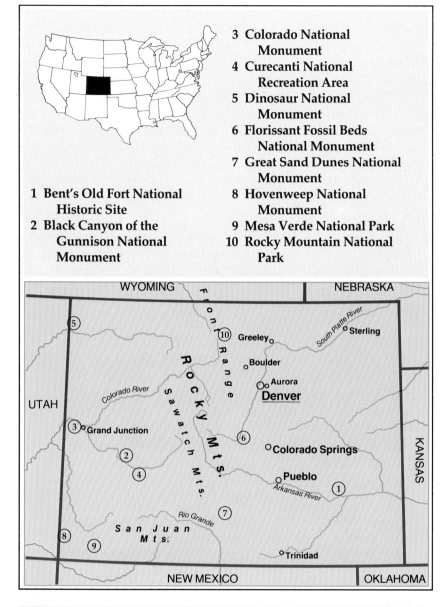

1. **Bent's Old Fort National Historic Site**
2. **Black Canyon of the Gunnison National Monument**
3. Colorado National Monument
4. Curecanti National Recreation Area
5. Dinosaur National Monument
6. Florissant Fossil Beds National Monument
7. Great Sand Dunes National Monument
8. Hovenweep National Monument
9. Mesa Verde National Park
10. Rocky Mountain National Park

Bent's Old Fort National Historic Site

35110 Highway 194 East, La Junta, CO 81050-9523
303/384-2596

8 miles east of La Junta, 15 miles west of Las Animas, on CO 194; 68 miles east of Pueblo; La Junta is served by Atchison, Topeka and Santa Fe Railroad. Visitor center, exhibits, guided tours, self-guiding tour of fort, picnicking, handicap access to restrooms; bookstore by Bent's Old Fort Historical Association. Accommodations in La Junta and Las Animas.

Bent's Old Fort, on the banks of the Arkansas River, was the principal Anglo-American outpost on the Southern Plains between 1833 and 1849; an important rendezvous point for Indians, traders and soldiers, and a significant fur-trading post on the Santa Fe Trail for trappers. The adobe fort has been reconstructed with rooms furnished in period style.

Black Canyon of the Gunnison National Monument

PO Box 1648, Montrose, CO 81402
303/240-6522

15 miles from Montrose, CO, on CO 347. Entrance fee; visitor center, exhibits, guided tours, self-guiding tours, picnicking, camping, backcountry permits, hiking, mountain climbing, fishing, handicap access to campgrounds/restrooms/visitor center; bookstore operated by Southwest Parks and Monuments Association. Food available in park; accommodations in Montrose.

Black Canyon is deeper than the Grand Canyon and in some respects more awesome. Its maximum depth is 2,700 feet, the narrowest width at the top is only 1,100 feet, and at one point the river channel is only 40 feet wide. No other canyon in North America combines the depth, narrowness, sheerness and somber countenance of this Black Canyon of the Gunnison. Carved by the Gunnison river as it hurries along to the Colorado, it is 53 miles long, but only the deepest, most spectacular 12 miles of the gorge lie within the national monument. Slanting rays of sunlight penetrate this deep and narrow canyon's dark walls of schist and gneiss that are shrouded in heavy shadows most of the day – hence "Black Canyon." East of the park the Gunnison river has been impounded and tamed behind three dams. In the Black Canyon, however, it remains one of the few unspoiled wild rivers in the country.

Left *The magnificent Rocky Mountain elk can stand five feet tall at the shoulders with antlers spreading six feet*

Right *Horseback riding, one of the many outdoor activities available amid the spectacular scenery of Rocky Mountain National Park*

Colorado National Monument

Fruita, CO 81521
303/858-3617

4 miles west of Grand Junction and 3½ miles south of Fruita, CO, on CO 340. Entrance fee; visitor center, exhibits, guided tours, self-guiding trail, picnicking, camping, hiking, horseback riding, bicycling, cross-country skiing, handicap access to restrooms/visitor center; bookstore by Colorado National Monument Association. Accommodations in Grand Junction and Fruita.

The national parks are full of surprises, and this is one. Deep canyons, towering monoliths, strange rock formations, dinosaur fossils, and the remains of a prehistoric Indian culture highlight this spectacularly beautiful country. Time and weather have scoured away great volumes of rocks in this land, remnants of which form today's dramatic landscape. The rocks' differing resistance to erosion has given rise to the varied landforms—here a rounded slope, there a sheer cliff and, beyond, a towering monolith – that grace the park. More than for any other reason, Colorado National Monument was established to preserve these scenic treasures. Fossils and other evidence help to date these rock layers, which spread across many other areas of the American southwest. Here, with the exception of those exposed on the deeper canyon floors, all the rocks were formed at various times during the Mesozoic era, 225 to 65 million years ago, dominated by the life forms we know as dinosaurs, perhaps not reptiles, but a form of life ancestral to today's birds.

Curecanti National Recreation Area

PO Box 1040, Gunnison, CO 81230
303/641-2337

Elk Creek Visitor Center on Blue Mesa Lake, 16 miles west of Gunnison via US 50. Visitor center, guided tours, self-guiding trail, picnicking, camping, group campsites, hiking, boating, fishing, hunting, snowshoe route, cross-country skiing, handicap access to campground/restrooms/visitor center. Food and supplies available in park; accommodations in Gunnison and Montrose area.

A chain of three dams and reservoirs form the Curecanti Unit of the Colorado River Storage Project and the national recreation area. Blue Mesa Lake, the focus of water sports, is Colorado's largest lake when filled to capacity. Morrow Point and Crystal lakes, narrow and deep with the canyon carved out by the Gunnison, suggest fjords. Boat tours in season on Morrow Point Lake provide an insight into the ancient sculpting work of time and the river. The old rock faces of the canyon walls reveal immense time spans which dwarf this landscape's human history of Ute Indians, Spanish explorers, fur traders, gold prospectors, miners, railroad builders and ranchers. Downstream, where the river still tumbles free, carving the ancient Precambrian rock, this two-million-year-old story continues to unfold in the Black Canyon of the Gunnison.

Dinosaur National Monument

PO Box 210, Dinosaur, CO 81610
303/374-2216

Headquarters on Colorado-Utah border 20 miles north of Dinosaur, CO; Quarry Visitor Center on UT 149, 7 miles north of Jensen. Visitor centers, exhibits, camping, fishing, backcountry permits, hiking; bookstore by Dinosaur Nature Association. Accommodations in Vernal, UT, 14 miles.

Spectacular canyons cut by the Green and Yampa rivers through upfolded mountains have revealed the world's largest concentrated deposit of petrified bones of dinosaurs and other ancient animals. The Dinosaur Quarry Visitor Center near Vernal, Utah, has been constructed around the face of a quarry where bones have been embedded in barren rock. Visitors can watch while scientists slowly chisel and chip in and around the exposed bones.

Florissant Fossil Beds National Monument

PO Box 185, Florissant, CO 80816
303/748-3253

35 miles southwest of Colorado Springs, via US 24. Visitor center, exhibits, guided tours, self-guiding trail, picnicking, hiking, handicap access to restrooms/visitor center; bookstore by Rocky Mountain Nature Association. Accommodations in Colorado Springs and Woodland Park.

Here is a treasure of paleontological history preserved by volcanic ash that has been continually studied since its discovery in 1874. Within the ancient mudflows is one of the world's richest plant, mammal, insect and bird fossil groupings, including the fossil remains of sequoia stumps 12 feet tall and 14 feet in diameter.

The museum contains about 500 specimens of fossils of all kinds.

Great Sand Dunes National Monument

Mosca, CO 81146
303/378-2312

US 160 east from Alamosa, CO, to CO 150 and the monument. Entrance fee; visitor center, exhibits, guided tours, self-guiding trails, picnicking, camping, backcountry permits, hiking, fishing, handicap access to campground/restrooms/visitor center; bookstore by Southwest Parks and Monuments Association. Supplies available in park; accommodations in Alamosa.

The Great Sand Dunes nestle against the Sangre de Cristo Mountains in the high-mountain San Luis Valley. An unexpected surprise, the dunes are products of the mountains, valley and climate. They probably began to form as the last ice age ended, when streams of glacial meltwater carried boulders, gravel, sand and silt from the mountains. Boulders and rocks dropped near the mountain's foot; lighter material was carried out onto the valley floor and as deposits built, the river shifted, leaving enormous sand deposits exposed to the wind.

The Sangre de Cristos tower 4,000 feet above the valley floor. The range's northern two-thirds forms a barrier to prevailing southwesterly winds. The southern third nearly parallels the wind and directs it to a pocket where the range shifts direction. Here the wind is funneled through three low passes. As it has for 15,000 years, the wind bounces and rolls the ancient river sand toward the mountain barrier where, through these passes, the wind loses energy, leaving the sand behind. Trillions of tons of sand have created a dune field of

150 square miles. The main dune field of 50 square miles, caught in a wind trap, is stable, but the dune surfaces change with each wind.

Hovenweep National Monument

c/o Mesa Verde National Park, CO 81330
303/529-4465

45 miles from Cortez, CO, on Utah-Colorado border; park can be reached only by dirt and gravel road, sometimes impassable in bad weather. Exhibits, self-guiding trail, picnicking, camping, hiking; bookstore by Mesa Verde Museum Association. Accommodations in Blanding and Bluff, UT and Cortez, CO.

Located in the Four Corners area (Colorado, New Mexico, Arizona, and Utah) west of Mesa Verde National Park, Hovenweep includes six groups of towers, pueblos, and cliff dwellings built by pre-Columbian Indians, representing the San Juan Anasazi Culture that occupied this land 700 years ago; two groups in Utah, four in Colorado.

Right *Evening in Great Sand Dunes National Monument, with the Rocky Mountains in the background*

Left *Great Sand Dunes National Monument, the largest and highest dunes in the country*

Mesa Verde National Park

Mesa Verde National Park, CO 81330
303/529-4465

Entrance on US 160, midway between Cortez and Mancos. Entrance fee; visitor center, museum, exhibits, guided tours, self-guiding trails, picnicking, camping, handicap access to campground/restrooms/ visitor center; bookstore by Mesa Verde Museum Association. Accommodations in park.

About 1,400 years ago a group of Indians living in the Four Corners region chose Mesa Verde for their home. For over 700 years their descendants lived and flourished here, eventually building elaborate stone cities in the sheltered recesses of the canyon wall. Then in the late 1200s, within the span of one or two generations, they abandoned their homes and moved away.

Mesa Verde National Park, which occupies part of a large plateau rising high above the Montezuma and Mancos valleys, preserves a spectacular remnant of their thousand-year-old culture. We call these people the Anasazi, from a Navajo word meaning "the ancient ones." Ever since local cowboys discovered the cliff dwellings a century ago archeologists have been trying to understand the life of these people but our knowledge is still sketchy. We will never know the whole story of their existence, for they left no written records and much that was important in their lives has perished. Yet for all their silence, these ruins speak with a certain eloquence. They tell of a people adept at building, artistic in their crafts, and skillful at wresting a living from a difficult land. They are evidence of a society that over the centuries accumulated skills and traditions and passed them on from one generation to another. By the twelfth and thirteenth centuries the Anasazi of Mesa Verde were the heirs of a vigorous civilization, with accomplishments in community living and the arts that rank among the finest expressions of human culture in ancient America.

Taking advantage of nature, the Anasazi built their dwellings

under the overhanging cliffs. Their basic construction material was sandstone, which they shaped into rectangular blocks about the size of a loaf of bread. The mortar between the blocks was a mix of mud and water. Rooms averaged about 6 feet by 8, space enough for two or three people. Isolated rooms in the rear and on the upper levels were generally used for storing crops.

It is these intriguing cliff houses that are the main feature of this national park, the only one of the 48 which has human culture as its central theme. Here, unfolded before your eyes, is a major city of the past – its busy streets and avenues, its skyscrapers, its community playgrounds; in the most simple terms, its heart and soul. Much of the daily routine took place in the open courtyards in front of the rooms you see. The women fashioned pottery there, while the men made various tools – knives, axes, awls, scrapers – out of stone and bone. The fires built in summer were mainly for cooking. In winter, when the cave rooms were damp and uncomfortable, fires probably burned throughout the village. Smoke-blackened walls and ceilings are reminders of the biting cold these people lived with for half the year.

Exhibits, interpretive talks and other special programs in the park help tune the mind to another age; but even without these it takes little to turn the imagination on, so vivid is the sense of history in this grand place.

Spruce Tree House, probably the best preserved of all the cliff dwellings, contains 114 rooms, of which eight are kivas, or small ceremonial rooms. Cliff Palace, the largest, perhaps most photographed and thus the best known, complex of houses has 200 rooms, 23 of which are kivas. There is Balcony House, Sun Point Pueblo, Sun Temple, and dozens of other interesting sights, not the least of which is Wetherill Mesa and its concentration of dwellings 12 miles from the main park visitor center.

Mesa Verde is a fragile park, and one that should not be visited fleetingly. One must linger, study, think; this is indeed ancient America – those who came before.

Spruce Tree House, carved out of the cliffs by native Americans centuries ago, is an extensive labyrinth of over a hundred rooms

Rocky Mountain National Park

Estes Park, CO 80517
303/586-2371

Access via Trail Ridge Road, which crosses the Continental Divide; access from east via US 34 and 36 to Estes Park; from southwest via US 34 to Grand Lake. Entrance fee; visitor centers, exhibits, self-guiding trails, picnicking, camping, backcountry permits, hiking, mountain climbing, horseback riding, fishing, snowmobile route, cross-country skiing; handicap access to campgrounds/restrooms/visitor centers; bookstore by Rocky Mountain Nature Association. Food available in park; accommodations in Estes Park.

The snow-mantled peaks of Rocky Mountain National Park rise above verdant alpine valleys and glistening lakes. A third of the park is above the tree line, and here tundra predominates – a major reason why these peaks and valleys have been set aside as a national park. This area was first traversed by settlers in 1859 when Joel Estes and his son Milton rode into the valley that bears their name. Few settlers came into this rugged country, and in about 1900 Enos Mills, a naturalist, writer and conservationist, began to campaign for preservation of this pristine area. Mills' campaign succeeded, and the area became Rocky Mountain National Park in 1915. A feature of the park is the marked differences found with the changing elevation. At lower levels open stands of ponderosa pine and juniper grow on the slopes facing the sun; on cooler north slopes are Douglas-fir. Gracing the stream sides are blue spruces intermixed with dense stands of lodgepole pines; here and there appear groves of aspen; wildflowers dot meadows and glades and above 9,000 feet forests of Englemann spruce and sub-alpine fir take over. Openings in these cool, dark forests produce wildflower gardens of rare beauty and luxuriance, where the blue Colorado columbine reigns. At the upper edges of this zone the trees are twisted, grotesque and hug the ground. Then the trees disappear and you are in alpine tundra – a harsh, fragile world. Here more than a quarter of the plants you will see can also be found in the Arctic. From the valleys to its mountain-tops Rocky Mountain National Park encompasses many worlds.

Long's Peak, Rocky Mountain National Park, the backdrop to typically spectacular scenery in the park

Right *Bear Lake in Rocky Mountain National Park, with a vast snow-covered peak rearing above the treeline*

Far right *Near Lake Haiyaha in Rocky Mountain National Park the classic alpine combination of peaks, snow, water and fir trees*

Below *Cross-country skiing in the Rocky Mountain National Park, only one of many different outdoor activities available at all seasons*

DISTRICT OF COLUMBIA

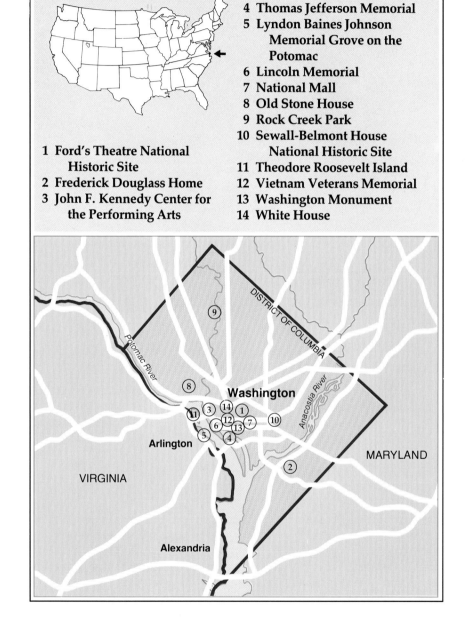

4 Thomas Jefferson Memorial
5 Lyndon Baines Johnson
   Memorial Grove on the
   Potomac
6 Lincoln Memorial
7 National Mall
8 Old Stone House
9 Rock Creek Park
10 Sewall-Belmont House
    National Historic Site
11 Theodore Roosevelt Island
12 Vietnam Veterans Memorial
13 Washington Monument
14 White House

1 Ford's Theatre National
   Historic Site
2 Frederick Douglass Home
3 John F. Kennedy Center for
   the Performing Arts

Frederick Douglass Home

1411 W Street, SE, Washington, DC 22020
202/426-5961

Anacostia Bridge from heart of Washington to Good Hope Road, then to 14th Street. Museum, exhibits, guided tours, self-guiding tour, picnicking, handicap access to restrooms/house; bookstore by Parks and History Association. Accommodations in Washington.

Frederick Douglass, outstanding nineteenth-century American black, remarkable orator and writer and noted abolitionist and antislavery editor, lived in this 14-room Victorian house, called Cedar Hill, from 1877 until his death in 1895.

Ford's Theatre National Historic Site

511 Tenth Street, NW, Washington, DC 20004
202/426-6924

Downtown Washington; Petersen House at 516 Tenth Street. Museum, exhibits, guided tours, self-guiding tours; bookstore by Parks and History Association. Accommodations in immediate area.

No other building in Washington has such a tragic history surrounding it; no other, so authentically restored, has so much charm, and none has been so wisely used by the National Park Service. Ford's Theatre, where President Abraham Lincoln was fatally shot on the evening of April 14, 1865, is a living theater, where small musicals, plays and one-person shows are performed in the spring, summer and fall. The Lincoln Museum is a splendid small museum devoted to Lincoln and artifacts of the assassination, including the assassin's pistol and the suit in which Mr. Lincoln died. The house where Lincoln died, the Petersen House, directly across Tenth Street from Ford's, has also been faithfully restored and is open to the public.

Thomas Jefferson Memorial

c/o National Park Service, 1100 Ohio Drive, SW, Washington, DC 20242
202/426-6841

South bank of Tidal Basin near downtown Washington. Guided tours, self-guiding tours, handicap access to restrooms. Accommodations in greater Washington area.

This popular circular colonnaded structure, in the classic style introduced to the country by Jefferson, memorializes the author of the Declaration of Independence and President of the United States from 1801 to 1809. The interior walls of the memorial are inscribed with his writings. A heroic statue of Jefferson stands in the center.

Above *The theater where Abraham Lincoln was fatally shot by John Wilkes Booth is a memorial to Lincoln and a living theater to this day*

Left *The classic dignity of the Thomas Jefferson's circular domed and pillared memorial*

Lyndon Baines Johnson Memorial Grove on the Potomac

c/o National Park Service, 1100 Ohio Drive, SW, Washington, DC 20242
202/285-2598

In Lady Bird Johnson Park on George Washington Memorial Parkway, west of I-95 and 14th Street Bridge. Picnicking, boating, fishing. Accommodations in Washington and vicinity.

A grove of 500 white pine trees and a slab of Texas granite with engraved quotations form a memorial to the thirty-sixth President on a 15-acre plot on the banks of the Potomac River.

John F. Kennedy Center for the Performing Arts

c/o National Park Service, 2700 D Street, NW, Washington, DC 20566
202/254-3760

At 2700 F Street, NW, on Potomac river. Exhibits, guided tours, handicap access to restrooms/theaters. Food available in Center; accommodations in immediate area.

The National Park Service is responsible for the maintenance and security of the Kennedy Center, which houses the national cultural center: the Concert Hall, Opera Hall, Eisenhower Theater, and the National Film Institute.

Lincoln Memorial

c/o National Park Service, 1100 Ohio Drive, SW, Washington, DC 20242
202/426-6841

Facing Washington Monument, at south end of Reflecting Pool. Guided tours, handicap access to restrooms; Abraham Lincoln bookstore by Parks and History Association. Accommodations in immediate area.

One of the most respected and probably the best known memorial in the country is this classical structure and its 19-foot marble statue of Abraham Lincoln by Daniel Chester French. The only spelunking tour in Washington, which is by reservation, takes you into the cave-like "basement" beneath the memorial where stalagmites and stalactites have been formed from water percolating through cracks in the memorial's limestone foundation.

National Mall

c/o National Park Service, 1100 Ohio Drive, SW, Washington, DC 20242
202/426-6841

Bordered by Constitution and Independence Avenues and Fourteenth Street and Capitol Plaza. Picnicking, handicap access to restrooms. Food available along Mall; accommodations in greater Washington area.

A key feature in the original L'Enfant plan for Washington, the Mall is that long sweep of grass extending from the base of the Capitol to the

The National Mall extends from the Washington Monument to the Capitol

north to the Washington Monument to the south, and includes the numerous buildings of the Smithsonian Institution. This is the site of the annual American Folklife Festival in July.

Old Stone House

3051 M Street, NW, Washington, DC 20007
202/426-6851

In Georgetown. Exhibits. Accommodations in immediate area.

Built in 1765, the Old Stone House is an excellent example of pre-Revolutionary architecture. It is the oldest house in Washington.

Rock Creek Park

5000 Glover Road, NW, Washington, DC 20002
202/426-6832

Nature Center at 5200 Glover Road, NW, south of Military Road and Oregon Avenue. Visitor center, exhibits, guided tours, self-guiding tours and trails, picnicking, hiking, horseback riding, fishing, bicycling, handicap access to restrooms/visitor center; bookstore by Parks and History Association. Accommodations in greater Washington area.

Rock Creek Park, some 4 miles long and 1 mile wide, is the largest natural park in an urban area in the country. Its wide range of natural, cultural, historical and recreational features is an oasis in the middle of the busy capital.

Sewall-Belmont House National Historic Site

144 Constitution Avenue, NE, Washington, DC 20002
202/546-3989

Near US Capitol. Exhibits, guided tours, self-guiding tours. Accommodations in greater Washington area.

Rebuilt after fire damage from the War of 1812, this 2½-story red brick house is one of the oldest on Capitol Hill. It has been the National Woman's Party headquarters since 1929 and commemorates the party's founder and suffrage leader, Alice Paul, and associates.

Theodore Roosevelt Island

c/o George Washington Memorial Parkway, Turkey Run Park, McLean, VA 22101
202/285-2601

In Potomac River in Washington, DC; reach parking area from northbound lanes of George Washington Memorial Parkway on Potomac's Virginia side; footbridge connects island to Virginia shore. Guided tours, self-guiding trails, aquatic life, bird and animal refuge. Accommodations in greater Washington area.

On this 88-acre wooded island sanctuary in the Potomac is an imposing statue of Roosevelt, the conservation-minded President. His tenets on nature, manhood, youth and the state are inscribed there.

The proud figure of one of America's most revered presidents looks gravely out on the capital

Vietnam Veterans' Memorial

c/o National Park Service, 900 Ohio Drive, SW, Washington, DC 20242
202/426-6841

In Constitution Gardens near Lincoln Memorial, just off Constitution Avenue at 23rd Street, NW. Accommodations in greater Washington area.

This striking but solemn memorial to the dead of the Vietnam War is composed of two 250-foot long black granite walls intersecting at a 130-degree angle. Inscribed on the walls are the names of 58,000 men and women who were killed or remain missing.

Washington Monument

c/o National Park Service, 1100 Ohio Drive, SW, Washington, DC 20242
202/426-6841

At south end of Mall, between Fifteenth and Seventeenth Streets. Guided tours, handicap access to restrooms; bookstore by Parks and History Association. Accommodations in greater Washington area.

This 555-foot obelisk honors the first President of the United States and is the dominating structure of Washington.

White House

c/o Director, White House Visitor Office, The White House, Washington, DC 20500
202/456-7041

1600 Pennsylvania Avenue. Exhibits, guided tours, handicap access to restrooms; book sales by the White House Historical Association. Accommodations in greater Washington area.

The White House has been the official residence of every President of the United States since November 1800. The cornerstone was laid on October 13, 1792, on a site selected by George Washington, who, incidentally, did not live there. The grounds of the White House are maintained and administered by the National Park Service.

Right The obelisk monument to George Washington seen from the Lincoln Memorial

Below The White House at 1600 Pennsylvania Avenue has been the home and office of the President of the United States since 1800

FLORIDA

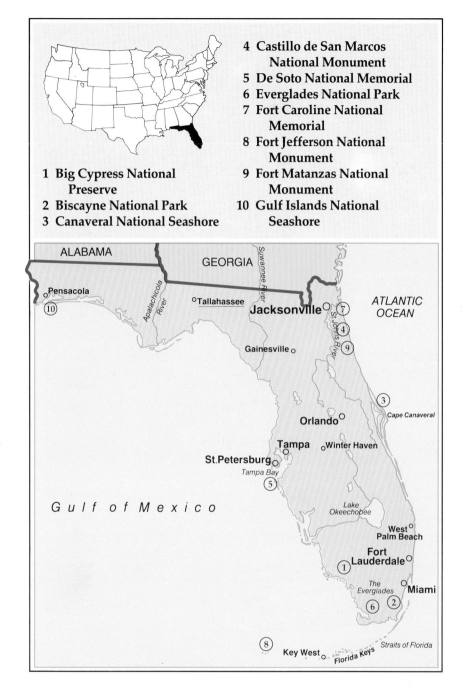

4 **Castillo de San Marcos National Monument**
5 **De Soto National Memorial**
6 **Everglades National Park**
7 **Fort Caroline National Memorial**
8 **Fort Jefferson National Monument**
9 **Fort Matanzas National Monument**
10 **Gulf Islands National Seashore**

1 **Big Cypress National Preserve**
2 **Biscayne National Park**
3 **Canaveral National Seashore**

Big Cypress National Preserve

Star Route Box 110, Ochopee, FL 33943
813/695-2000

Headquarters approximately 35 miles east of Naples, behind Golden Lion Motel on US 41, Satinwood Drive. Picnicking, camping, hiking, fishing, hunting. Accommodations available in park.

Adjoining the northwest section of Everglades National Park, this large area provides a freshwater supply crucial to the Everglades' survival. Subtropical plant and animal life abounds in this ancestral home of the Seminole and Miccosukee Indians.

Biscayne National Park

PO Box 1369, Homestead, FL 33090-1369
305/247-2044

Headquarters at Convoy Point, 9 miles east of Homestead, on SW 328 Street. Visitor center, exhibits, guided tours, self-guiding trail, picnicking, camping, group campsites, backcountry permits, hiking, swimming, bathhouse, boating, fishing, handicap access to campground/restrooms; bookstore by Florida Natural History Association. Accommodations in Homestead.

Biscayne is Florida's other, lesser known, national park. Established as a national monument in 1968, it is 21 miles east of the Everglades. In 1980 it was enlarged to 175,000 acres and designated as a national park to protect a rare combination of terrestrial and undersea life, preserve a scenic subtropical setting and provide an outstanding spot for recreation and relaxation.

In most parks land dominates the scenery, but at Biscayne water and sky overwhelm the scene in every direction, leaving the bits of low-lying land looking remote and insignificant. This is a paradise for marine life, water birds, boaters, fishermen, snorkelers and divers alike. The water is clean and extraordinarily clear. Only the maintenance of the natural interplay between the mainland, Biscayne Bay, keys and reefs and the Atlantic Ocean keeps it that way.

The region's Caribbean-like climate provides year-round warmth, generous sunshine and abundant rainfall. Tropical life thrives. The land is filled to overflowing with an unusual collection of trees, ferns, vines, flowers and shrubs. Forests are lush, dark, humid, evergreen. Many birds, butterflies and other animals live in these woods.

No less odd or diverse is Biscayne's underwater world. At its center are the coral reefs. The shallow water reefs are inundated with light and life. Brilliantly colorful tropical fish and other curious creatures populate them. Their appearances and behavior are as exotic as their names – stoplight parrotfish, finger garlic sponge, goosehead scorpionfish, princess venus, peppermint goby.

Above *Tropical birds like this roseate spoonbill are returning to the Everglades as a result of conservation measures*

Left *Waterfowl at a dried up pond, seen against the Kennedy Space Center*

Canaveral National Seashore

PO Box 6447, Titusville, FL 32780
305/867-4675

Access via major highways between Jacksonville and West Palm Beach – US 1, I-95, I-4, I-75. Visitor center, exhibits, guided tours, self-guiding trails, picnicking, hiking, swimming, boating, fishing, handicap access to restrooms/visitor center; bookstore by Eastern National Park and Monument Association. Food available in park; private campgrounds in vicinity. Accommodations in Titusville and New Smyrna Beach.

Twenty-five miles of undeveloped barrier island preserve the natural beach, dune, marsh and lagoon habitats for a variety of wildlife, including many species of birds. The Kennedy Space Center occupies the southern end of the island and occasionally the seashore is closed for launches. The area includes a portion of 140,393-acre Merritt Island National Wildlife Refuge, administered by the Fish and Wildlife Service.

Castillo de San Marcos National Monument

1 Castillo Drive, St. Augustine, FL 32084
904/829-6506

Downtown St. Augustine. Entrance fee; visitor center, exhibits, guided tours, self-guiding trail, handicap access to restrooms. Accommodations in St. Augustine.

The construction of this oldest masonry fort in the continental United States was started in 1672 by the Spanish to protect St. Augustine, the first permanent settlement by Europeans in the continental US in 1565. The floor plan is the result of modernization in the eighteenth century.

Deep in the Everglades. The apparently stagnant water is in fact a very slow-moving river

De Soto National Memorial

75th Street, NW, Bradenton, FL 33529
813/792-0458

On Tampa Bay, 5 miles west of Bradenton; 40 miles south of Tampa, off FL 64. Visitor center, exhibits, self-guiding trail, fishing, handicap access to visitor center; bookstore by Eastern National Park and Monument Association. Accommodations in Bradenton.

This small park commemorates the sixteenth-century Spanish explorer Hernando de Soto, who led the first extensive exploration by Europeans into what is now the southern United States (1539-42).

Everglades National Park

PO Box 279, Homestead, FL 33030
305/247-6211

Main visitor center 12 miles southwest of Homestead on FL 27. Entrance fee; visitor centers, exhibits, guided tours, self-guiding trails, picnicking, camping, backcountry permits, hiking, boating, boat rental, boat ramp, fishing, bicycling, cabin rental, handicap access to campgrounds/restrooms/visitor centers; bookstores by Florida Natural History Association. Accommodations in park and in Homestead, Key Largo and Everglades City.

Tropical life from Caribbean islands blends with temperate species in the Everglades. The result is a rich mixture of plants and animals in a unique setting. Give this park half a chance, take the time, and you will discover wonder itself. You can drive through its skinny pine trees and miss its forests, or drive through its sawgrass and miss the glades. Many take such a hurried look. But try it another way. Talk and walk with a ranger. Slow down.

A freshwater river 6 inches deep and 50 miles wide creeps seaward through the Everglades on a riverbed that slopes ever so gradually. Everglades... the name means a marshy land covered with scattered tall grasses. The national park's 1.5 million acres contain only part of the watery expanse for which it is named.

Despite the park's size, its environment is threatened by the possibly disruptive activities of agriculture, industry and urban development around it. There is no guarantee that the endangered species protected in the park since its establishment in 1947 will survive. The importance and uniqueness of the Everglades ecosystem have been recognized by its designation as an International Biosphere Reserve and a World Heritage Site, but it will take both human concern and prudent management to preserve the park's natural treasures.

The Everglades' subtropical climate governs its life. The nearly uniform warm, sunny weather makes the park a year-round attraction, but there are two distinct seasons. Summer is wet, winter dry. Heavy rains fall during intense storms from late May through October. Warm, humid conditions bring abundant insects, including mosquitoes, which are important to intricate food webs. Precipitation can exceed 50 inches a year.

Life hangs by a delicate thread in the Everglades. The problem is water, fresh water, the life-blood of the Everglades. It appears to be everywhere, but man has drastically blocked its free flow through southern Florida. Conflicting demands compete for this precious water, leaving the Everglades, at Florida's southernmost tip, struggling to survive. Despite an apparent lush richness, water supplies are critical and porous limestone underlies the entire park. Rooting plants have only a thin mantle of marl and peat on this limestone for their support.

Agriculture development and the continued mushrooming of metropolitan Miami demand increasing amounts of water, depleting water supplies. This, in turn, increases the threat of fire, which can destroy thin soils, inviting the invasion of exotic plants and animals that upset natural habitats. Native vegetation vital to Everglades ecology is depleted and the diversity and complexity protecting the fabric of life are diminished. When rainfall is ample few problems arise, but in drought years agreements for sharing the limited amount of water have been required. Man is as much a part of the Everglades as the alligator, but our conflicting actions as consumers and conservers have irrevocably changed southern Florida and altered the Everglades ecosystem.

Concern for protecting rookeries of herons, ibis and other wading birds from commercial plume hunting and other human impacts motivated creation of the park. Ironically, millions of people now seek sanctuary here. Ultimately places like the Everglades may be the last refuge, not just of eagles, crocodiles and wood storks, but of people too.

The alligator, once nearly hunted to extinction for its hide, is protected in the Everglades, where its numbers are increasing

Fort Caroline National Memorial

12713 Fort Caroline Road, Jacksonville, FL 32225
904/641-7155

East of downtown Jacksonville, via FL 10. Visitor center, exhibits, self-guiding trail, picnicking, hiking, handicap access to restrooms/visitor center; bookstore by Eastern National Park and Monument Association. Accommodations in Jacksonville.

Fort Caroline overlooks the site of a French Huguenot colony of 1564-65, the second French attempt at settlement within the present United States. Here French and Spaniards began two centuries of European colonial rivalry in North America.

The Florida cougar is an elusive creature: it is a rare treat to sight one even in the Everglades, a known habitat

Left *The marshy Everglades make an ideal home for the egret, a long-legged wading bird which feeds on water creatures such as fish and frogs*

Right *Sea oats thrive in the sandy soil of Gulf Islands National Seashore*

Fort Jefferson National Monument

c/o US Coast Guard Base, Key West, FL 33040
305/247-6211

68 miles west of Key West; access only by boat or air taxi from Key West area. Exhibits, self-guiding tour, underwater nature trail, picnicking, camping, swimming, boating, fishing, handicap access to campground/restrooms; bookstore by Florida Natural History Association. Accommodations at Key West.

Built in 1856 to help control the Florida Straits, this is the largest of a ring of masonry coastal defense forts constructed in the United States. It stands on an island in the Gulf of Mexico's Dry Tortugas group, named to warn mariners of the lack of fresh water. During and after the Civil War the fort was used as a federal military prison.

Fort Matanzas National Monument

Route 1, Box 105, St. Augustine, FL 32084
904/471-0116

On Anastasia Island, 14 miles south of St. Augustine, via FL A1A. Visitor center, exhibits, guided tours, self-guiding trail, swimming, fishing, handicap access to visitor center; bookstore by Eastern National Park and Monument Association. Accommodations in St. Augustine.

This Spanish fort was built in 1740-42 to protect St. Augustine from the British.

Gulf Islands National Seashore

PO Box 100, Gulf Breeze, FL 32561 (see also Mississippi)
904/932-5302

Access via FL 992 southwest from Pensacola. Entrance fee; visitor center, exhibits, guided tours, self-guiding trails, picnicking, camping, hiking, swimming, boating, fishing, bicycling, handicap access to campgrounds; bookstore by Eastern National Park and Monument Association. Food and supplies available in park; accommodations in Pensacola and Fort Walton Beach.

Offshore islands and keys have both sparkling white sand beaches and historic forts and batteries. The mainland features of this Florida unit, which is near Pensacola, include the Naval Live Oaks Reservation, beaches and military forts.

Right *Some curious vegetation has adapted itself to the sandy soils of Gulf Islands National Seashore*

Inset *A beach morning glory sends tendrils into the sand for moisture and nourishment*

Below *The Naval Live Oaks Reservation area in the Florida Unit of Gulf Islands National Seashore*

GEORGIA

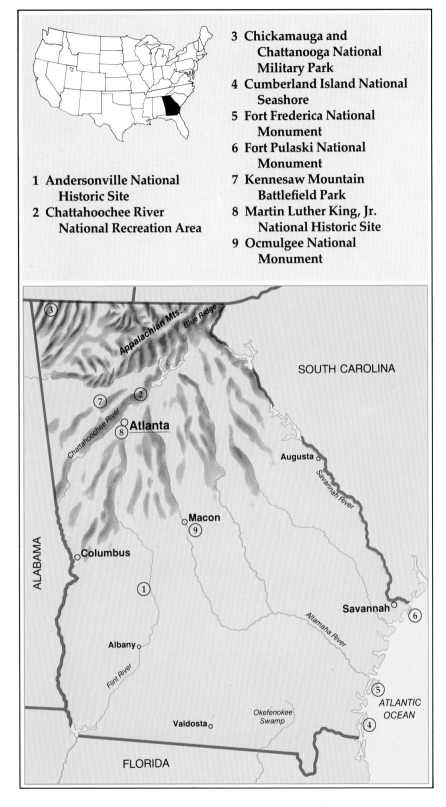

1 Andersonville National Historic Site	**3 Chickamauga and Chattanooga National Military Park**
2 Chattahoochee River National Recreation Area	**4 Cumberland Island National Seashore**
	5 Fort Frederica National Monument
	6 Fort Pulaski National Monument
	7 Kennesaw Mountain Battlefield Park
	8 Martin Luther King, Jr. National Historic Site
	9 Ocmulgee National Monument

Andersonville National Historic Site

Andersonville, GA 31711
912/924-0343

9 miles northeast of Americus. Visitor center, exhibits, self-guiding tour, picnicking, handicap access to restrooms/visitor center; bookstore by Eastern National Park and Monument Association. Food in Andersonville; accommodations in Americus and Montezuma.

It was known as Camp Sumter when 45,000 Union soldiers were imprisoned here; 12,912 of them died under the most terrible conditions. The Andersonville story is not a pleasant one, but it has become an important chapter of our Civil War history. Now Andersonville National Historic Site and its National Cemetery honors soldiers from all America's wars.

The Iowa monument honoring the men who died at Andersonville Prison in Georgia during the Civil War

Chattahoochee River National Recreation Area

1900 Northridge Road, Dunwoody, GA 30338
404/394-7912

Paces Mill Unit accessible from north side of Atlanta off US 41. Guided tours, picnicking, backcountry permits, hiking, horseback riding, swimming, handicap access to restrooms; bookstore by Eastern National Park and Monument Association. Food available in park; accommodations in greater Atlanta area.

A series of sites along a 48-mile stretch of the Chattahoochee river, extending into Atlanta, has been preserved for public enjoyment of the scenic, recreational and historical values.

Chickamauga and Chattanooga National Military Park

PO Box 2128, Fort Oglethorpe, GA 30742
404/866-9241

Visitor center on US 27, off I-75, 10 miles south of Chattanooga. Visitor centers, exhibits, self-guiding tours, picnicking, hiking, horseback riding, handicap access to restrooms/visitor centers; bookstore by Eastern National Park and Monument Association. Accommodations in Fort Oglethorpe and Chattanooga.

The struggle for control of Chattanooga in the Civil War resulted in two major victories, one for each side, within nine weeks in 1863 on these fields, now a 5,000-acre park on the Georgia/Tennessee border. The Confederate and Union armies first met on September 18-20 along Chickamauga Creek; it was one of the worst defeats for the North. Two months later, on November 24, Ulysses S. Grant took Lookout Mountain and on the following day George H. Thomas stormed and took Missionary Ridge in some of the most fierce fighting of the Civil War, involving some 120,000 men.

The main visitor center houses the Fuller Gun Collection, one of the finest displays of small arms in the country.

Over 15,700 slain lie buried at Andersonville

Georgia

Cumberland Island National Seashore

PO Box 806, St. Mary's, GA 31558
912/882-4335

Visitor center at St. Mary's River front, end of GA 40; park accessible only by concessioner-operated boat. Visitor center, guided tours, self-guiding tours, picnicking, camping, backcountry permits, hiking, swimming, fishing, handicap access to restrooms/visitor center; bookstore by Eastern National Park and Monument Association. Accommodations in mainland communities.

Magnificent and unspoiled beaches and dunes, marshes and fresh-water lakes make up this largest of Georgia's Golden Isles.

Fort Frederica National Monument

Route 4, Box 286-C, St. Simons Island, GA 31522
912/638-3639

On St. Simons Island, 12 miles from Brunswick; reached via Brunswick-St. Simon toll causeway. Visitor center, exhibits, self-guiding tour, handicap access to restrooms/visitor center. Accommodations in Brunswick and on St. Simons Island.

The fort was built by General James E. Oglethorpe in 1736-48 during the Anglo-Spanish struggle for control of what is now the southeastern United States.

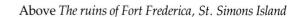

Above *The ruins of Fort Frederica, St. Simons Island*

Left above and below *Cumberland Island's pristine beaches and sand dunes survive the ravages of wind and tide and provide one of our finest and least used national seashores*

93

Fort Pulaski National Monument

PO Box 98, Tybee Island, GA 31328
912/786-5785

13 miles east of Savannah, off US 80. Entrance fee; visitor center, exhibits, self-guiding tour, picnicking, hiking, fishing; bookstore by Eastern National Park and Monument Association. Accommodations in greater Savannah area.

Bombardment of this early nineteenth-century fort by Federal rifled cannon in 1862 first demonstrated the ineffectiveness of old-style masonry fortifications.

Kennesaw Mountain Battlefield Park

PO Box 1167, Marietta, GA 30061
404/427-4686

3 miles north of Marietta, short distance off US 41. Visitor center, exhibits, self-guiding trails, picnicking, hiking, horseback riding, handicap access to restrooms/visitor center; bookstore by Kennesaw Mountain Historical Association. Accommodations in Marietta.

On June 27, 1864, in his march toward Atlanta, Union General William T. Sherman defeated Confederate Joseph E. Johnston's Army of Tennessee here.

The Stars and Stripes fly over Fort Pulaksi

Martin Luther King, Jr, National Historic Site

522 Auburn Avenue, NE, Atlanta, GA 30312
404/331-5190

Downtown Atlanta. Exhibits, guided tours, self-guiding tours. Accommodations in greater Atlanta area.

The birthplace, church and grave of Dr. Martin Luther King, Jr, American civil rights leader, make up this park. The neighborhood also includes the Martin Luther King, Jr. Center for Nonviolent Social Change, Inc. The surrounding preservation district includes Sweet Auburn, the economic and cultural center of Atlanta's black community during most of the twentieth century. There are no federal facilities, but several key sites, run by private organizations, are open to the public.

Ocmulgee National Monument

1207 Emery Highway, Macon, GA 31201
912/742-0447

On east edge of Macon, off I-16. Visitor center, exhibits, guided tours, self-guiding tours; summer program includes Indian handicraft demonstrations; bookstore by Ocmulgee National Monument Association. Accommodations in Macon.

Traces of 10,000 years of southeastern Indian prehistory are preserved here, including the massive temple mounds of a Mississippian Indian ceremonial complex abandoned in about 1100.

The Colonel Patrick Ferguson monument at Kennesaw Mountain Battlefield Park

HAWAII

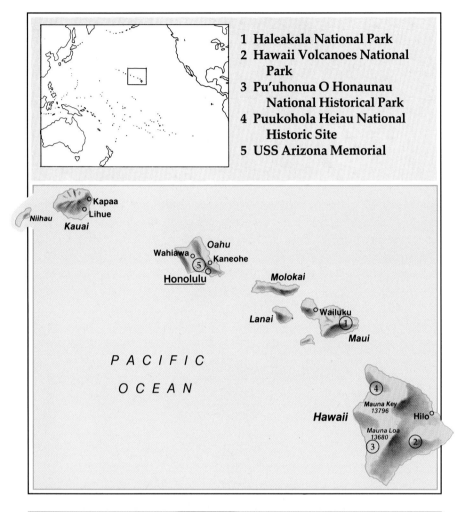

Haleakala National Park

PO Box 369, Makawao, HI 96768
808/572-9177

Access from Kahului via HI 36, 37, 377, or 378. Visitor center, exhibits, self-guiding trails, picnicking, camping, backcountry permits, hiking, horseback riding, swimming, hunting, cabin rental, handicap access to restrooms/visitor center; bookstore by Hawaii Natural History Association. Accommodations in Pukalaui.

Maui, one of the younger islands in this chain, began as two separate volcanoes on the ocean floor; after eons of eruptions the volcano heads emerged from the sea. Lava, wind-blown ash and alluvium eventually joined the two by an isthmus or valley, forming Maui, "The Valley Isle." Finally Haleakala, the larger eastern volcano, reached its greatest height, 12,000 feet above the ocean – some 30,000 feet from its base on the ocean floor.

For a time volcanic activity ceased and erosion created large amphitheater-like depressions near the summit. Ultimately these two valleys met, creating a long erosional "crater." At the same time a series of ice age submergences and emergences of the shoreline occurred; the final submergence formed the four islands of Lanai, Molikai, Kahoolawe and Maui.

When volcanic activity resumed near the summit lava nearly filled the valleys. More recently cinders, ash, volcanic bombs and spatter were blown from the numerous young vents in the "crater" forming multicolored symmetrical cones as high as 600 feet. Thus this water-carved basin became partially filled with lava and cinder cones and it came to resemble a true volcanic crater.

Several hundred years have passed since the last volcanic activity, probably because of the constant northwestward movement of the Pacific tectonic plate. As the oldest islands on the northwest end of the chain have moved farther away from the plume – the source of new lava – they have ceased to grow and wind, rain and time have reduced them to sandbars and atolls.

Maui has shifted a few miles from the plume's influence, and Haleakala, too, is destined to become extinct. Though dormant since about 1790, earthquake records indicate that internal adjustments are still taking place in the earth's crust, but no volcanic activity is visible in the crater or elsewhere on Maui. Perhaps Haleakala could erupt again; we just don't know.

Left *Masked booby duck chick and adult on Hawaii*

Right *The serrated ridge of the Koolan mountain range*

*Small craters of more recent eruptions within the huge
ancient crater of Haleakala*

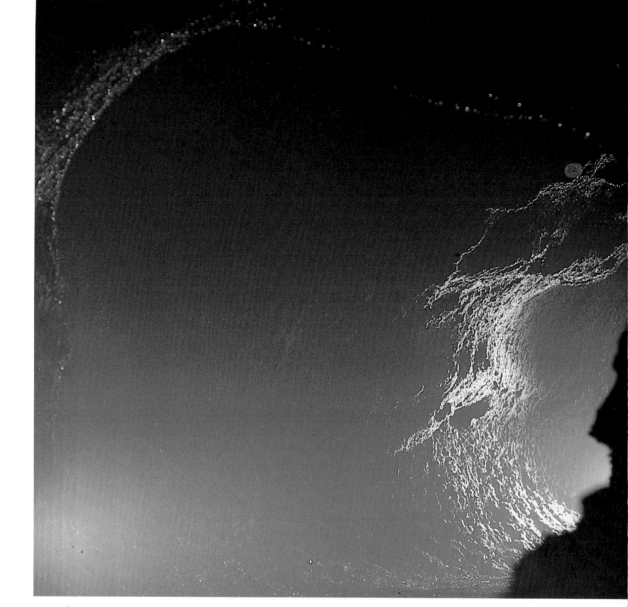

Left *At Volcanoes National Park there are sensational walks through lava tubes*

Right *Clouds drifting into Haleakala crater, Haleakala National Park*

Below *Luxuriant vegetation covers the dramatic mountains formed by volcanic activity*

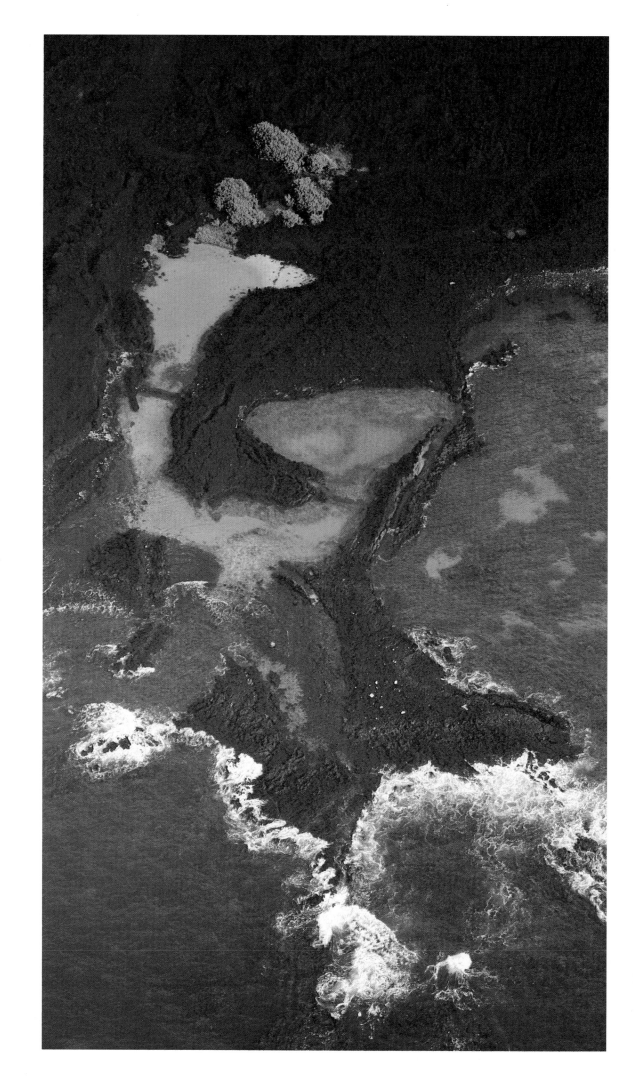

Right *Lava from Haleakala meets the sea*

Far right *A startling remnant of volcanic activity on Maui*

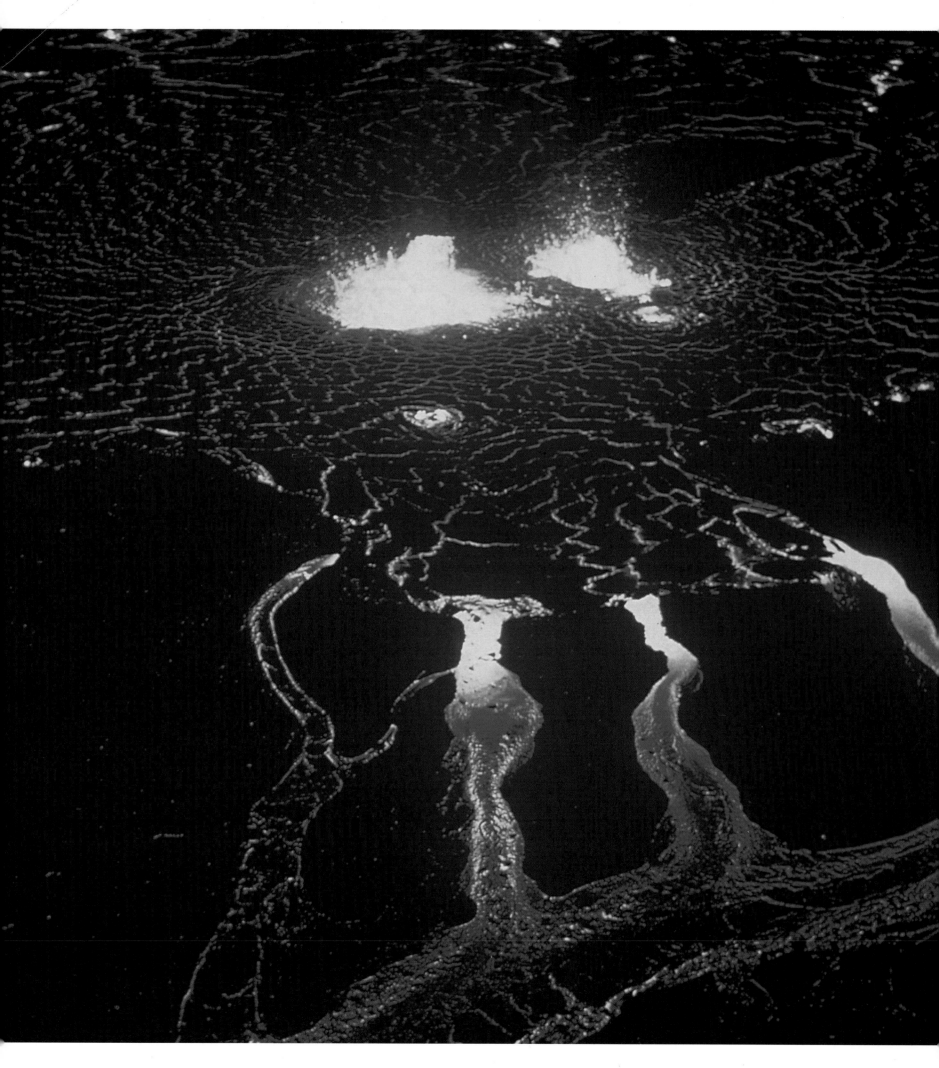

Hawaii Volcanoes National Park

Hawaii Volcanoes National Park, HI 96718
808/967-7311

Visitor centers at Kilauea and Wahaula; Kilauea 29 miles southwest of Hilo, off HI 11. Visitor centers, exhibits, self-guiding trails, picnicking, camping, backcountry permits, hiking, mountain climbing, cabin rental, handicap access to campgrounds/restrooms/visitor centers; bookstore by Hawaii Natural History Association. Accommodations in park and in Hilo.

By far the largest island in the Hawaiian archipelago, Hawaii is also one of earth's most prodigious volcanic constructions, as most vividly demonstrated within Hawaii Volcanoes National Park. Ever since man has watched and studied volcanic eruptions, Hawaii's two most active volcanoes, Mauna Loa and Kilauea, have obliged.

The ocean floor lies more than 18,000 feet below Hawaii's beaches, the highest point on Mauna Kea is 13,796 feet above sea level and Mauna Loa is 13,667 feet high. Measured from the ocean floor these shield volcanoes are considered the greatest mountain masses on earth. Geologists also tell us that it took Mauna Loa about three million years to attain its size – two million to reach the surface of the ocean and perhaps another million to make that vast mound of stone now visible above sea level.

Left *At night a network of fiery channels of lava spill out of a crater*

Below *Almost as spectacular by day as night, the awesome force of an erupting volcano*

Although Mauna Loa appears to be so much bigger, Kilauea is an impressive shield volcano in its own right. It rises about 22,000 feet above the ocean floor; its height above sea level is slightly more than 4,000 feet. Both are counted among the earth's most active volcanoes.

Kilauea erupted in 1969 in one of its more spectacular shows, spewing molten lava some 1,800 feet into the air. Eruptions continued intermittently for some five years and then again in 1977, 1979, April 1982 and, in front of 25,000 spectators for 16 hours, in September 1982. Repeated eruptions since have damaged property extensively within the park and added tons of lava to the island.

Mauna Loa added one billion tons of lava to the island in 23 days of eruptions in 1950 and was then dormant for a quarter-century. On July 5, 1975, it erupted in a six-mile curtain of fire at the Mokiaweoweo Crater, and again in 1984 and 1985.

Active though they are, Hawaii's volcanoes are relatively gentle. Violent outbursts – characterized by tremendous explosions, destructive earthquakes, clouds of poisonous gases, showers of hot mud and rains of erupted rocks – have occurred only twice in recorded history. Both happened at Kilauea, one about 1790 the other in 1924. In general Kilauea's eruptions are mild, producing mostly slow-moving lava.

Today this national park, created primarily to preserve the natural setting of Mauna Loa and Kilauea, is also a refuge for those native plants and animals that still survive the encroachments of civilization. Here too scientists can study the processes and effects of volcanism. Kilauea has been studied more intensively than any other volcano and so is one of the best understood. In studying Kilauea during its periods of quiet as well as during eruptions experts are learning more about how the earth was born and its parts were formed, how continents and islands have been made and destroyed and improving methods for predicting volcanic eruptions.

Pu'uhonua O Honaunau National Historical Park

PO Box 128, Honaunau, Kona, HI 96726
808/328-2326

30 miles south of Keahole Airport on HI 160. Visitor center, exhibits, self-guiding tours, picnicking, backcountry permits, hiking, swimming, fishing, handicap access to restrooms/visitor center; bookstore by Hawaii Natural History Association. Accommodations at Captain Cook.

Until 1819 vanquished Hawaiian warriors, noncombatants and kapu breakers could escape death by reaching this sacred ground. The park encompasses prehistoric house sites, royal fishponds, coconut groves, and spectacular shore scenery.

Puukohola Heiau National Historic Site

PO Box 4963, Kawaihae, HI 96743
808/882-7218

Northwestern shore. Visitor center, self-guiding tours, handicap access to restrooms/visitor center; bookstore by Hawaii Natural History Association. Accommodations at Waimea.

Preserved here are the ruins of Puukohola Heiau (temple on the hill of the whale), built by King Kamehameha the Great during his rise to power.

USS *Arizona* Memorial

1 Arizona Memorial Place, Honolulu, HI 96818
808/422-2771

Off elevated freeway above Kamehameha Highway. Visitor center, exhibits, guided tours, handicap access to restrooms/visitor center; bookstore by Arizona Memorial Museum Association. Food available in park; accommodations in greater Honolulu area.

USS *Arizona*, sunk at Pearl Harbor on December 7, 1941, remains at the bottom of the harbor with its crew of sailors and marines. Spanning the battleship is the USS *Arizona* Memorial, a gleaming white 184-foot-long concrete-enclosed, bridge-like structure. A white marble wall within the memorial lists the names of the 1,177 *Arizona* men who died in the Japanese attack that drew the United States into World War II.

Right *Steam from volcanic activity seeps out among the lush tropical vegetation of the National Park*

Left *The east rift zone of Kilauea Volcano ablaze with volcanic activity*

Inset *Detail of solidified lava*

IDAHO

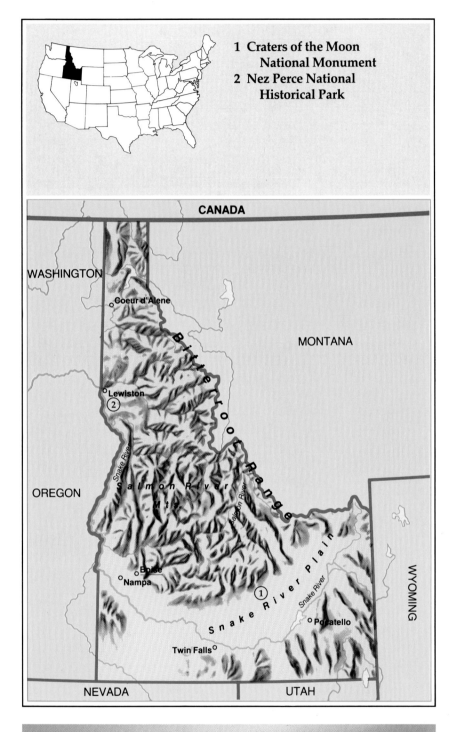

1 Craters of the Moon
   National Monument
2 Nez Perce National
   Historical Park

Craters of the Moon National Monument

PO Box 29, Arco, ID 83213
208/527-3257

18 miles southwest of Arco on US 20, 26 and 93. Entrance fee; visitor center, exhibits, guided tours, self-guiding trails, picnicking, camping, backcountry permits, hiking, cross-country skiing, handicap access to restrooms/visitor center; bookstore by Craters of the Moon Natural History Association. Accommodations in Arco.

Fissure eruptions, volcanic cones, craters, lava flows, caves and other volcanic phenomena make this one of the most bizarre landscapes in America. It literally does resemble the surface of the moon and little wonder, for its origins may well be quite similar to the moon's. Although the last volcanic eruptions were perhaps 2,000 years ago, such activity had probably been going on for a million years before. Some 200 species of plant and a number of animals have successfully braved these harsh conditions and seem to survive in an otherwise barren and sterile land.

Nez Perce National Historical Park

PO Box 93, Spalding, ID 83551-0093
208/843-2261

Park headquarters at Spalding, 11 miles east of Lewiston, on US 95.
Visitor center, exhibits, self-guiding trail, picnicking; bookstore by
Pacific Northwest National Parks and Forests Association.
Accommodations in Lewiston.

This park comprises 24 historic sites in north central Idaho, four
administered by the National Park Service and 20 managed cooper-
atively with federal, tribal, state and private agencies. Some sites
relate to westward expansion, settlement and the 1877 war; others
relate to Nez Perce religion and legends.

Far left *Plants which can survive the inhospitable conditions in Craters of the
Moon National Monument are tenacious and hardy*

Left *The eerie landscape of Craters of the Moon National Monument*

Right *Life as lived by the native Indians of America is preserved at Nez Perce
National Historical Park*

Below *St. Joseph's Mission, one of the sites of Nez Perce National Historical Park*

ILLINOIS

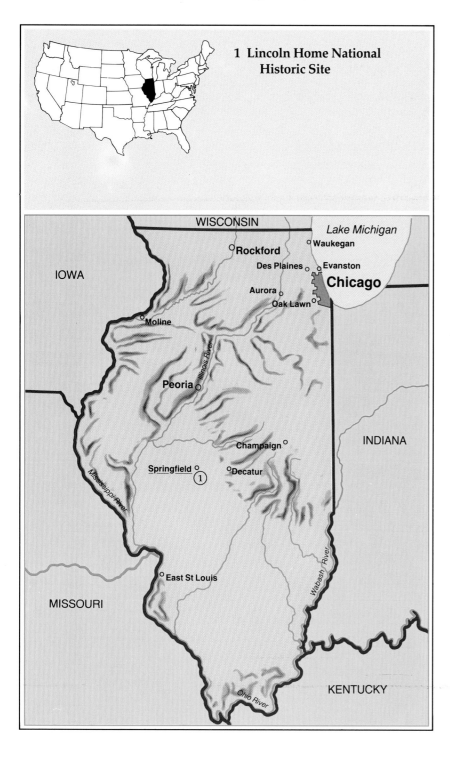

1 Lincoln Home National Historic Site

Lincoln Home National Historic Site

426 South Seventh Street, Springfield, IL 62703
217/492-4241

Visitor center one block west of Lincoln Home in downtown Springfield.
Visitor center, exhibits, guided tours, self-guiding tours, handicap access to restrooms/visitor center; bookstore by Eastern National Park and Monument Association. Accommodations in Springfield.

This was the only house Lincoln ever owned. He lived here with his family from 1844 to 1861, when he left for Washington to become President of the United States. The site includes four city blocks and twelve homes of Mr. Lincoln's Springfield neighbors.

Above *The first floor sitting room of the Lincoln Home, Springfield, in which the Lincoln family gathered each evening – Mr and Mrs Lincoln to read, the children to play*

Right *The gracious exterior of one of America's most famous presidents' home*

INDIANA

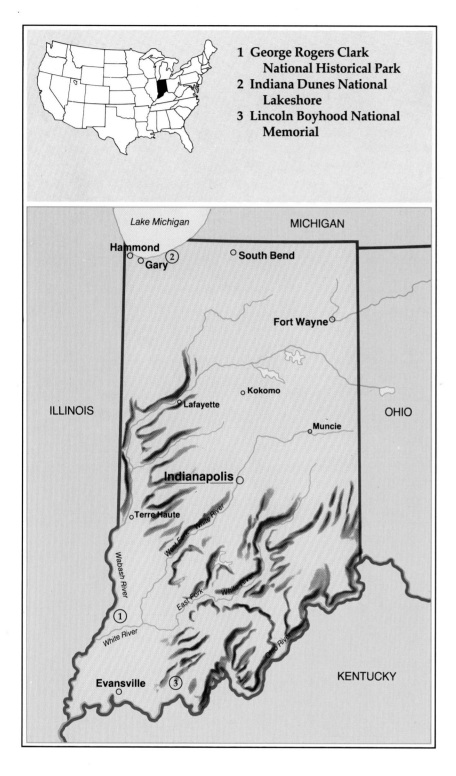

1 George Rogers Clark
   National Historical Park
2 Indiana Dunes National
   Lakeshore
3 Lincoln Boyhood National
   Memorial

George Rogers Clark National Historical Park

401 South Second Street, Vincennes, IN 47591
812/882-1776

At junction of US 50 and 41 in southwestern Indiana. Visitor center, exhibits, handicap access to restrooms/visitor center; bookstore by Eastern National Park and Monument Association. Accommodations in Vincennes.

This classic memorial stands on the site of old Fort Sackville, which the frontier army under Lt. Col. George Rogers Clark captured from the British in 1779. This won the old northwest for the United States.

Right *The imposing statue of George Rogers Clark at the historic site named in his honor at Vincennes*

Far right *The famous and popular dunes of Indiana Dunes National Lakeshore on Lake Michigan*

Indiana Dunes National Lakeshore

1100 North Mineral Springs Road, Porter, IN 46304
219/926-7561

Access via US 12 and 20, I-80, I-90, I-94 and IN 49. Visitor center, exhibits, guided tours, self-guiding trails, picnicking, hiking, horseback riding, swimming, boating, fishing, bicycling, handicap access to restrooms/visitor center; bookstore by Eastern National Park and Monument Association. Food available in park; accommodations in Michigan City and Gary.

It has been said that the Indiana Dunes are to the Midwest what the Grand Canyon is to Arizona and Yosemite to California. It is certainly a unique place along the southern shore of Lake Michigan.

Dunes are created when a plentiful supply of sand combines with wind blowing mostly from one direction, and a natural trap causes the wind to drop the sand. A short distance inland from this place plants and hilly terrain slow the wind so that it drops its cargo, creating shoreline sand dunes.

The Dunes, as this place is affectionately called, has been the subject of preservation movements since the early 1900s when proposals to make it a national park were put before the Congress. Indiana Dunes State Park was established in 1925; the national lakeshore was authorized in 1966 and formally established in 1972. Not only does this protect a very special ecological environment, but the recreational facilities for the people living in the Chicago, Illinois, to Michigan City, Indiana, area are boundless.

Lincoln Boyhood National Memorial

Lincoln City, IN 47552
812/937-4757

On IN 162, 2 miles east of Gentryville, 4 miles south of Dale, 5 miles west of Santa Claus. Visitor center, exhibits, self-guiding tours, handicap access to restrooms/visitor center; bookstore by Eastern National Park and Monument Association. Accommodations in Dale.

On this southern Indiana farm Abraham Lincoln grew from youth into manhood. His mother, Nancy Hanks Lincoln, is buried here.

The Lincoln boyhood farm in Indiana, where our sixteenth President grew to manhood

IOWA

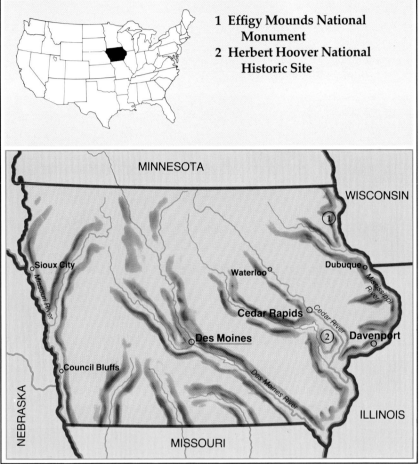

1 **Effigy Mounds National Monument**
2 **Herbert Hoover National Historic Site**

Effigy Mounds National Monument

PO Box K, McGregor, IA 52157
319/873-2356

4 miles north of McGregor and Marquette, Iowa, on Highway 76. Visitor center, exhibits, self-guiding trail, hiking, guided tours; bookstore. Accommodations in McGregor.

Along the bluffs of the Mississippi near Marquette, Iowa, stand the remains of an Indian society. These are outstanding examples of Indian burial mounds in the shape of birds and other creatures.

Herbert Hoover National Historic Site

PO Box 607, West Branch, IA 52358
319/643-2541

Visitor center on Parkside Drive at intersection with Main Street; West Branch 10 miles east of Iowa City. Visitor center, museum, exhibits, guided tours, self-guiding tours, picnicking, hiking, handicap access to restrooms/visitor center; museum, bookstore. Accommodations in West Branch.

Herbert Hoover, the 31st President of the United States, was born and spent his first 10 years in the two-room cottage preserved in this small park. Across from the cottage there is a reconstructed blacksmith shop similar to the one run by Hoover's father, and here also is the Hoover Presidential Library-Museum and the graves of Mr and Mrs Hoover.

The Mississippi from the high bluff of Effigy Mounds

The reconstructed blacksmith's shop at the Herbert Hoover Historic Site

KANSAS

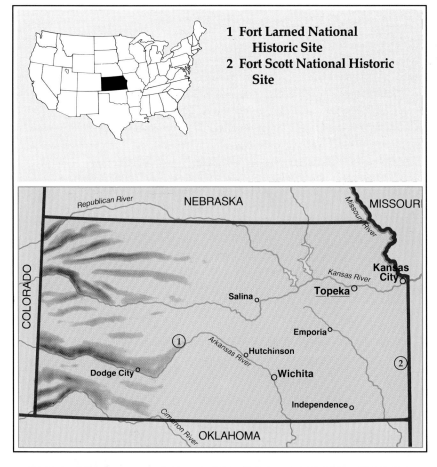

1 **Fort Larned National Historic Site**
2 **Fort Scott National Historic Site**

Fort Larned National Historic Site

Route 3, Larned, KS 67550
316/285-3571

7 miles west of Larned, on US 156. Visitor center, exhibits, guided tours, self-guiding tour, picnicking, handicap access to restrooms/ visitor centers; bookstore by Southwest Parks and Monuments Association. Accommodations in Larned and Great Bend.

Fort Larned was a key military post against the Plains Indians in the 1868-69 wars, and served as an Indian agency in the 1860s. From 1859 to 1878 it protected traffic on the Santa Fe Trail. Nine original military buildings still stand.

Fort Scott National Historic Site

Old Fort Boulevard, Fort Scott, KS 66701
316/223-0321

90 miles south of Kansas City, on north edge of Fort Scott. Visitor center, exhibits, guided tours, self-guiding tours, picnicking, handicap access to restrooms/visitor center; bookstore by Southwest Parks and Monuments Association. Accommodations in town of Fort Scott.

In its brief but varied life Fort Scott mirrored the course of western settlement along the middle border. From 1842-53 troops from this post helped keep peace on the Indian frontier; between 1854 and 1861, the years of "Bleeding Kansas," the fort and town were caught up in the violent struggle between "free-soilers" and slave-holders; during the Civil War the fort became an important supply center for Union armies in the West and in the 1870s the US Army returned to Fort Scott to protect workers building a railroad across disputed land. Twenty-one historic military buildings, 13 furnished, are open to the public.

The golden-mantled ground squirrel has a white stripe bordered with black on its sides and resembles a large chipmunk

KENTUCKY

1 Cumberland Gap National Historical Park
2 Abraham Lincoln Birthplace National Historic Site
3 Mammoth Cave National Park

Cumberland Gap National Historical Park

PO Box 840, Middlesboro, KY 40965
606/248-5766

Visitor center ½ mile south of Middlesboro on US 25E. Visitor center, exhibits, self-guiding tours, picnicking, camping, backcountry permits, hiking, handicap access to campgrounds/restrooms/visitor center; bookstore by Eastern National Park and Monument Association. Accommodations in Middlesboro.

Some 20,000 acres in Kentucky, Tennessee and Virginia form this site commemorating the opening of a trail to the western frontier by Daniel Boone and 30 men, who for two years in the mid-1770s blazed the Wilderness Trail from Cumberland Gap into Kentucky. By the end of the Revolutionary War some 12,000 hardy souls had crossed into the new territory. By 1792 Kentucky's population was over 100,000 and it was admitted to the Union.

Cumberland Gap

Abraham Lincoln Birthplace National Historic Site

RFD 1, Hodgenville, KY 42748
502/358-3874

---

3 miles south of Hodgenville, on US 31E, KY 61. Visitor center, exhibits, self-guiding tours, picnicking, handicap access to restrooms/visitor center; bookstore by Eastern National Park and Monument Association. Accommodations in Hodgenville.

A large granite and marble building encloses a log cabin representing Lincoln's birthplace. This was the site of the Thomas Lincoln home for the first 2½ years of Abraham Lincoln's life.

Mammoth Cave National Park

Mammoth Cave, KY 42259
502/758-2251

Visitor center 9 miles northwest of Park City off I-65 via KY 255 or 70. Visitor center, exhibits, guided tours, self-guiding tours, picnicking, camping, backcountry permits, hiking, boating, fishing, cabin rental, handicap access to campground/restrooms/ visitor center; bookstore by Eastern National Park and Monument Association. Accommodations in park and at Bowling Green, Glasgow, Horse Cave, Park City and Cave City.

In 1935 the mummified body of a native American was found in Mammoth Cave. It was estimated that "Lost John," as he became known, was mining gypsum there in about 420 BC. His clothing, sandals, even his last meal, were all perfectly preserved. Of course, "John" was not the only clue to the earliest explorations of this silent underground world. Footprints, remnants of torches and hundreds of other traces left behind have given scientists a date of about 2,000 BC for when the first human stepped into the cave.

The first known white man to enter Mammoth Cave was Valentine Simons in 1798. Simons bought some 200 acres of land surrounding the cave and began mining for nitrate, a basic ingredient of saltpeter, used to make gunpowder. When travelers stopped for a look, the seeds of a mighty tourist industry were planted. It was some years before sightseeing began in earnest, however, for Simons did virtually no exploring.

In 1838 Franklin Gorin, who was said to be the first white man born in this region, bought the cave from Simons and set one of his slaves, Stephen Bishop, to exploring. Before he died in 1857 Bishop had become America's first great cave explorer. He had seen and mapped more than eight miles of passageways, rooms, streams and rivers in Mammoth, and gained an international reputation.

What Bishop and his many followers saw was a geological phenomenon quite unlike any in the world, and it attracted the curious from all over; Edwin Booth recited Shakespeare in what is now called Booth's Amphitheatre; Jenny Lind once gave a concert here, and even Jesse James held up the old Mammoth stage filled with tourists and relieved them of a few hundred dollars.

Some 300 million years ago, so geologists say, the seas that covered what is now west central Kentucky deposited layer upon layer of mud, shells and sand, which all hardened into the limestone and sandstone we see today. Then as the land around uplifted the seas drained away, seeping through cracks in the earth's crust and eroding away the underground stone. Eons of this abrasive action created hundreds of caves and passageways, and from the ceilings, where ground-water has percolated through, myriad colorful stalactites.

A hundred and fifty miles of Mammoth Cave have been explored, and there may well be hundreds more that link this great system to others in this section of the country. The cave was designated a national park in 1926 after years of controversy over land acquisitions, and attitudes in these Kentucky hills still reflect the bitter disputes between the federal government and private enterprise.

"The Rotunda" in Mammoth Cave

LOUISIANA

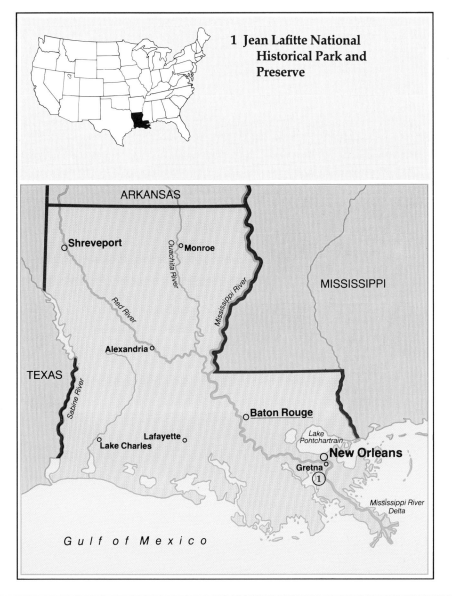

1 Jean Lafitte National Historical Park and Preserve

ARKANSAS

Shreveport

Monroe

Ouachita River

Red River

Mississippi River

MISSISSIPPI

Alexandria

TEXAS

Sabine River

Baton Rouge

Lafayette
Lake Charles

Lake Pontchartrain

New Orleans

Gretna
①

Mississippi River Delta

Gulf of Mexico

Jean Lafitte National Historical Park

c/o Municipal Auditorium, 1201 St. Peter's Street, New Orleans, LA 70116
504/589-3882

French Quarter Unit visitor center at 527 St. Ann Street on Jackson Square, New Orleans; complex directions to other units available. Visitor centers, exhibits, guided tours, self-guiding tours/trails, picnicking, hiking, boating, fishing, hunting, bicycling, handicap access to restrooms/visitor centers; bookstore by Eastern National Park and Monument Association. Accommodations in greater New Orleans area.

This park preserves significant examples of natural and historical resources of the Mississippi delta. The Chalmette Unit, where American forces were victorious in the Battle of New Orleans in the War of 1812, contains the Chalmette National Cemetery. The French Quarter Unit provides an introduction to the culture of the Mississippi Delta region and includes a visitor center on Jackson Square. The Barrataria Unit, 15 miles south of New Orleans, focuses on the ecology of the Mississippi river delta.

Bustling present day naval activity on the Mississippi contrasts with a gracious relic of a bygone age at Jean Lafitte National Historical Park and Preserve

MAINE

1 Acadia National Park
2 Appalachian National Scenic Trail

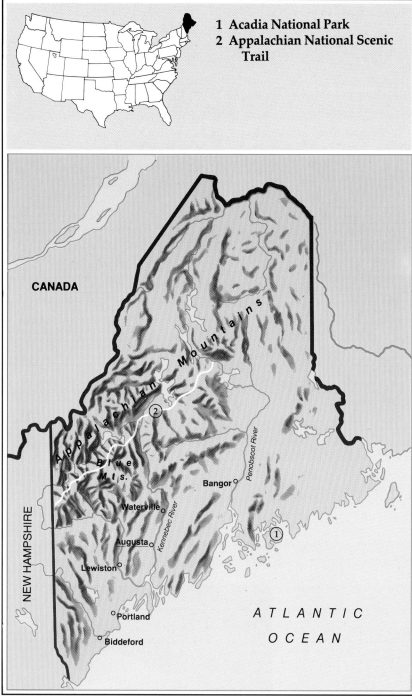

CANADA

Appalachian Mountains

Blue Mts.

NEW HAMPSHIRE

Bangor

Penobscot River

Waterville

Kennebec River

Augusta

Lewiston

Portland

Biddeford

ATLANTIC OCEAN

One of the many moods of sea and shore at Acadia National Park

Acadia National Park

PO Box 177, Bar Harbor, ME 04609
207/288-3338

On ME 3, 47 miles southeast of Bangor, Schoodic Peninsula; only part of the park on the mainland is accessible via ME 186. Visitor center, exhibits, guided tours, self-guiding trails, picnicking, camping, hiking, mountain climbing, horseback riding, swimming, boating, fishing, bicycling, snowmobile route, cabin rental, handicap access to campgrounds/restrooms/visitor center; bookstore by Eastern National Park and Monument Association. Food and supplies available in park; accommodations at Bar Harbor, Northeast Harbor, Ellsworth and Southeast Harbor.

Acadia, as the name suggests, was French before it was English and then American. French frigates hid from English men-of-war in Frenchman Bay, screened by the Porcupine Islands. The French and English battled for possession of North America from 1613 until 1760. French explorer Samuel de Champlain sailed into the bay in 1604 and named this Mount Desert Island because of its landmark bare top. Between the sea and the forested mountains here is the small, fascinating, almost nether world of the tidal zone. Twice daily

exposed to air and drowned by sea water, it is a world of specially adapted organisms. Tidepools, pockets of seawater stranded in rock basins, are microhabitats brimming with life and exposed to view. In these natural aquariums you can watch marine animals going about their business. This life zone is amplified here by Acadia's tides, which vary from 9 to 14 feet, averaging 11 to 12 feet. It is the primeval meeting place of earth and water.

Behind the sea lie Acadia's forests and mountains, made easy for exploring by the 43-mile system of carriage paths. They offer stunning views of Somes Sound and Frenchman Bay; and they lead you along beaver-dammed brooks. The grades are gentle, but the vistas are long. The loop road around Eagle Land is a bicycle path.

The story of the people who lived on this island when Champlain first saw it is told in the Abbe Museum at Sieur de Monts Spring with Indian artifacts and exhibits. The Islesford Museum, on Little Cranberry Island, reveals life in the nineteenth and early twentieth centuries with ship models, tools and pictures.

Villages near the park present the variety of life-styles on the island today. Northeast Harbor shelters sailboats, large and small, and a summer colony. Bar Harbor caters to tourists, offering many accommodations and amusements. Bass Harbor and Southwest Harbor and Winter Harbor at Schoodic retain more of the traditional flavor of Maine coastal villages. Those who earn livings from the sea – whether lobstering, fishing, building boats, or guarding the coast – tie up here. And canneries, lobster pounds, and boatyards have not yet been replaced by summer homes and motels.

This national park is unusual because it was neither carved out of public lands nor bought with public funds. It was envisioned and donated through the efforts of private citizens. Many people loved Mount Desert Island, Schoodic Peninsula, and the nearby islands. Maine residents and summer visitors alike donated their time and resources to preserve Acadia's beauty.

Mountain laurel, Acadia National Park

Acadia National Park is ideal for an "away-from-it-all" vacation

Appalachian National Scenic Trail

Appalachian Trail Conference, PO Box 807, Harpers Ferry, WV 25425
304/535-6331

Contact the Appalachian Trail Conference for information.

The ancient Appalachian Trail runs some 2,000 miles from Mount Katahdin in Maine, through New Hampshire, Massachusetts, Vermont, Connecticut, New York, New Jersey, Pennsylvania, Maryland, West Virginia, Virginia, Tennessee and North Carolina to Springer Mountain in Georgia.

The rocky coast of Maine at Acadia National Park

MARYLAND

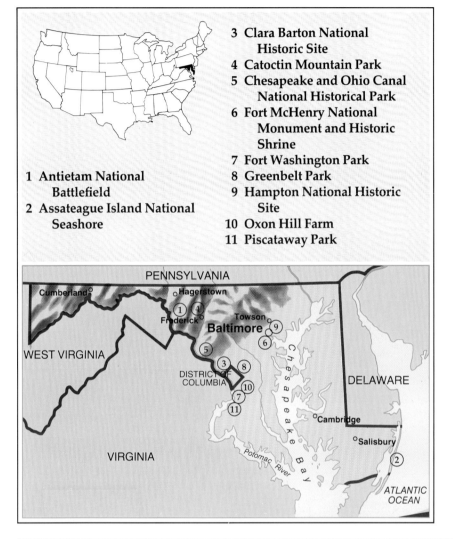

3 Clara Barton National
   Historic Site
4 Catoctin Mountain Park
5 Chesapeake and Ohio Canal
   National Historical Park
6 Fort McHenry National
   Monument and Historic
   Shrine
7 Fort Washington Park
8 Greenbelt Park
9 Hampton National Historic
   Site
10 Oxon Hill Farm
11 Piscataway Park

1 Antietam National
  Battlefield
2 Assateague Island National
  Seashore

Antietam National Battlefield

PO Box 158, Sharpsburg, MD 21782
301/432-5124

On MD 65, north of Sharpsburg. Visitor center, exhibits, guided tours, self-guiding tours, picnicking, camping, hiking, bicycling, handicap access to campground/restrooms/visitor center; bookstore by Parks and History Association. Accommodations in Keedysville, 3 miles north of park on MD 34, and along nearby US 40.

This lovely and serene park commemorates the bloodiest single day of the Civil War, September 17, 1862, when more than 26,000 men were killed or wounded in a ferocious but inconclusive all-day struggle in the Battle of Antietam (or Sharpsburg). Some 41,000 southerners under General Robert E. Lee were pitted against the 87,000-man Federal Army of the Potomac under General George B. McClellan.

Lee's failure to carry the war to the enemy's territory made Great Britain postpone recognizing the Confederate government. The battle also gave President Abraham Lincoln the opportunity to issue the Emancipation Proclamation, which on January 1, 1863, declared free all slaves in states still in rebellion against the Union. From that point on the Civil War had a dual purpose – to preserve the Union and to end slavery.

Below left *The wild ponies of Assateague Island National Seashore*

Below right *A rail fence along Bloody Lane on the Antietam National Battlefield in Maryland, site of the bloodiest single day of the American Civil War*

Assateague Island National Seashore

Route 2, Box 294, Berlin, MD 21811
301/641-1441; 804/336-6577 for Virginia District office

Visitor center at extreme ends of island – on north near Ocean City, MD, on south opposite Chincoteague Island. Visitor centers, exhibits, guided tours, self-guiding trails, picnicking, camping, backcountry permits, swimming, boating, fishing, hunting, handicap access to campgrounds/restrooms/visitor centers; bookstore by Eastern National Park and Monument Association. Accommodations at Chincoteague, VA and Ocean City, MD.

Assateague is a 37-mile-long, low barrier island, named by native Americans, roamed by wild ponies and filled with magnificent dunes, bird sanctuaries and grasslands and marshes. Assateague is a product of the sea, made of sand raised from a gently sloping ocean floor by the action of waves. The island's origins and continued reshaping give it a restless, distant mood akin to the sea more than the mainland.

Visitors to Assateague soon take to the lure of sparkling beaches, mild surf and moderate temperatures; forests and bayside marshes invite discovery. Birdwatchers, fishermen, canoeists and beachcombers are drawn here year-round – indeed spring and autumn, with brisk nights and placid days, give you a chance to avoid the crowds of summer beachgoers. Seashells and other cast-offs from the ocean washed up by winter storms are a part of the excitement and intrigue of Assateague.

Legend long attributed the famed Assateague ponies to horses that swam ashore from a wrecked Spanish galleon. Recent research reveals that the original horses were much smaller, but they interbred with those that were imported from the mainland by Eastern Shore planters in the mid-seventeenth century to graze on the island. During three centuries nature selected those animals best adapted to the island's harsh environment. Today's ponies are still smaller than horses, shaggy and very sturdy, and they are a very popular attraction, particularly when it comes to round-up time in July in the Virginia section.

The flat landscape, sturdy plant life clinging to the sandy soil and grazing wild ponies typify Assateague Island

Clara Barton National Historic Site

5801 Oxford Road, Glen Echo, MD 20812
301/492-6246

Adjacent to Glen Echo Park. Guided tours; bookstore by Parks and History Association. Accommodations in greater Washington area, eight miles away.

Built in 1891, this 38-room home of American Red Cross founder Clara Barton was the headquarters of that organization for seven years. Miss Barton lived her last twenty years here at Glen Echo on the outskirts of Washington.

Catoctin Mountain Park

Thurmont, MD 21788
301/824-2574

Visitor center on MD 77, 3 miles off US 15 north of Frederick. Visitor center, museum, exhibits, guided tours, self-guiding trails, picnicking, camping, hiking, mountain climbing, fishing, cross-country skiing, cabin rental, handicap access to campgrounds/restrooms/visitor center; bookstore by Parks and History Association. Accommodations at Thurmont.

On Catoctin Mountain one can read the story of a group of people and the effect they had on the land written in old stone fences, logging roads and the growth that now covers the land. This wonderful mountain retreat is filled with the spirits of early American pioneers, where now there are campsites, hiking trails, conducted nature walks, all for those who get away from the busy metropolitan areas nearby.

Chesapeake and Ohio Canal National Historical Park

PO Box 4, Sharpsburg, MD 21782
301/739-4200

Visitor centers at Great Falls Tavern, 11710 MacArthur Boulevard, Potomac, MD; 108 West Main Street, Hancock, MD; North Branch, 6 miles south of Cumberland, off MD 51. Visitor centers, museum, exhibits, guided tours, self-guiding trails, picnicking, camping, hiking, horseback riding, boating, fishing, ice skating, bicycling, handicap access to restrooms/visitor center; bookstore by Parks and History Association. Accommodations in Washington, DC, Hancock, MD, Cumberland, MD and other communities along I-70.

The Chesapeake and Ohio Canal was begun as a proposed waterway along the established Potomac and trans-Allegheny trade route from Georgetown in the District of Columbia to the Ohio river through the Potomac Valley. Construction was started on July 4, 1828, but on the same day work was also started on the Baltimore and Ohio Railroad. By 1850 the canal had only reached Cumberland; the B&O had won and further construction on the canal was stopped. It stayed in use until 1924, however, bringing coal and other goods down to Washington.

Until 1938, when it was turned over to the National Park Service, the canal suffered greatly from decay and storm damage. While hurricanes and floods still take their toll, the entire canal and its towpath have been stabilized and enlarged. The towpath is used for hiking, jogging and in the lower sections for canal boat rides with mules pulling the boats along as they did years ago.

Left *The charmingly sited museum of the history of the Chesapeake and Ohio Canal*

Below *Kayaking, one of the water-borne sports to be enjoyed on the Chesapeake and Ohio Canal*

Fort McHenry National Monument and Historic Shrine

East Fort Avenue, Baltimore, MD 21230
301/962-4290

Access via East Fort Avenue, 3 miles from center of Baltimore. Visitor center, museum, exhibits, guided tours, self-guiding tours, picnicking, handicap access to restrooms/visitor center. Accommodations in Baltimore.

The successful American defense of this fort in the War of 1812, September 13-14, 1814, inspired Francis Scott Key to write "The Star Spangled Banner." Key, who had gone to a British ship in the Patapsco river to secure the release of a friend, was trapped when the 25-hour bombardment began. The next morning, seeing the Stars and Stripes still flying from the fort, so the story goes, Key wrote the words to the song which later became the national anthem.

Fort Washington Park

c/o National Capital Parks-East, 1900 Anacostia Drive, SE, PO Box 38104, Washington, DC 20020
301/292-2112

On Fort Washington Road, 3 miles from Indian Head Highway. (MD 210), off I-495. Visitor center, exhibits, guided tours, self-guiding tours; bookstore by Parks and History Association. Accommodations in greater Washington area.

Fort Washington occupies the site of an earlier fortification erected for the defense of Washington. Altered only slightly since 1824, it exemplifies early nineteenth-century coastal defense.

Greenbelt Park

6501 Greenbelt Road, Greenbelt, MD 20770
301/344-3948

Take Exit 23 off I-95 on the Capital Beltway at Kenilworth Avenue (MD 201) toward Bladensburg and follow signs to park. Guided tours, self-guiding trails, picnicking, camping, hiking, handicap access to campgrounds/restrooms. Accommodations in greater Washington.

Greenbelt Park, 12 miles northeast of Washington, provides a rural retreat and a refuge for native plants and animals. It has 12 miles of marked trails in 1,100 acres of forested land, with facilities for hiking and camping.

Hampton National Historic Site

535 Hampton Lane, Towson, MD 21204
301/823-7054

Hampton Lane is off Dulaney Valley Road (MD 146) at Towson, just off I-695, the Baltimore Beltway. Exhibits, guided house tours, self-guiding tours; bookstore by Historic Hampton, Inc. Tearoom serves lunch, accommodations in Towson and greater Baltimore.

One of the largest and more ornate of the preserved mansions of the post-Revolution period (1790), with a complex of historic outbuildings, English formal gardens and specimen trees on a 60-acre tract occupied by the Maryland Ridgely family from 1788 until 1948.

Oxon Hill Farm

c/o National Capital Parks-East, 1900 Anacostia Drive, SE, Washington, DC 20020
301/839-1177

Access via Exit 3-A (Oxon Hill Road) off I-95. Exhibits, picnicking. Accommodations in the greater Washington area.

Especially attractive to children, Oxen Hill Farm is typical of the Maryland and Virginia farms at the end of the nineteenth century. It includes pastures, woodland, farm buildings and equipment and animals.

Piscataway Park

c/o National Capital Parks-East, 1900 Anacostia Drive, SE, Washington, DC 20020
301/472-9227

Access from Capital Beltway (I-495) exit 3-A; go south on Indian Head Highway (Route 210) for 10 miles to Bryan Point Road, then west 4 miles to Potomac river. Visitor center, farm animals, woodland foot trail, picnicking at Saylor Memorial Grove, fishing pier. Accommodations available throughout Maryland suburbs of Washington.

Preserves the tranquil view of the Potomac river's Maryland shore as seen from Mount Vernon, George Washington's home. National Colonial Farm, an agricultural-historical project of Accokeek Foundation, provides exhibits and demonstrations of farming methods, crops and livestock of a modest tidewater farm in the mid-eighteenth century.

The Chesapeake and Ohio Canal as it runs along the Potomac River from Georgetown in the District of Columbia to Cumberland, Maryland

MASSACHUSETTS

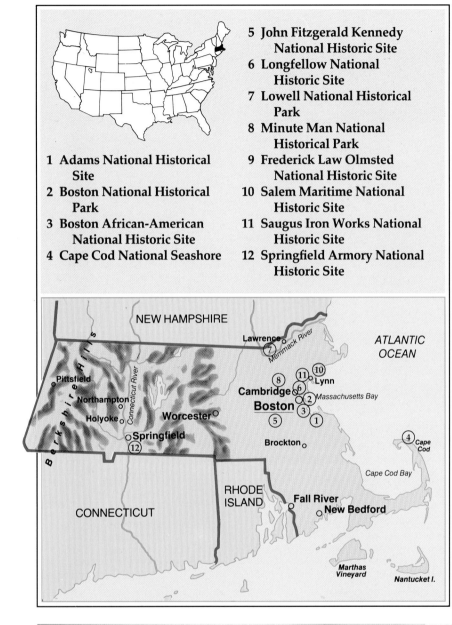

1 **Adams National Historical Site**
2 **Boston National Historical Park**
3 **Boston African-American National Historic Site**
4 **Cape Cod National Seashore**
5 **John Fitzgerald Kennedy National Historic Site**
6 **Longfellow National Historic Site**
7 **Lowell National Historical Park**
8 **Minute Man National Historical Park**
9 **Frederick Law Olmsted National Historic Site**
10 **Salem Maritime National Historic Site**
11 **Saugus Iron Works National Historic Site**
12 **Springfield Armory National Historic Site**

Adams National Historic Site

135 Adams Street, Quincy, MA 02269
617/773-1177

Adams Street and Newport Avenue, just off Quincy Center. Park open April 19 to November 10. Entrance fee; guided tours. Accommodations in Quincy and greater Boston areas.

The home of Presidents John Adams and John Quincy Adams, of US Minister to Great Britain Charles Francis Adams, and of the writers and historians Henry Adams and Brooks Adams, this house reflects the influence of each of these distinguished men. The park also includes the birthplaces of the two presidents and the United First Parish Church, built by the Adams family.

Boston African-American National Historic Site

c/o National Park Service, 15 State Street, Boston, MA 02109
617/242-5625

Information available at National Park Service headquarters, 15 State Street. Guided tours offered by Museum of Afro American History, Box 5, Roxbury, MA 02119.

Established in 1980 as a national historic site, the African Meeting House (1806) is the oldest black church building standing in this nation. The 1½-mile Black Heritage Trail connects the church with 14 other buildings associated with Boston's early black community.

Four generations of the Adams family lived here, beginning with the second president of the United States

Boston National Historical Park

Charlestown Navy Yard, Boston, MA 02129
617/242-5644

Museums, exhibits, guided tours, self-guiding tours, picnicking, handicap access to restrooms and some sites; bookstore at 15 State Street (National Park Service headquarters) by Eastern National Park and Monument Association. Accommodations in immediate area.

Eight major historic sites in the heart of Boston make up this complex park. They are all operated and maintained by public and private organizations, but coordinated and managed according to National Park Service regulations.

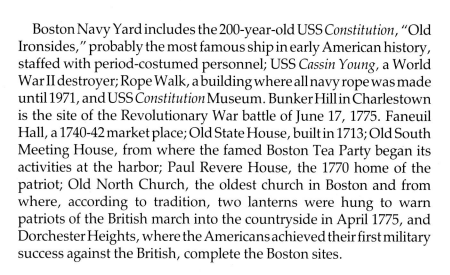

Boston Navy Yard includes the 200-year-old USS *Constitution*, "Old Ironsides," probably the most famous ship in early American history, staffed with period-costumed personnel; USS *Cassin Young*, a World War II destroyer; Rope Walk, a building where all navy rope was made until 1971, and USS *Constitution* Museum. Bunker Hill in Charlestown is the site of the Revolutionary War battle of June 17, 1775. Faneuil Hall, a 1740-42 market place; Old State House, built in 1713; Old South Meeting House, from where the famed Boston Tea Party began its activities at the harbor; Paul Revere House, the 1770 home of the patriot; Old North Church, the oldest church in Boston and from where, according to tradition, two lanterns were hung to warn patriots of the British march into the countryside in April 1775, and Dorchester Heights, where the Americans achieved their first military success against the British, complete the Boston sites.

"Old Ironsides," the USS Constitution, *built in 1797, is docked in the Charlestown Navy Yard (Boston Naval Shipyard), and outfitted, complete with sailors in period uniform, as it appeared in 1803 action*

Cape Cod National Seashore

South Wellfleet, MA 02663
617/349-3785

Visitor centers at Salt Pond in Eastham on MA 6 and Province Lands in Provincetown on Race Point Road. Entrance fee; visitor centers, guided tours, self-guiding trails, picnicking, backcountry permits, hiking, horseback riding, swimming, boating, fishing, hunting, bicycling, snowmobiling, handicap access to restrooms/visitor centers; bookstore by Eastern National Park and Monument Association. Food and supplies available in park; accommodations in areas serving the park.

Cape Cod is many things to many people – swimming and sunbathing, fishing and whaling, clams and cranberries, writers and artists, cottages and shops, Pilgrims and Indians. All are part of the ambience and charm that attract thousands of tourists to the Cape each year. To help protect this environment the National Seashore was established in 1961 between Chatham and Provincetown.

The Cape is a glacial deposit that is constantly undergoing natural changes as winds and water move sand along the shorelines, tearing away one place and building another. One can get a good sense of how quickly the land is diminishing at the Marconi Wireless Station site at Wellfleet, where the Cape is only a mile wide. Much of the cliff has eroded away since Guglielmo Marconi first built his towers there in 1901. Another place to sense nature's power is near Provincetown where giant dunes are encroaching on the highway. Changing too, though at a much slower pace, is the Cape Cod Bay shoreline. Great Island, where whalers used to congregate, is now connected to the peninsula; it can be explored by a trail.

Cape Cod's human history is just as rich as its natural history. In the Provincetown area one can see where the Prilgrims landed in 1620 before sailing on across the bay to Plymouth. Five lighthouses within the Seashore attest to a long tradition of lifesaving activities, and the Eastham home of Edward Penniman denotes the once profitable whaling business, another chapter in the Cape Cod story.

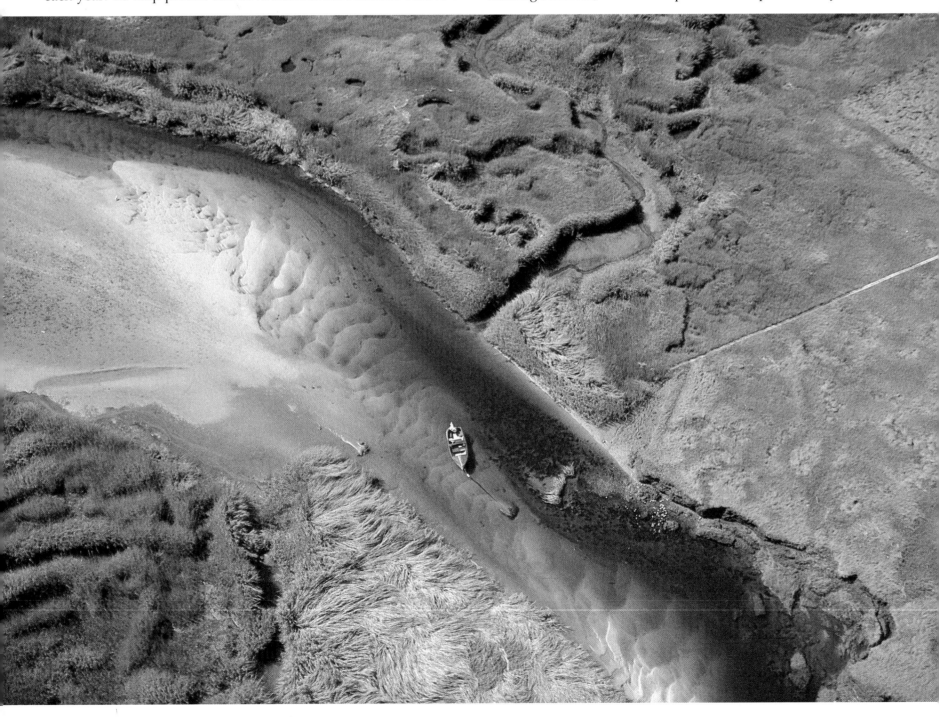

Right *Plant life is slowly returning to Cape Cod's fragile environment, which had been damaged by human abuse*

Below left *A shallow inlet on the sandy Cape Cod seashore to which sturdy plant life clings*

Below *Aerial view of the marshes and sand spit at Cape Cod*

John Fitzgerald Kennedy National Historic Site

83 Beals Street, Brookline, MA 02146
617/566-7937

Entrance fee; exhibits, guided tours; bookstore by Eastern National Park and Monument Association. Accommodations in greater Boston area.

This house is the birthplace and boyhood home of the thirty-fifth President. The family lived here until 1921.

Right *Built in 1759 by a wealthy Loyalist, this house was used as headquarters for the Continental Army by George Washington in 1775. Henry Wadsworth Longfellow lived here from 1837 to 1882*

Below *President John Fitzgerald Kennedy was born in this house on May 29, 1917, and spent the first four years of his childhood here*

Longfellow National Historic Site

105 Brattle Street, Cambridge, MA 02138
617/876-4491

Entrance fee; exhibits, guided tours; bookstore by Eastern National Park and Monument Association. Accommodations in Cambridge.

The poet Henry Wadsworth Longfellow lived here from 1837 to 1882 while professor of modern languages at Harvard. Built in 1759, the house had been General Washington's headquarters during the siege of Boston in 1775-76. It is furnished with mid- to late nineteenth-century pieces.

Lowell National Historical Park

171 Merrimack Street, Lowell, MA 01852
617/459-1000

Visitor center at 246 Market Street. Visitor center, exhibits, guided tours, self-guiding tours, picnicking, handicap access to restrooms/ visitor center; bookstore by Eastern National Park and Monument Association. Accommodations in Lowell.

America's first planned industrial community is commemorated by this park at the heart of the city. Elements of Lowell's factories, canal system, and the lifestyle of its people are preserved here.

Minute Man National Historical Park

PO Box 160, 174 Liberty Street, Concord, MA 01742
617/369-6993

North Bridge visitor center off Liberty Street in Concord; Battle Road visitor center off MA 2A in Lexington. Entrance fee; visitor centers, museum, exhibits, guided tours, self-guiding tours; bookstore by Eastern National Park and Monument Association. Accommodations in Concord, Lexington, Acton and Bedford.

This is the site of the fighting on April 19, 1775, that opened the American Revolution. The park includes North Bridge, the Minute Man statue by Daniel Chester French, four miles of Battle Road between Lexington and Concord, and "The Wayside," home of Nathaniel Hawthorne.

Frederick Law Olmsted National Historic Site

99 Warren Street, Brookline, MA 02146
617/566-1689

Just off MA 9 at Warren and Dudley Streets in Brookline, 4 miles from downtown Boston. Visitor center, exhibits, guided tours, bookstore by Eastern National Park and Monument Association. Accommodations in greater Boston area.

The great conservationist, landscape architect and founder of city planning lived and worked here at "Fairstead." An archival collection of more than 63,000 original photographs with 150,000 drawings and plans is housed at the site.

Salem Maritime National Historic Site

Custom House, Derby Street, Salem, MA 01970
617/744-4323

Visitor center at Custom House; park is 20 miles northeast of Boston.
Visitor center, exhibits, guided tours, self-guiding tours, bicycling;
bookstore by Eastern National Park and Monument Association.
Food available in park; accommodations at Salem, Beverly,
Marblehead, and Boston's North Shore area.

Structures preserved here date from the era when Salem ships opened
trade with ports of the Far East. Some of these of maritime significance
include the Custom House where Nathaniel Hawthorne worked,
Derby Wharf, the Bonded Warehouse and the West India Goods
Store.

Far left top *Daniel Chester French's famous statue of the "Minute Man" stands
guard at the North Bridge, Concord*

Far left bottom *It was here at the Old North Bridge that the first British soldier
fell in the American Revolution on April 19, 1775*

Below *Salem Maritime National Historic Site represents New England's gateway
to the world in the late 18th century when foreign trade was the very heart of the
nation's economic structure*

Saugus Iron Works National Historic Site

244 Central Street, Saugus, MA 01906
617/233-0050

2 blocks from Saugus Center. Visitor center, museum, exhibits, guided tours, self-guiding tours, handicap access to visitor center; bookstore by Eastern National Park and Monument Association. Accommodations on US 1, 1 mile from park.

This reconstruction of the first integrated iron works in North America begun in 1646 includes the iron works, furnace, forge and rolling and slitting mill.

Springfield Armory National Historic Site

1 Armory Square, Springfield, MA 01105
413/734-6477

Off State Street, in downtown Springfield. Visitor center, museum, exhibits, handicap access to restrooms. Accommodations in immediate area.

From 1794 to 1968 the Springfield Armory was a center for the manufacture of US military small arms and the scene of many important technological advances. A large weapons museum is now housed in the original Main Arsenal Building.

Below *Financed by the American Iron and Steel Institute, the National Park Service has reconstructed a large portion of this 17th century iron works-village*

Right *The Saugus blast furnace very much as it was from about 1648 to 1670*

MICHIGAN

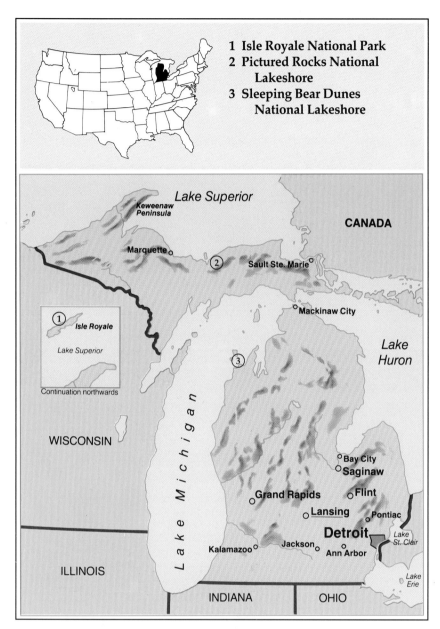

1 Isle Royale National Park
2 Pictured Rocks National Lakeshore
3 Sleeping Bear Dunes National Lakeshore

Isle Royale National Park

87 North Ripley Street, Houghton, MI 49931
906/482-3310

Access by boat from Houghton, May to October. Visitor center, exhibits, guided tours, self-guiding trails, picnicking, camping, backcountry permits, hiking, swimming, boating, fishing, cabin rental, handicap access to campgrounds/restrooms/visitor center; bookstore by Isle Royale Natural History Association. Accommodations available in park and in Houghton.

Isle Royale is an island in many ways: it is an island of wilderness and home to wolves in a modern world, an island in time, where you operate on natural time and experience the rhythms of light and dark. Days are measured by footsteps, possibly under a backpack. Walking the island you are struck by its striated layout. Its elongated forested-rock and lake patterns that parallel its backbone, the Greenstone

Ridge. The island, it seems, must have been forcibly combed from northeast to southwest. The surface visible from the island's heights is the product of 10,000 years of natural sculpting, soil-building, and plant-pioneering and succession. Beneath the ponds, the forests, and the light soil covering, however, is a story which must be told not in increments of centuries, but in millions and billions of years. The ridge-and-trough pattern of the rocks is the work of millions of years, predating even the formation of Lake Superior and its islands. Some 1.2 billion years ago a great rift in the earth's crust, which may have extended from here southward to the Gulf of Mexico, poured forth molten lava covering thousands of square miles and the land along the rift zone sank to form the Superior Basin, which has shaped all subsequent geological events in the region. The rock record of this cataclysmic happening – the volcanics, sandstones, and conglomerates – forms Isle Royale's bedrock today. Clues to the island's past abound. Smoothed, rounded and even grooved rocks witness the crushing power of the last major glaciation, known as the Wisconsin. It ended here only a few thousand years ago.

On the southwestern part of the island, where this glacier paused in its retreat, are small linear hills made of its deposits. On the Stoll Trail out toward Scoville Point you pass three small pits in the rock, a clue to the Indians who mined copper on the island. The Indians came to the island only in mild seasons, taking what resources they could, and leaving before winter. The Indians were mining here by about 2000 BC, continuing for 1,000 years, and Isle Royale and Superior area copper made its way by trade as far as New York, Illinois and Indiana. Indians were probably most active from 800 to 1600. By the 1840s the only Indian encampments white miners encountered were a maple sugaring camp on Sugar Mountain and a seasonal fishing camp on Grace Island.

Aquatic environments abound both on and around the island. In fact some 80 percent of the national park is under water, as shallow warm ponds, streams, and rivers, and the deep, cold forbidding Lake Superior waters. Commercial fishing has been one of the main economic activities on the island since before 1800. Since about 1840 it has been a largely individual enterprise. The major economic species were lake trout, whitefish, and herring lurking in the range of water depths and bottoms along miles of Isle Royale shoreline. Most of the commercial fishing enterprises had closed by mid-century; that world is now preserved by a few fishermen and in historical programs conducted by the National Park Service. Sport fishing has now replaced it: anglers catch lake, brook and rainbow trout; northern pike; walleye and yellow perch. Spring and fall produce the biggest catches, but fishing is considered good throughout the season.

Isle Royale is indeed an island of superlatives for wilderness and beauty.

Right above *The shores of Lake Ritchie in the heart of Isle Royale National Park, Lake Superior*

Right *Pictured Rocks National Lakeshore, one of America's jewels on the largest freshwater lake in the world, Lake Superior. Here multicolored sandstone cliffs rise to heights of 200 feet*

Pictured Rocks National Lakeshore

PO Box 40, Munising, MI 49862
906/387-2607

Southeast of Marquette on M 28. Visitor center, exhibits, self-guiding trails, picnicking, camping, backcountry permits, hiking, swimming, boating, fishing, hunting, snowmobile route, cross-country ski trail, handicap access to restrooms/visitor center; bookstore by Eastern National Park and Monument Association. Accommodations at Munising and Grand Marais.

The multicolored sandstone cliffs, broad beaches, sand dunes, waterfalls, inland lakes, ponds and marshes all make Pictured Rocks a marvelous scenic area on Lake Superior. The Pictured Rocks, for which the park is named, rise directly from the lake to heights of 50 to 200 feet and stretch 15 miles along the lake to northeast of the town of Munising. This wall of rock has been sculpted into caves, arches and formations that for all the world loom like castles and fortresses. The play of light on the layers of rock and cliffs changes with each passing hour. The ramparts of the Pictured Rocks give way to a sand and pebble strand known as Twelve-Mile Beach. The waters of Lake Superior remain cold the year round and only the hardiest souls venture into the lake, and then only briefly.

Sleeping Bear Dunes National Lakeshore

400 Main Street, Frankfort, MI 49635
616/352-9611

On MI 22, on the shores of Lake Michigan, north of Frankfort. Visitor center, exhibits, guided tours, self-guiding trails, picnicking, camping, backcountry permits, hiking, swimming, boating, fishing, hunting, cross-country ski trail; bookstore by Eastern National Park and Monument Association. Food available in park; accommodations in Frankfort and Glen Arbor.

On the northwestern shore of Michigan's lower peninsula lies Sleeping Bear Dunes National Lakeshore, a hilly region fringed with massive coastal sand dunes and dotted with clear lakes. It is a diverse landscape, embracing quiet, birch-lined streams, dense beech-maple forests and rugged bluffs towering as high as 460 feet above Lake Michigan. Several miles offshore, surrounded by the unpredictable waters of Lake Michigan, sit the Manitou Islands, tranquil and secluded.

Right *A lighthouse at Sleeping Bear, a vital beacon to travelers on the vast and moody waters of Lake Michigan*

Below *More than 31 miles of towering sand dunes along the shores of Lake Michigan are protected here; the most prominent feature is a massive dune whose appearance gives the site its name*

MINNESOTA

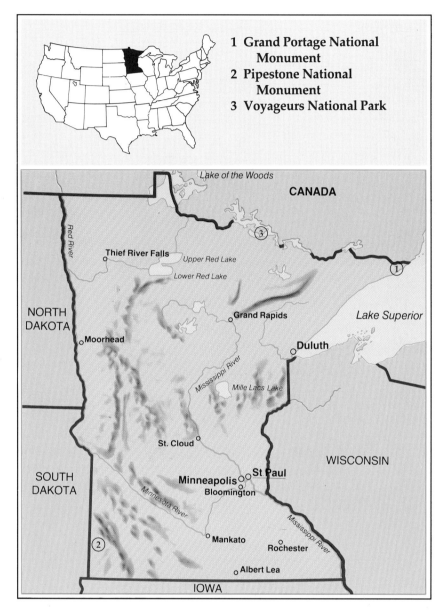

1 Grand Portage National
   Monument
2 Pipestone National
   Monument
3 Voyageurs National Park

Grand Portage National Monument

PO Box 666, Grand Marais, MN 55604
218/387-2788

*On the Grand Portage Chippewa Reservation, off US 61, 36 miles
northeast of Grand Marais, MN.* Visitor center, exhibits, guided tours,
self-guiding trails, picnicking, backcountry permits, hiking, fishing,
cross-country ski trails, handicap access to restrooms/visitor center;
bookstore by Eastern National Park and Monument Association.
Accommodations in Grand Portage and Grand Marais.

The gateway to the northern plains and woodlands for explorers and
traders, this was the "great depot," established in 1778 near the
Canadian border. The monument preserves the strategic 8½-mile
Grand Portage and the Lake Superior post of the North West
Company. The reconstruction here includes the Great Hall of 1797,
operating kitchen and pack warehouse housing three birchbark
canoes.

Pipestone National Monument

PO Box 717, Pipestone, MN 56164
507/825-5463

On US 75, MN 23 and 30, near north boundary of Pipestone. Visitor
center, exhibits, self-guiding trail, handicap access to restrooms/
visitor center; bookstore and pipe sales by Pipestone Indian Shrine
Association. Accommodations in Pipestone.

The red stone quarry preserved by this park is a sacred place to a large
portion of the Indian population of the north central United States.
Called "catlinite," honoring the famed artist-explorer George Catlin
who brought the quarries to the attention of the world in 1836, the red
stone is still used to make ceremonial peace pipes and religious items.
Native Americans demonstrate their craft in the visitor center, where
elaborate peace pipes are sold.

Left *The gray wolf, one of whose habitats is Voyageurs National Park*

Right *The lakes and forest of the north country make Voyageurs National Park one of the unique wilderness areas of the United States*

Voyageurs National Park

PO Box 50, International Falls, MN 56649
218/283-9821

On US 53, north from Duluth. Visitor center, exhibits, guided tours, picnicking, camping, backcountry permits, hiking, swimming, boating, fishing, cross-country ski trail, handicap access to restrooms/visitor center; bookstore by Lake States Interpretive Association. Accommodations in park and at International Falls, Kabetogama Lake, Ash River and Crane Lake.

The name of this national park honors the unique breed of man who came into the north country looking for the beaver in the eighteenth and nineteenth centuries. It is, of course, much more than just a monument to an important chapter in American history, for the trails and forts and camps associated with these extraordinary frontiersmen have long since disappeared. But the lakes and forests they traveled have been little disturbed and here in northern Minnesota, just east of International Falls and along the Canadian border, are more than 200,000 acres of pristine land and sparkling clear water as they saw it.

Much of this land is undeveloped and accessible only by boat and is one of those last vestiges of wilderness America, a microcosm, in effect, of the whole northern region of the country and of the route traveled by the voyageur.

This splendid, unspoiled land is built on the most solid foundation, ancient Precambrian rock laid down billions of years ago and shaved off by giant glaciers. It is a land like no other, interwoven by waterways, lakes of all sizes and shapes, islands big and small, framed by great vertical cliffs and huge boulders dropped by the melting ice of ancient times.

Voyageurs National Park is new and is still being developed as a full-scale park, but everything one could want is here.

Right *A fitting form of transport in the vast wilderness of Voyageurs*

The densely forested islands in the lakes of Voyageurs National Park are unblemished by human development

MISSISSIPPI

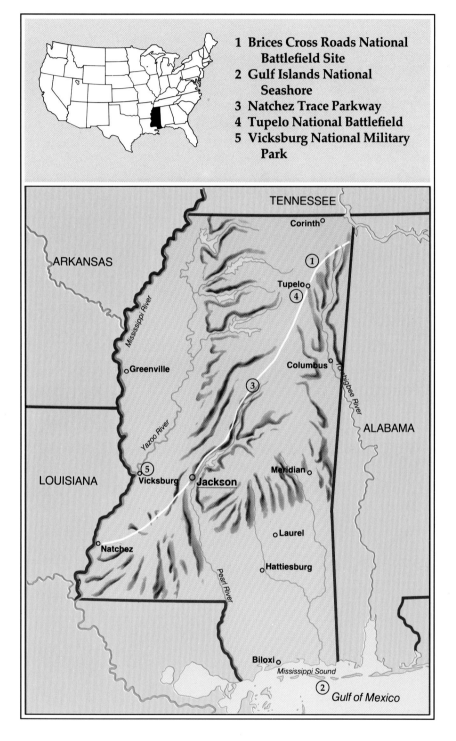

1 Brices Cross Roads National
   Battlefield Site
2 Gulf Islands National
   Seashore
3 Natchez Trace Parkway
4 Tupelo National Battlefield
5 Vicksburg National Military
   Park

Brices Cross Roads National Battlefield Site

c/o Natchez Trace Parkway, Rural Route 1, NT-143, Tupelo, MS 38801
601/842-1572

On MS 370, 6 miles west of Baldwyn. Exhibits; no visitor facilities. Accommodations at Tupelo and Booneville.

One of the smallest sites in the national park system, this one-acre plot commemorates the scene of General Nathan Bedford Forrest's tactical Civil War victory over a large Union force on June 10, 1864.

Gulf Islands National Seashore

3500 Park Road, Ocean Springs, MS 39564 (see also Florida)
601/875-9057

To reach Davis Bayou on mainland in Ocean Springs, follow the signs for the park along US 90. Concession boat trips to West Ship Island from Gulfport and Biloxi. See the Florida Unit for complete information on activities for both the Florida and Mississippi units.

Sparkling beaches, historic ruins and wildlife sanctuaries accessible only by boat can be found on the offshore islands of this unit near Pascagoula and Biloxi, MS. On the mainland there is an urban park with a nature trail, picnic area and a campground at Ocean Springs.

Far right top *Sunset on the grassy marshes of Gulf Island National Seashore*

Far right *The sand on the beach of Horn Island in the Mississippi unit of Gulf Islands National Seashore can give an illusion of being frosted over*

Right *A monument to the Civil War battle on June 10, 1864, at Brices Cross Roads*

Natchez Trace Parkway

(Mississippi, Alabama, Tennessee)
Rural Route 1, NT 143, Tupelo, MS 38801
601/842-1572

Visitor center 5 miles north of Tupelo at intersection of Natchez Trace Parkway and US 45N. Visitor center, exhibits, guided tours, self-guiding trails, picnicking, camping, hiking, horseback riding, swimming, boating, fishing, handicap access to campgrounds/restrooms/visitor center; bookstore by Eastern National Park and Monument Association. Supplies available in park; accommodations at Natchez, Port Gibson, Jackson, Tupelo, and Cherokee.

The story of Natchez Trace is the story of the people who used it – the Indians who traded and hunted along it; the "Kaintuck" boatmen who pounded it into a rough wilderness road on their way back from trading expeditions to Spanish Natchez and New Orleans; and the post riders, government officials and soldiers who from 1800 to 1830 made it a link between Mississippi Territory and the fledgling United States. Natchez Trace Parkway preserves a good part of the original frontier road. When completed the 450-mile parkway will roughly follow the trace through the States of Mississippi, Alabama and Tennessee, connecting the cities of Natchez, Jackson, Tupelo and Nashville.

Tupelo National Battlefield

c/o Natchez Trace Parkway, Rural Route 1, NT-143, Tupelo, MS 38801
601/842-1572

On MS 6, within city limits of Tupelo. Exhibits; no visitor facilities. Accommodations in immediate area.

This one-acre tract in Tupelo honors both Union and Confederate soldiers who died in the battle to protect Sherman's supply line during the famed march to Atlanta in July 1864.

Vicksburg National Military Park

PO Box 349, Vicksburg, MS 39180
601/636-0583

On US 80, just outside Vicksburg. Visitor center, exhibits, self-guiding trail, picnicking, handicap access to restrooms/visitor center; bookstore by Eastern National Park and Monument Association. Accommodations in immediate area.

Between Cairo, Illinois, and the Gulf of Mexico the Mississippi river meanders over a course nearly 1,000 miles long. During the Civil War control of this stretch of the river was of vital importance to the federal government, giving passage for Union troops and supplies into the South and isolating Texas and Arkansas and most of Louisiana, comprising nearly half the land area of the Confederacy and a region on which the South depended heavily for supplies and recruits.

In the spring of 1863 General Ulysses S. Grant, in an attempt to split the Confederacy, moved against Vicksburg, which eventually surrendered in June.

Below and below left *The old Natchez Trace, the Indian and pioneer trail that linked Nashville, Tennessee and Natchez, Mississippi*

MISSOURI

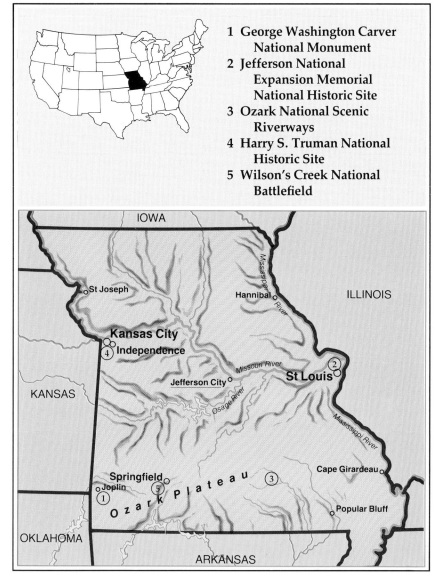

1 George Washington Carver National Monument
2 Jefferson National Expansion Memorial National Historic Site
3 Ozark National Scenic Riverways
4 Harry S. Truman National Historic Site
5 Wilson's Creek National Battlefield

George Washington Carver National Monument

PO Box 38, Diamond, MO 64840
417/325-4151

On County Highway V, 3 miles from Diamond; 65 miles west of Springfield, MO. Visitor center, exhibits, self-guiding trail, picnicking, handicap access to restrooms/visitor center; bookstore by George Washington Carver Birthplace District Association. Accommodations in Diamond and Joplin; campground nearby.

This is the birthplace and childhood home of George Washington Carver, who rose from slavery to become one of America's great pioneer agronomists, botanists and conservationists.

Jefferson National Expansion Memorial National Historic Site

11 North 4th Street, St. Louis, MO 63102
314/425-4465

On waterfront, a short walk from downtown St. Louis. Visitor center, museum, exhibits, handicap access to restrooms/visitor center; visitors may ascend the 630-foot-high arch via elevator cars for an incredible view of the city and the river; bookstore by Jefferson National Expansion Historical Association. Accommodations in area.

The magnificent expression of inner beauty and wisdom on the sculptured face of George Washington Carver

Here, near Gateway Arch, the Missouri river empties into the Mississippi. That is why young Pierre LaClede founded the village of St. Louis here in 1764. He intended it to be a trading center, and the Missouri water highway was vital to any plan to tap the wealth of the west. His judgement proved sound.

In 1803 Lewis and Clark outfitted here for their epic exploration of the Louisiana Purchase. Three years later they returned and reported that the western part of the continent was a fabulous land, thick with beaver. Soon St. Louis became fur trader to the world, and the pleasant park where the arch now stands was an exotic and busy place. This was the gateway to the west. Eero Saarinen's prize-winning, stainless-steel gateway arch now commemorates the pioneers who made their way from the Mississippi into the new uncharted western territory. In the nearby courthouse, Dred Scott sued for freedom in the historic slavery case.

Ozark National Scenic Riverways

PO Box 490, Van Buren, MO 63965
314/323-4236

Visitor center at Powder Mill, 35 miles north of Van Buren, off MO 106. Visitor center, exhibits, guided tours, self-guiding trails, picnicking, camping, hiking, horseback riding, swimming, boating, fishing, hunting, cabin rental, handicap access to campgrounds/restrooms/ visitor center; bookstore by Ozark National Riverways Historical Association. Accommodations in Eminence, Van Buren, Salem, Ellington, Mountain View, Winona and Birch Tree.

For about 140 miles the Current and Jacks Fork rivers flow through a quiet world of bountiful nature. The most notable features of this unique park land are the huge freshwater springs and numerous caves along the way.

Harry S. Truman National Historic Site

c/o Harry S. Truman Library, Independence, MO 64050

On Truman Road, west from I-435 or east from Noland Road. Information center, exhibits, guided tours. Accommodations in Independence.

With the exception of his years in Washington, Harry S. Truman lived in this Victorian house from his marriage in 1919 until his death in 1972. It served as the Summer White House from 1945 until 1953. Mrs. Truman lived here until her death. It was opened to visitors in May 1984.

Wilson's Creek National Battlefield

521 North Highway 60, Republic, MO 65738
417/732-2662

3 miles east of Republic via MO 182. Visitor center, exhibits, self-guiding tours, picnicking, hiking, handicap access to restrooms/ visitor center; bookstore by Eastern National Park and Monument Association. Accommodations in Springfield.

The Confederate victory here on August 10, 1861 was the first major engagement west of the Mississippi, a bitter struggle for the control of Missouri with severe losses on both sides.

The tranquil stretches of the Ozark National Scenic Riverways are ideal for leisurely boating

MONTANA

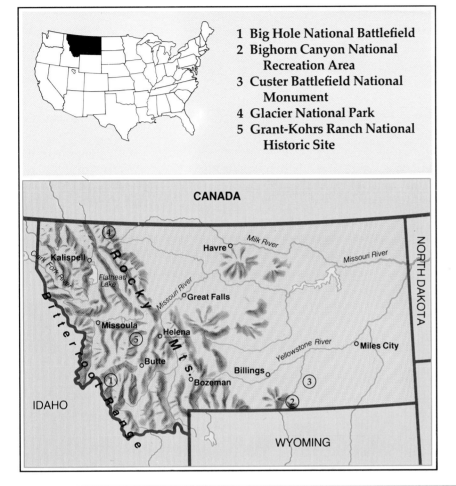

1 Big Hole National Battlefield
2 Bighorn Canyon National Recreation Area
3 Custer Battlefield National Monument
4 Glacier National Park
5 Grant-Kohrs Ranch National Historic Site

Big Hole National Battlefield

PO Box 237, Wisdom, MT 59761
406/689-3155

On MT 43, 10 miles west of Wisdom. Visitor center, exhibits, self-guiding trail, picnicking, fishing; bookstore by Yellowstone Association. Accommodations at Wisdom; Forest Service and private campgrounds nearby.

This is the site of the turning point in the great Indian war of 1877 between the Nez Perce and the US 7th Infantry, when Indian women and children, as well as Indian warriors, were slain by American soldiers. Led by Chief Joseph, the Nez Perce were trapped here as they made their epic march from Idaho. The visitor center offers a panoramic view of the battlefield.

Hidden Lake in the Heart of Glacier National Park

Bighorn Canyon National Recreation Area

PO Box 458, Fort Smith, MT 59035
406/666-2412

Follow MT 313 from Hardin to Yellowtail Dam; 96 miles southeast of Billings. Visitor centers near Lovell, WY, and near Fort Smith, MT. Visitor centers, exhibits, guided tours, self-guiding trails, picnicking, camping, backcountry permits, hiking, swimming, boating, fishing, hunting, snowshoeing, handicap access to campgrounds/restrooms/visitor centers; bookstore by Bighorn Canyon Natural History Association. Supplies available in park; accommodations in Lovell, WY, and in Hardin and Fort Smith, MT.

The 525-foot-high Yellowtail dam on the Bighorn river creates a 71-mile-long reservoir that extends 47 miles through spectacular Bighorn Canyon, which cuts a chasm between the Pryor Mountains on the west and the Bighorn Mountains on the east.

Custer Battlefield National Monument

PO Box 39, Crow Agency, MT 59022
406/638-2522

17 miles from Hardin, via I-90; 70 miles east of Billings. Visitor center, exhibits, guided tours, self-guiding tours, handicap access to visitor center; bookstore by Custer Battlefield Historical and Museum Association. Accommodations in Hardin.

The arrogant and flamboyant George Armstrong Custer, along with five companies of the Seventh Cavalry, died here in the well-known battle of the Little Big Horn in June 1876. The Sioux and Cheyenne reigned supreme on those two fateful summer days, but it was to be their last victory in their struggle against the white man. It was the end of Custer, but the beginning of a myth about the man that has now grown beyond all realistic proportions to his place in history.

Glacier National Park

West Glacier, MT 59936
406/888-5441

On US 2 and 89, and near US 91 and 93. Entrance fee; visitor centers, exhibits, guided tours, self-guiding trails, picnicking, camping, backcountry permits, hiking, mountain climbing, horseback riding, swimming, boating, fishing, cross-country skiing, cabin rental, handicap access to campgrounds/restrooms/visitor centers; bookstore by Glacier Natural History Association.
Accommodations in park and at St. Mary, West Glacier and East Glacier.

The mountains of Glacier National Park are a part of the Rockies, that upheaval of mountain building that began about 75 million years ago and extended from South America through Mexico and the United States and Canada into Alaska and the Aleutians. This vast scenery of rugged peaks, cascading waterfalls, glacial snow masses, clear streams and lakes and lush primitive forests make Glacier one of the great wilderness sanctuaries.

Glacier National Park contains more than a million acres, where bighorn sheep, mountain goat, mule deer, moose and elk roam freely; where hawks and eagles glide majestically overhead; where thousands of species of trees, plants and wildflowers blanket the hills and valleys; and where miles and miles of trails lead visitors into a backcountry filled with wonders. And here is one of the last strongholds of the grizzly bear.

Four great ice ages have worked their way through these mountains, leaving glaciers in the park today which are, alas, rapidly melting away.

Peter Fidler, a scout for the Hudson's Bay Company in 1792, was the first European to see the Glacier area. He found that the Piggan Indian had been here long before and, no doubt, other prehistoric Indians before that. Settlement was slow and tedious through the nineteenth century as rugged terrain and fierce Indian reluctance to yield territory presented barriers, but the coming of the Great Northern Railroad hastened the development of Glacier National Park. Politicians and conservationists joined with the railroad to preserve the area in its natural state. Glacier became a national park on May 11, 1910.

Nowhere is the work of glaciers quite so evident as here in Montana, a place of extraordinary beauty. It has been called the "Crown of the Continent," where the mountains unfold into a panorama of cathedral-like spires.

Grant-Kohrs Ranch National Historic Site

PO Box 790, Deer Lodge, MT 59722
406/846-2070

ON I-90, at the north edge of Deer Lodge, MT. Visitor center, exhibits, guided tours, self-guiding tours, handicap access to restrooms/visitor center; bookstore by Glacier Natural History Association.
Accommodations available in Deer Lodge.

The only fully functional ranch in the national park system, Grant-Kohrs north of Yellowstone preserves a complete cattle ranch headquarters of the type operated in the west between 1850 and 1910: an elegant Victorian ranch house, bunkhouse, granaries, carriage sheds, along with early ranch implements, wagons and sleighs. Summer programs recreate late nineteenth-century ranch activities.

Far left *Iceberg Creek in Glacier National Park displays the distinctive characteristics of a landscape created by the mighty forces of the ice ages*

Left *Mountain goats, seldom-glimpsed inhabitants of Glacier National Park*

NEBRASKA

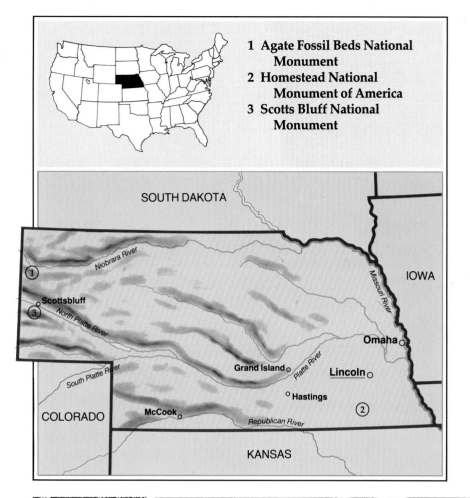

1 Agate Fossil Beds National
   Monument
2 Homestead National
   Monument of America
3 Scotts Bluff National
   Monument

SOUTH DAKOTA

IOWA

Niobrara River

Scottsbluff

North Platte River

Missouri River

Omaha

Grand Island

Platte River

Lincoln

Hastings

South Platte River

COLORADO

McCook

Republican River

KANSAS

Agate Fossil Beds National Monument

c/o Scotts Bluff National Monument, PO Box 427, Gering,
NE 69341
308/668-2211

Off NE 29, near Agate; 30 miles south of Harrison. Visitor center,
exhibits, self-guiding trail, hiking, handicap access to restrooms/
visitor center; bookstore by Oregon Trail Museum Association.
Accommodations in Harrison.

Here are the 20-million-year-old fossils of Miocene mammals, some
exposed in such fashion that one can see them along a self-guiding
foot trail to University and Carnegie hills.

Right *A look at the valley floor from Scotts Bluff, a landmark on the Oregon Trail
in Nebraska*

Below *Agate Fossil Hills with (inset) fossilized remains*

Homestead National Monument of America

Route 3, Beatrice, NE 68310
401/223-3514

Off NE 4, 4½ miles northwest of Beatrice; 50 miles south of Lincoln.
Visitor center, exhibits, guided tours, self-guiding tours, hiking, handicap access to restrooms/visitor center; bookstore by Eastern National Park and Monument Association. Accommodations in Beatrice.

Daniel Freeman was one of the first of a million American citizens who, in 1862, rushed to take advantage of free land offered in the Homestead Act. This monument stands on 160 acres of Freeman's original tract near Beatrice, Nebraska, and commemorates through its buildings and furnishings the struggle to establish a new life on the unknown frontier. The Freeman School is a furnished one-room schoolhouse that served the local community for nearly a century before it was added to the monument.

Scotts Bluff National Monument

PO Box 427, Gering, NE 69341
308/436-4340

On NE 92, 3 miles west of Gering. Entrance fee; visitor center, exhibits, self-guiding tours, hiking, bicycling, handicap access to restrooms/visitor center; bookstore by Oregon Trail Museum Association. Accommodations in Gering and Scotts Bluff.

An 800-foot rocky promontory above the North Platte Valley stood as a landmark for thousands of pioneers as they worked their way west on the Oregon Trail in the mid-1800s. Ruts of the old wagon trail are still visible as they pass Scotts Bluff, named for Hiram Scott, a fur trapper who died in the vicinity about 1828. The Oregon Trail museum tells the story of the westward migration.

The bluff was once a part of the ancient High Plains. Erosion over long periods has cut down the surrounding valleys to their present level, leaving Scotts Bluff and the adjoining hills as remnants of the unbroken plains which now lie farther to the west.

NEVADA

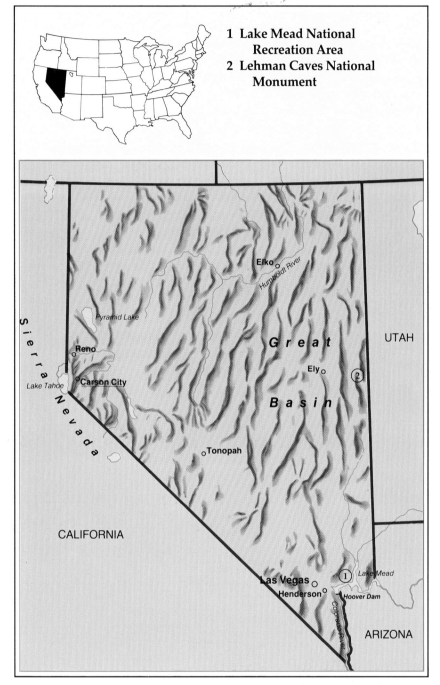

1 Lake Mead National
  Recreation Area
2 Lehman Caves National
  Monument

Elko
Humboldt River
Pyramid Lake
Reno
Great
Ely
Carson City
Lake Tahoe
Basin
Sierra Nevada
Tonopah
UTAH
CALIFORNIA
Las Vegas
Henderson
Lake Mead
Hoover Dam
Colorado River
ARIZONA

Lake Mead National Recreation Area

(Nevada, Arizona)
601 Nevada Highway, Boulder City, NV 89005
702/293-4041

Alan Bible Visitor Center near west end of Lake Mead, on US 93, 6½ miles east of Boulder City. Visitor center, exhibits, guided tours, self-guiding tours, picnicking, camping, hiking, swimming, boating, fishing, hunting, handicap access to campgrounds/restrooms/visitor center; bookstore by Southwest Parks and Monuments Association. Accommodations in park and in Boulder.

Lake Mead National Recreation Area exhibits a startling contrast of desert and water, mountains and canyons, primitive backcountry and modern technology. Two powerful forces created this fantastic place: nature, working slowly over millions of years, built the foundation and man, working feverishly over the last few decades, remodeled and built a landscape that better suited his needs, desires and senses. In one of the hottest, driest regions on earth, two huge lakes were created. Lake Mead and Lake Mohave emerged as the center of the country's first national recreation area. Today thousands of visitors enjoy the facilities of the man-made lakes. Drawn by water, they find many other unexpected rewards. There is the quiet and the stark, desolate beauty of the desert. There are imposing scenes of the ancient, twisted mountains of the basin and range province and the colorful vertical walls and high plateaus of the Grand Canyon. There is raw, untouched backcountry, and there is Hoover Dam, a towering symbol of what human genius can achieve. The range of experiences is as broad as the lakes and land are big.

Before the creation of Lake Mead few people set foot in this region. Those who did quickly became aware of the hostile, unforgiving character of this dry, brutally hot, rugged land. Some left; others stayed to meet the challenges. The first to stay behind were ancient Indians. Fur trappers, Mormon settlers, prospectors and riverboat captains followed. Explorers like John Wesley Powell penetrated deep into the uncharted territory of the Grand Canyon and other remote areas. With the twentieth century came modern-day pioneers who built a 726-foot-high dam on the Colorado river – higher than any built before. Hoover Dam changed the nature of this country forever. It created an abundance of water and power for the southwest, calmed the floodwaters of the Colorado, and turned a once uninviting landscape into one that today attracts thousands of visitors year after year.

Top right *Morning mist over Lake Mead National Recreation Area*

Right *Lake Mead sparkles in the barren Nevada landscape*

Left *A great day for sailing on Lake Mead*

Lehman Caves National Monument

Baker, NV 89311
702/234-7331

At terminus of NV 488; from US 6 and 50, take NV 487 south to NV 488 west. Visitor center, exhibits, guided tours, self-guiding tours, picnicking, handicap access to restrooms/visitor center; bookstore by Lehman Caves Natural History Association. Accommodations in park and at Baker.

This one-square-mile park deceives the eye. While the land is covered with wildflowers in spring and summer, the real attraction is the limestone caves with their beautiful and intriguing formations, including columns 22 feet high.

Right *A great blue heron stands motionless, saving its energy to spear a victim with its sharp bill*

Below *Hoover Dam, whose building formed Lake Mead*

NEW HAMPSHIRE

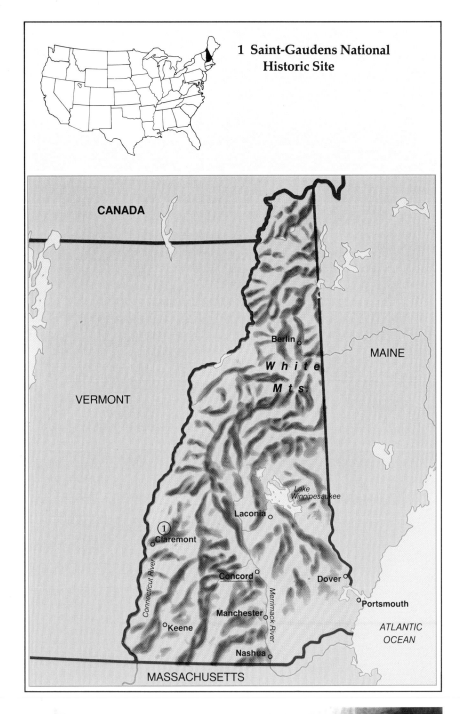

1 Saint-Gaudens National Historic Site

Saint-Gaudens National Historic Site

RR#2, Box 73, Cornish, NH 03745
603/675-2175

Off NH 12A, in Cornish. Entrance fee; visitor center, exhibits, guided tours, self-guiding tours, picnicking, handicap access to restrooms/visitor center; bookstore by Eastern National Park and Monument Association. Accommodations in surrounding area.

This is the home and studio of sculptor Augustus Saint-Gaudens. Today at this site, with its well-kept house, its carefully designed gardens and the studios that retain a touch of their master's hand, one can relive for a moment an age gone by. Many of Saint-Gaudens' portraits, busts and casts are displayed in the studio.

Augustus Saint-Gaudens, whose studio and home are preserved as a national historic site

NEW JERSEY

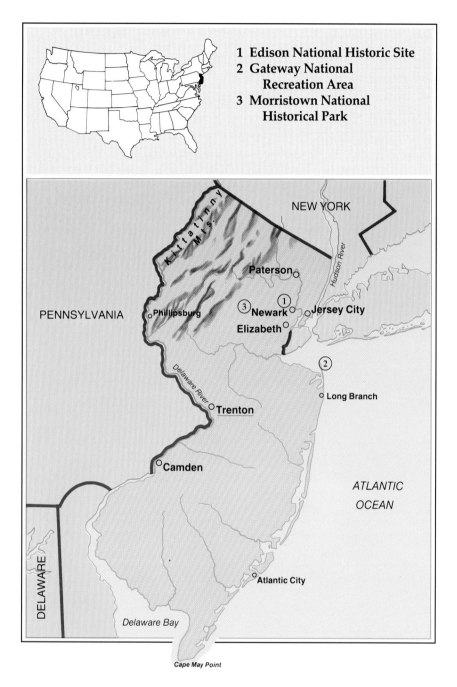

1 Edison National Historic Site
2 Gateway National
  Recreation Area
3 Morristown National
  Historical Park

Edison National Historic Site

Main Street and Lakeside Avenue, West Orange, NJ 07052
201/736-0550

Lakeside Avenue and Main Street in West Orange. Entrance fee; visitor center, museum, exhibits, guided tours of laboratory, handicap access to restrooms/visitor center; bookstore by Eastern National Park and Monument Association. Accommodations in surrounding area.

A busy urban area has grown up around Edison's West Orange laboratories, and all but one of the poured-concrete factory buildings that surrounded them are gone, but the old complex remains a quiet enclave where it is easy to feel the spirit of new ideas, the excitement of new technology, that drove Thomas Edison and his staff. This is the place where Edison invented the early electric light and power equipment, including the tinfoil phonograph of 1877 and the 1889 Strip Kinetograph and other motion picture apparatus. The buildings include his office and library, the Black Maria, a reconstruction of Edison's motion picture studio, and Glenmont, Edison's home.

On the beach at Gateway National Recreation Area, a haven from the metropolitan bustle of New York

Gateway National Recreation Area (Sandy Hook Unit)

PO Box 437, Highlands, NJ 07732 (see also New York)
212/338-3575

Sandy Hook Unit accessible via NJ 36. Visitor center, exhibits, guided tours, self-guiding tours, picnicking, hiking, swimming, fishing, bicycling, handicap access to visitor center; bookstore by Eastern National Park and Monument Association. Food available in park; accommodations in Sandy Hook area.

The sand dunes here protect portions of the Sandy Hook uplands against sea winds and enable the growth of plant life. The growth culminates in a holly forest unsurpassed on the eastern seaboard. Sandy Hook also has a number of important historic sites. The lighthouse is the oldest operating one in the country. Fort Hancock is the last of several forts erected on Sandy Hook to protect the shipping channels into New York harbor. Here also was established one of the first stations of the US Lifesaving Service.

A hovercraft comes to rest at Gateway National Recreation Area

Morristown National Historical Park

Washington Place, Morristown, NJ 07960
201/539-2016

Access via I-287; use Exit 32 for Washington's headquarters and Ford Mansion; use Exit 26B for Jockey Hollow; also accessible via US 303 or NJ 24. Entrance fee; visitor center, museum, exhibits, guided tours, self-guiding tours, hiking, handicap access to restrooms/visitor center; bookstore by Eastern National Park and Monument Association. Accommodations at Morristown.

During two critical winters of the American Revolution Morristown sheltered the main encampment of the Continental Army. In 1777 George Washington overcame desertion and disease to rebuild an army capable of taking the field against veteran Redcoats. In 1779-80 – the hardest winter in anyone's memory – the military struggle was almost lost amid starvation, nakedness and mutiny on the bleak hills of Jockey Hollow.

Among the outstanding features of this lovely park, all on a self-guiding tour route, are the Ford Mansion, Washington's head-quarters; the Jockey Hollow encampment area of 1779-80, the home of 10,000 soldiers living in 1,000 simple log huts; the Pennsylvania Line; the Grand Parade area; the Wick Farm, used as General Arthur St. Clair's headquarters; and Fort Nonsense.

NEW MEXICO

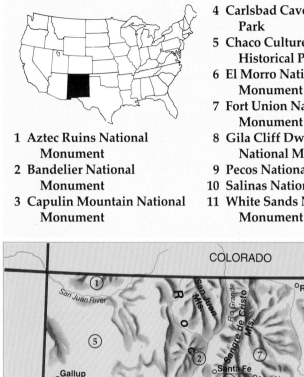

4 **Carlsbad Caverns National Park**

5 **Chaco Culture National Historical Park**

6 **El Morro National Monument**

7 **Fort Union National Monument**

1 **Aztec Ruins National Monument**

2 **Bandelier National Monument**

3 **Capulin Mountain National Monument**

8 **Gila Cliff Dwellings National Monument**

9 **Pecos National Monument**

10 **Salinas National Monument**

11 **White Sands National Monument**

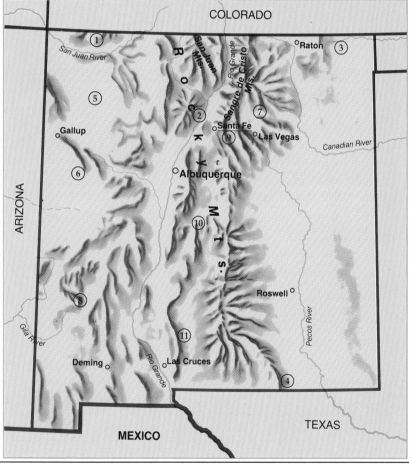

Aztec Ruins National Monument

PO Box U, Aztec, NM 87410
505/334-6174

On the outskirts of Aztec. Entrance fee; visitor center, exhibits, self-guiding tours, picnicking; bookstore by Southwest Parks and Monuments Association. Accommodations in Aztec.

Aztec Ruins National Monument in fact has nothing to do with the Aztecs of ancient Mexico. A century ago early pioneer settlers in the Animas river valley speculated about the large ruins they found here and incorrectly guessed that the Aztecs had built them. They gave the name "Aztec" to both the ruins and to the town they founded.

These ruins, near the Navajo Reservation in the Four Corners country, were discovered in 1859; the first description and drawings of the structures were published in 1887. In 1916 the American Museum of Natural History began to excavate the ruins and they were stabilized in the 1930s. A self-guiding tour takes visitors through the west pueblo, site of the restored Great Kiva, and to the Hubbard Ruin.

Right *15th century Pueblo Indian ruins at Bandelier National Monument*

Center right *Ladder leading to a Kiva at Bandelier National Monument*

Far right *The scale of only one of the Carlsbad Caverns is merely hinted at here*

Bandelier National Monument

Los Alamos, NM 87544
505/672-3861

On NM 4, 7 miles southwest of White Rock, 10 miles south of Los Alamos, 46 miles west of Santa Fe; visitor center is 3 miles into park. Entrance fee; visitor center, exhibits, guided tours, self-guiding tours, picnicking, camping, hiking, handicap access to visitor center; bookstore by Southwest Parks and Monuments Association. Food available in park; accommodations at White Rock, Los Alamos, and Santa Fe.

Bandelier, an area crossed only by trails, covers nearly 50 square miles. It was named in honor of Adolph F.A. Bandelier, the distinguished Swiss-American scholar, who carried on an extensive survey of prehistoric ruins in the region and studied the Pueblo Indians around Santa Fe between 1880 and 1886.

The most accessible features of the monument are the ruins of Frijoles Canyon. Cliff ruins, or talus villages, extend along the base of the northern walls of the canyon for approximately two miles. These houses of masonry are irregularly terraced, from one to three stories high, and have many cave rooms gouged out of the solid cliff.

Capulin Mountain National Monument

Capulin, NM 88414
505/278-2201

On NM 325, 3 miles north of town of Capulin. Entrance fee; visitor center, exhibits, self-guiding trails, picnicking, hiking, handicap access to restrooms/visitor center; bookstore by Southwest Parks and Monuments Association. Accommodations at Capulin, Des Moines, Clayton and Raton.

Capulin Mountain is one of the few places in the world where you can walk into a volcano – the cone of a volcano that was active only about 10,000 years ago. This mountain represents the last stage of a great period of volcanism that began about two million years earlier.

Carlsbad Caverns National Park

3225 National Parks Highway, Carlsbad, NM 88220
505/885-8884

On US 62 and US 180, 20 miles southwest of Carlsbad, NM; visitor center is 7 miles west of highway at the end of NM 7. Visitor center, exhibits, guided tours, self-guiding tours, picnicking, backcountry permits, hiking, handicap access to restrooms/visitor center; bookstore by Carlsbad Caverns Natural History Association. Food available in park; accommodations in Carlsbad.

On the northeastern slope of the Guadalupe Mountains in southern New Mexico is Carlsbad Caverns. Unlike many other natural parks, it reaches deep within the earth to preserve and interpret a subterranean wonderland. On the surface the land is harsh and rugged, with steep rock-strewn ridges covered with cactus and other spiny plants; temperatures are often extreme and rainfall is sparse. But below ground huge galleries lavishly decorated with delicate stone formations are always cool and moist.

Some 70 caves are preserved in the 46,753-acre park. Carlsbad, the largest, has one room with a floor area equal to 14 football fields and enough height for the US Capitol building in one corner.

More than a thousand years ago native Indians left paintings on the entrance wall of Carlsbad Cavern and cooked agave and other desert plants in a rock pit outside. Later Apache Indians also used the cavern.

More permanent settlers arriving after the Civil War were attracted to the cavern by what appeared to be smoke against the sky; from nearer the cave they discovered that the dark cloud consisted of literally millions of bats streaming out of the opening. Later, finding huge guano deposits, valuable as natural fertilizer, beneath the bat roost the settlers' interest in the cave became commercial. Mining claims were filed on the "Bat Cave" and more than 100,000 tons of guano were removed in 10 years.

James Larkin White, a young cowboy who was fascinated by the cavern and its bats, became a foreman for the guano mining companies and spent more than 20 years exploring, building trails and escorting people through portions of the cavern. His efforts, along with those of others, led to a visit by Robert Holley of the General Land Office and a six-month National Geographic Society expedition under Dr. Willis T. Lee; and finally his work led to designation of the cave as a national monument in 1923; it became a national park in 1930.

For thousands of years bats that winter in Mexico have used a portion of the main cavern as a summer home. From late spring until the first major frost in October or early November, these tiny flying mammals spiral out of the cavern entrance in incredible numbers at sunset each evening. They fly southeastward over the escarpment rim to feed at night on flying insects along the Black and Pecos rivers. Before sunup the colony returns to the cavern where the bats sleep during the day. Up to 5,000 bats per minute may boil up through the cavern opening, depending on the weather and the insect food supply.

Inset *The entrance of the vast subterranean complex of Carlsbad Caverns*

Below *"The Dolls Theatre," just one of dozens of prominent features in Carlsbad Caverns*

Chaco Culture National Historical Park

Star Route 4, Box 6500, Bloomfield, NM 87413
505/786-5384

On NM 57, 64 miles south of Aztec, NM. Visitor center, exhibits, guided tours, self-guiding tours, picnicking, camping, backcountry permits, hiking, handicap access to campgrounds/restrooms/visitor center; bookstore by Southwest Parks and Monuments Association. Accommodations in Aztec.

Chaco Canyon in northwestern New Mexico is the site of a highly developed prehistoric community of Pueblo Indians, encompassing some of the most significant Indian ruins in the United States. A thousand years ago this valley was a center of urban life. Pueblo Indians farmed the lowlands and built great masonry towns that connected with other villages over a far-reaching network of roads. In architecture, in complexity of community life and in social organization the Anasazi of Chaco Canyon reached heights rarely matched and never surpassed by their kindred only a few hundred miles away in the Four Corners area. During classic times, Chaco was the center of a far-flung trading network. Evidence abounds in the pottery and jewelry found in recent excavations. Beginning in the tenth century, like the other great Anasazi communities of the southwest, Chaco succumbed to the speculated drought during the twelfth century and the people disappeared, leaving behind for modern archeology a treasure of early American life.

El Morro National Monument

Ramah, NM 87321
505/783-5132

58 miles southeast of Gallup, NM, via NM 32 and 53. Entrance fee; visitor center, exhibits, guided tours, self-guiding tours, camping, hiking, handicap access to campgrounds/restrooms/visitor center; bookstore by Southwest Parks and Monuments Association. Accommodations in Grants and Gallup.

Rising some 200 feet above the valley floor, El Morro is a massive mesa-point of sandstone, forming a striking landmark. It was named by the Spanish conquistadors who used the place, with its large natural basin of rain and melted snow, as a camping spot in the seventeenth century: *morro* meaning headland or bluff. These sheltered coves also served later American travelers to the West. Many of the travelers left a record of their passage by cutting inscriptions into the soft sandstone, thus giving the landmark its other name, "Inscription Rock." Two years before the founding of Jamestown, and 15 years before the Pilgrims landed at Plymouth Rock, the Spanish inscription was made by Don Juan de Onate in April 1605.

The Spaniards were not the first to record their presence, however: on the very top of El Morro lie ruins, still largely unexcavated, of Zuni Indian pueblos abandoned long before the coming of the Spaniards. Carved on the rock itself are hundreds of petroglyphs left by these ancient people.

A watering hole at El Morro National Monument

Fort Union National Monument

Watrous, NM 87753
505/425-8025

90 miles north of Santa Fe, via I-25 and NM 477; 26 miles north of Las Vegas, NM. Visitor center, self-guiding tours, handicap access to restrooms/visitor center; bookstore by Southwest Parks and Monuments Association. Accommodations in Las Vegas, NM.

Fort Union, on the route of the Santa Fe Trail, was the largest military post guarding the nineteenth-century southwestern frontier. The first of three forts that occupied this site in 1851 consisted of shabby log buildings. For a decade it served as a military base and the principal quartermaster depot for the southwest, receiving supplies from the east and forwarding them to posts throughout the territory. When Civil War came in 1861 earthwork fortifications were erected for an expected Confederate invasion of New Mexico; this was the second Fort Union. The final and more modern structures were begun once the Union had New Mexico secured during the Civil War. It was finally abandoned in 1891. Only the walls and chimneys now stand and one's imagination must provide the picture of a bustling time when hundreds of men prepared for battles against the Indians and the Confederates. A self-guiding trail roams the tall sentinels of a former time.

Gila Cliff Dwellings National Monument

Route 11, Box 100, Silver City, NM 88061
505/534-9344

44 miles north of Silver City, via NM 15. Visitor center, exhibits, self-guiding tours, handicap access to restrooms/visitor center; bookstore by Southwest Parks and Monuments Association. Limited accommodations at Gila Hot Springs; more extensive at Silver City.

The term "cliff dwellers" refers to Pueblo people of the Mongollon culture, who built their homes in natural caves. This monument preserves the ruins of pithouses dating from about AD 100 to 400 to cliff dwellings dating to the late 1200s and early 1300s. Several natural caves are found in the southeast-facing cliff of a side canyon; five of these caves contain the ruins of cliff dwellings, a total of about 40 rooms. The Pueblo people left their homes in about 1400; the site was then occupied first by nomadic bands of Apaches, and later by Spanish colonists, who settled areas east and south of the monument.

Pecos National Monument

PO Drawer 11, Pecos, NM 87552
505/757-6414

25 miles southeast of Santa Fe, via I-25. Visitor center, exhibits, guided tours, self-guiding tours, picnicking, handicap access to restrooms/visitor center; bookstore by Southwest Parks and Monuments Association. Accommodations in Pecos and Santa Fe.

When Spanish explorers arrived here in 1540 they discovered a five-story communal structure with 2,000 inhabitants. By the early 1600s they had established a Franciscan mission; a second mission was built after 1680. It is the ruins of the second that are visible today,

along with the ruins of the convento. Mysteries abound in this small but complex monument, but the story of early pueblo and later Spanish occupation is slowly being pieced together to form a fascinating picture of the Pecos people.

Salinas National Monument

PO Box 496, Mountainair, NM 87036
505/847-2770

Off US 60 and NM 14, 75 miles southeast of Albuquerque. Visitor center, exhibits, guided tours, self-guiding tours, picnicking, handicap access to restrooms/visitor center; bookstore by Southwest Parks and Monuments Association. Accommodations at Mountainair.

The name "Salinas," from the Spanish word for this region of salt lagoons, has been given to the people who lived here in communal stone and adobe homes, the earliest of which were concentric circles of wedge-shaped rooms surrounding a kiva. These were later covered by rectangular complexes with hundreds of rooms for living and storage. The monument preserves a large portion of this community, abandoned in the 1670s.

White Sands National Monument

PO Box 458, Alamogordo, NM 88310
505/437-1058

On US 70 and 82, 15 miles southwest of Alamogordo. Entrance fee; visitor center, exhibits, self-guiding trails, picnicking, backcountry permits, hiking, handicap access to visitor center; bookstore. Accommodations in Alamogordo.

Great wavelike dunes of gypsum sand grace the floor of the Tularosa Basin of southern New Mexico. In this harsh, constantly changing environment, plants and animals have evolved unique forms of survival. This national monument preserves a vast undulating land-scape of brilliant white sand, the most impressive part of the world's largest gypsum dune field.

Right *Yucca plants stand starkly against the wind-formed dunes of White Sands National Monument*

Below *Constantly changing shapes and forms in the heart of the dune field at White Sands National Monument are a perpetual source of fascination*

NEW YORK

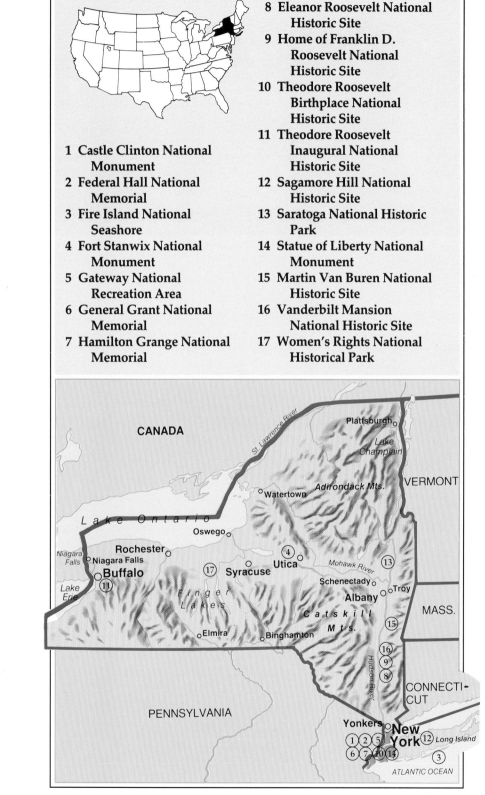

8 **Eleanor Roosevelt National Historic Site**
9 **Home of Franklin D. Roosevelt National Historic Site**
10 **Theodore Roosevelt Birthplace National Historic Site**
11 **Theodore Roosevelt Inaugural National Historic Site**
12 **Sagamore Hill National Historic Site**
13 **Saratoga National Historic Park**
14 **Statue of Liberty National Monument**
15 **Martin Van Buren National Historic Site**
16 **Vanderbilt Mansion National Historic Site**
17 **Women's Rights National Historical Park**

1 **Castle Clinton National Monument**
2 **Federal Hall National Memorial**
3 **Fire Island National Seashore**
4 **Fort Stanwix National Monument**
5 **Gateway National Recreation Area**
6 **General Grant National Memorial**
7 **Hamilton Grange National Memorial**

Right Federal Hall, where George Washington took his oath of office as President of the United States

Far right A peaceful stretch of Fire Island's 32 miles of seashore

Castle Clinton National Monument

c/o National Park Service Manhattan Sites, 26 Wall Street, New York, NY 10005
212/344-7220

In Battery Park in New York City. Exhibits, guided tours, self-guiding tours, handicap access to building; bookstore by Eastern National Park and Monument Association. Accommodations in greater New York City area.

Built in 1808-11 this structure served successively as a defense for New York harbor, a promenade and entertainment center and an immigration depot through which more than eight million people entered the United States from 1855 to 1890.

Federal Hall National Memorial

c/o National Park Service Manhattan Sites, 26 Wall Street, New York, NY 10005
212/264-8711

On Wall Street, in lower Manhattan. Exhibits, guided tours, self-guiding tours, handicap access to restrooms and building; bookstore by Eastern National Park and Monument Association. Accommodations in greater New York City area.

This graceful building is on the site of the original Federal Hall where the trial of John Peter Zenger, involving freedom of the press, was held in 1735; the Stamp Act Congress convened in 1865; the Second Continental Congress met in 1785; Washington took the oath as first US President and the Bill of Rights was adopted in 1789. The present building was completed in 1842 as a federal customs house.

Fire Island National Seashore

120 Laurel Street, Patchogue, NY 11772
516/289-4810

Access by car only to eastern and western ends of park; ferries operate from mainland to park from May to November. Visitor center, exhibits, guided tours, self-guiding trails, picnicking, camping, hiking, swimming, boating, fishing, hunting, handicap access to campground/restrooms/visitor center; bookstore by Eastern National Park and Monument Association. Accommodations in park and on mainland.

Fire Island stretches 32 miles from Democrat Point on the west to Moriches Inlet on the east. This barrier island faces the Atlantic, protecting the waters of Great South Bay and the mainland of Long Island behind it. People have created 17 separate communities on Fire Island primarily for summer recreation, but efforts have been made to preserve the natural life, too, whether it be a hidden hardwood grove or long-legged herons stalking stiffly through grassy wetlands. Here, too, wild geese including brant fly over the salt marsh and occasionally a startled deer dashes off through the thicket. Yet, this national seashore is almost within sight of New York City's skyscrapers.

Fort Stanwix National Monument

112 East Park Street, Rome, NY 13440
315/336-2090

In downtown Rome, at intersection of NY 26, 46, 49, 69, and 365. Exhibits, guided tours, self-guiding tours, handicap access to restrooms and the fort; bookstore by Eastern National Park and Monument Association. Accommodations in immediate area.

The American stand here in August 1777 was a major factor in repulsing the British invasion from Canada. Fort Stanwix was also the site of the treaty with the Iroquois, November 5, 1768. This is one of the little-known jewels of the National Park Service. Stanwix has been totally reconstructed and, with its costumed demonstrations, makes any visit an exciting one.

The Fire Island lighthouse on Fire Island National Seashore, an unexpected delight within miles of New York's urban hubbub

Gateway National Recreation Area

Floyd Bennett Field Building 69, Brooklyn, NY 11234 (see also New Jersey)
212/338-3575

Detailed directions to all units available by writing to the individual sites or to the headquarters above. Visitor centers, exhibits, guided tours, self-guiding trails, picnicking, camping, hiking, horseback riding, swimming, boating, fishing, bicycling, handicap access to campgrounds/restrooms/visitor centers; bookstores by Eastern National Park and Monument Association. Food available in park; accommodations in greater New York City area.

At the entrance to the great New York-New Jersey estuary two arms of land stretch across the water toward each other, forming a natural gateway to the nation's greatest port. This is the gateway through which millions of immigrants have entered the New World and which has given its name to a new national park site – Gateway National Recreation Area.

One of these land arms is Sandy Hook, the New Jersey unit of Gateway; the other is the Rockaway Peninsula in New York, site of the park's Breezy Point unit. The other Gateway units, Staten Island and Jamaica Bay, lie within the arms. Together the four units contain 26,000 acres of land and water – ocean beaches, dunes, wooded uplands, bays, a holly forest, the Jamaica Bay Wildlife Refuge, three forts, two historic airfields and the nation's oldest operating lighthouse. Besides its natural and historic features Gateway provides tremendous opportunities for recreation: swimming, fishing, basketball, softball, football, soccer and jogging are just a few of the sports in which you can engage at the park. Or you may wish to do nothing but relax, and let the noise and bustle drain away as you watch birds fly by and waves roll in. Gateway is a place of both activity and relaxation.

In New York are the Breezy Point Unit, Fort Tilden, NY 11695; Jamaica Bay Unit, Floyd Bennett Field, Brooklyn, NY 11234; Staten Island Unit, PO Box 37, Staten Island, NY 10306.

Left *Ellis Island, the immigration port into the United States from 1892 to 1954*

Below *Fort Wadsworth, one of three forts which used to protect New York and are now preserved within Gateway National Recreation Area*

General Grant National Memorial

c/o National Park Service Manhattan Sites, 26 Wall Street,
New York, NY 10005
212/283-5154

At Riverside Drive and 122nd Street, and Henry Hudson Parkway, overlooking Hudson River. Exhibits, guided tours; bookstore by Eastern National Park and Monument Association. Accommodations in greater New York City area.

This, the largest mausoleum in America, is the burial place of President Ulysses S. Grant and his wife Julia. Grant signed the act establishing the first national park, Yellowstone, in 1872.

Hamilton Grange National Memorial

c/o National Park Service Manhattan Sites, 26 Wall Street,
New York, NY 10005
212/283-5154

At 287 Convent Avenue. Exhibits, guided tours, self-guiding tours, handicap access to restrooms. Accommodations in greater New York City area.

"The Grange," named after his grandfather's estate in Scotland, was the home of Alexander Hamilton, American statesman and first Secretary of the Treasury.

Eleanor Roosevelt National Historic Site

249 Albany Post Road, Hyde Park, NY 12538
914/229-9422

Entrance off NY 9G in Hyde Park; the site is about 3 miles from Franklin Roosevelt Home on NY 9 via St. Andrew's Road. Guided tours. Accommodations in Hyde Park.

Mrs. Roosevelt used her "Val-Kill" estate as a retreat from her busy life. The pastoral setting of the cottage, built for her by her husband in 1925, includes fields, trees, swamps and ponds. She also used the estate to entertain friends and dignitaries and to promote the many causes in which she was interested.

Home of Franklin D. Roosevelt National Historic Site

249 Albany Post Road, Hyde Park, NY 12538
914/229-9115

On NY 9 at Hyde Park. Entrance fee; exhibits, guided tours, self-guiding tours, handicap access to restrooms; bookstore by Hyde Park Historical Association. Accommodations at Hyde Park.

This was the birthplace, lifetime residence, and Summer White House of the 32nd President. The gravesites of President and Mrs. Roosevelt are in the Rose Garden.

Left The largest mausoleum in the United States, the tomb of President Ulysses S. Grant and his wife

Below The Dresden Room of the Franklin D. Roosevelt Home National Historic Site, Hyde Park

Theodore Roosevelt Birthplace National Historic Site

c/o National Park Service Manhattan Sites, 26 Wall Street, New York, NY 10005
212/260-1616

20 East 20th Street, New York City. Entrance fee; exhibits, guided tours, self-guiding tours; bookstore by Eastern National Park and Monument Association. Accommodations in greater New York City area.

The 26th President was born in a brownstone house here on October 27, 1858. Demolished in 1916, it was reconstructed in the 1920s to include a museum and period rooms.

Theodore Roosevelt Inaugural National Historic Site

641 Delaware Avenue, Buffalo, NY 14202
716/884-0095

On Delaware Avenue, near North Street in North Buffalo. Entrance fee; exhibits, guided tours, self-guiding tours. Accommodations in Greater Buffalo area.

Theodore Roosevelt took the oath of office as President of the United States on September 14, 1901, here in the Ansley Wilcox House, after the assassination of President William McKinley.

Far left *Sagamore Hill, the home of conservationist President Theodore Roosevelt*

Left *Saratoga Battlefield is often the scene of living history demonstrations, when people in colonial and military costume relive the days of America's struggle with Britain*

Sagamore Hill National Historic Site

Box 304, Cove Neck Road, Oyster Bay, NY 1171
516/922-4447

On Cove Neck Road, 3 miles east of Oyster Bay, Long Island. Entrance fee; exhibits, self-guiding tours, handicap access to house. Accommodations on Long Island.

This estate was the home of Theodore Roosevelt from 1885 until his death in 1919. Used as the Summer White House from 1901 until 1908, it contains original furnishings.

Saratoga National Historical Park

RD 2, Box 33, Stillwater, NY 12170
518/664-9821

30 miles north of Albany on US 54 and NY 32. Visitor center, exhibits, guided tours, self-guiding tours, picnicking, bicycling, handicap access to restrooms/visitor center; bookstore by Eastern National Park and Monument Association. Accommodations in Stillwater.

The American victory here over the British in 1777 was the turning point of the Revolution. The park includes the country home of Maj. Gen. Philip Schuyler.

Right *The Statue of Liberty, recently renovated, celebrated its centennial birthday in 1986*

Far right *One of the many bedrooms in this 54-room "country home," built in 1898 by Frederick Vanderbilt, grandson of Cornelius Vanderbilt*

Statue of Liberty National Monument

(New York, New Jersey)
Liberty Island, New York, NY 10004
212/732-1236

On Liberty Island, accessible only by ferry. Circle Line Ferries leave Battery Park in Lower Manhattan every hour and more frequently during the summer. Visitor center, exhibits, guided tours, self-guiding tours, handicap access to visitor center. Food available in park; accommodations in greater New York area.

The famous 152-foot copper statue bearing the torch of freedom was a gift of the people of France in 1886 to commemorate the alliance of the two nations in the American Revolution. The monument includes the American Museum of Immigration, in the base of the statue, and Ellis Island, an immigration port from 1892 to 1954. It has recently undergone a complete renovation.

Martin Van Buren National Historic Site

PO Box 545, Route 9H, Kinderhook, NY 12106
518/758-9689

Off NY 9H south of Kinderhook Village. Exhibits, guided tours; bookstore by Eastern National Park and Monument Association. Accommodations in nearby villages.

The Lindenwald estate was the home of the eighth President of the United States for 21 years until his death in 1862. Built in 1797, the house belonged to his life-long friends, the Van Ness family. Van Buren bought it in 1839 while President. His grave is in nearby Kinderhook Village.

Vanderbilt Mansion National Historic Site

249 Albany Post Road, Hyde Park, NY 12538
914/229-9115

On US 9 at Hyde Park. Entrance fee; exhibits, guided tours, self-guiding tours, picnicking, handicap access to mansion; bookstore by Eastern National Park and Monument Association. Accommodations at Hyde Park.

This palatial mansion is a fine example of homes built by nineteenth-century millionaires.

Women's Rights National Historical Park

PO Box 70, Seneca Falls, NY 13148
315/568-2991

Visitor center at 116 Fall Street near State Street, in center of Historic District; Stanton Home at 32 Washington Street; park near junction of NY 414 and 20. Visitor center, exhibits, guided tours, self-guiding tours, handicap access to restrooms/visitor center; bookstore by Eastern National Park and Monument Association. Accommodations in villages in the Finger Lakes section of upstate New York.

This park in Seneca Falls commemorates the beginning of the women's struggle for equal rights and includes the Wesleyan Methodist Chapel, the site of the 1848 Women's Rights Convention and the homes and offices of Elizabeth Cady Stanton, Amelia Jenks Bloomer, and other notable early women's rights activists.

NORTH CAROLINA

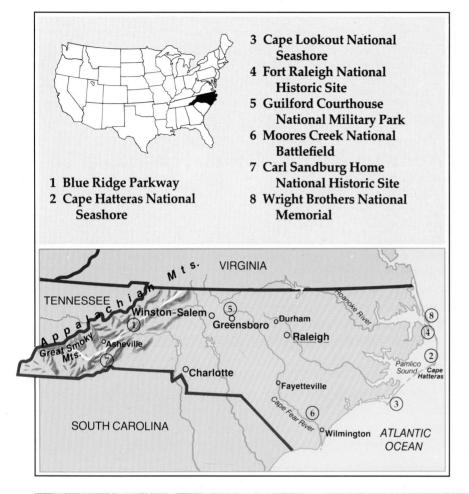

3 **Cape Lookout National Seashore**
4 **Fort Raleigh National Historic Site**
5 **Guilford Courthouse National Military Park**
6 **Moores Creek National Battlefield**
7 **Carl Sandburg Home National Historic Site**
8 **Wright Brothers National Memorial**

1 **Blue Ridge Parkway**
2 **Cape Hatteras National Seashore**

Blue Ridge Parkway

(North Carolina, Virginia)
700 Northwestern Bank Building, Asheville, NC 28801
704/259-0717

Access via many major US and State highways, including I-64, I-77, I-40, and I-26. Visitor centers, exhibits, guided tours, self-guiding trails, picnicking, camping, hiking, boating, fishing, cross-country skiing, cabin rental, handicap access to campgrounds/restrooms/visitor centers; bookstores by Eastern National Park and Monument Association. Accommodations in park and on both sides of parkway.

The Blue Ridge Parkway extends 469 miles along the crests of the southern Appalachians and links two eastern national parks – Shenandoah and Great Smoky Mountains. The parkway follows the Appalachian Mountain chain and provides seemingly endless views of many parallel ranges connected by cross ranges and scattered hills. From Shenandoah National Park the parkway follows the Blue Ridge Mountains, eastern rampart of the Appalachians, for 355 miles. Then, for the remaining 114 miles, it skirts the southern end of the massive Black Mountains, weaves through the Craggies, the Pisgahs and the Balsams, and ends in the Great Smoky Mountains.

Right *The Blue Ridge Mountains of North Carolina from the Blue Ridge Parkway*

Below *Mabry Mill, a water-powered gristmill grinding corn and buckwheat, along the Blue Ridge Parkway*

Cape Hatteras National Seashore

Route 1, Box 675, Manteo, NC 27954
919/473-2111

Whalebone Junction Information Center at intersection of US 158 and NC 12, due south of Nags Head. Visitor centers, exhibits, guided tours, self-guiding trails, picnicking, camping, hiking, swimming, boating, fishing, hunting, handicap access to restrooms/visitor centers; bookstores by Eastern National Park and Monument Association. Food available in park; accommodations in several nearby communities.

Between broad, shallow sounds to the west and the foaming surf of the Atlantic to the east lie the windswept Outer Banks of North Carolina – a string of barrier islands where wind, sea and sand have contended with each other for ages. Here long stretches of beach, sand, dunes and marshlands have been set aside as Cape Hatteras National Seashore, a park offering many opportunities for outdoor recreation and rewarding exploration in nature and history. Here you can swim and fish and sunbathe, climb the tower of an 1870 lighthouse and see a variety of wildlife.

When in 1524 the Italian navigator Giovanni da Verrazano reported to the King of France, his royal employer, that he had discovered an isthmus separating the Atlantic and Pacific oceans, he had actually seen only the Outer Banks of North Carolina, the sound was so wide that the mainland was invisible beyond. Unlike Fire Island and Assateague, which hug the New York and Maryland shores so closely, the Carolina Outer Banks curve out to sea by as much as 30 miles to form a 175-mile-long bulging chain of narrow islands from the Virginia border just south of Norfolk to Cape Lookout. Constantly and erratically widening and narrowing, the Outer Banks, barely a mile wide in some places, have become one of the east's favourite playgrounds.

Left *The toll of wrecks off the dangerous sands of Cape Hatteras would have been even higher without this lighthouse beaming a warning*

Below *The skeletal remains of one of the many ships to have been wrecked on the treacherous sandbars off Cape Hatteras*

Cape Lookout National Seashore

PO Box 690, Beaufort, NC 28516
919/778-2121

Headquarters on Front Street, in Beaufort. Visitor center, guided tours, picnicking, hiking, swimming, boating, fishing, hunting; bookstore. Accommodations in Beaufort.

Cape Lookout National Seashore is a low, narrow ribbon of sand running from Ocracoke Inlet on the northeast to Beaufort Inlet on the southwest. These 55-mile long barrier islands consist mostly of wide, bare beaches with low dunes covered by scattered grasses, flat grasslands bordered by dense vegetation and large expanses of salt marsh alongside the sound.

Wind, waves and currents are continually at work reshaping these low-lying islands; one strong storm can create extensive changes. In such an environment only the most tenacious plants can survive. Of the plants, the grasses are the most important, for their deep roots help to anchor the sand. For this reason sea oats, a large grass with a grain-like head, is protected by law.

Human beings, too, have found this environment difficult to deal with but also protective and bountiful. One of the earliest maps that shows Cape Lookout dates from 1590 and calls the area "promontorium tremendum" – horrible headland – in acknowledgement of the area's treacherous shoals. Behind the islands, however, are several sheltered anchorages that can shield a vessel from a northeaster or, as in World War II, an enemy submarine. Fishing and whaling have for centuries been an important industry on the Outer Banks. In the nineteenth century the small settlement of Diamond City on Shackleford Banks became famous for the excellent salted mullet it shipped. Commercial fishing continues today as the forces of nature continue to shape and alter these islands.

Fort Raleigh National Historic Site

Route 1, Box 675, Manteo, NC 27954
919/473-5772

On US 64 and 264, 3 miles north of Manteo. Visitor center, exhibits, guided tours, self-guiding tours, handicap access to restrooms/ visitor center. Accommodations in Manteo.

Fort Raleigh, named for Sir Walter Raleigh, is on the site of the first English attempt to colonize the New World during the 1580s. This is the site of the "Lost Colony," the fate of which remains a mystery.

Guilford Courthouse National Military Park

PO Box 9806, Greensboro, NC 27408
919/288-1776

Visitor center near intersection of Old Battleground Road and New Garden Road, just north of Greensboro. Visitor center, exhibits, self-guiding tours, handicap access to restrooms/visitor center; bookstore by Eastern National Park and Monument Association. Accommodations in Greensboro.

The battle fought here on March 15, 1781, opened the campaign that led to Yorktown and the end of the Revolution.

Moores Creek National Battlefield

PO Box 69, Currie, NC 28435
919/283-5591

23 miles northwest of Wilmington, via US 421 and NC 210. Visitor center, exhibits, self-guiding tours, picnicking, handicap access to restrooms/visitor center; bookstore by Eastern National Park and Monument Association. Accommodations in Wilmington.

The battle on February 27, 1776, between North Carolina Patriots and Loyalists is commemorated here. The Patriot victory advanced the revolutionary cause in the South, with North Carolina becoming the first colony to vote for independence.

Carl Sandburg Home National Historic Site

PO Box 395, Flat Rock, NC 28731
704/693-4178

3 miles south of Hendersonville; turn off US 25 onto Little River Road at Flat Rock Playhouse. Exhibits, guided tours, self-guiding tours, handicap access to restrooms; bookstore by Eastern National Park and Monument Association. Accommodations at Hendersonville.

"Connenara" was the farm home of the noted poet-author for the last 22 years of his life. Several of his books were published while he lived here. The park includes the house, barns, and other outbuildings, surrounded by rolling pastures, mountainside woods and lakes and flowering gardens.

Wright Brothers National Memorial

Cape Hatteras Group, Route 1, Box 675, Manteo, NC 27954
919/441-7430

On US 158, 18 miles northeast of Manteo. Visitor center, exhibits, guided tours, self-guiding tours, handicap access to restrooms/visitor center; bookstore by Eastern National Park and Monument Association. Accommodations in Manteo.

The first sustained flight in a heavier-than-air machine was made here on December 17, 1903, by Orville Wright.

Kitty Hawk, North Carolina, where the Wright Brothers made the first ever airplane flight

NORTH DAKOTA

1 **Fort Union Trading Post**
   National Historic Site
2 **Knife River Indian Villages**
   National Historic Site
3 **Theodore Roosevelt**
   National Park

Fort Union Trading Post National Historic Site

Buford Route, Williston, ND 58801
701/572-9083

On County Road 4, off US 2, 25 miles southwest of Williston. Visitor center, exhibits, guided tours, self-guiding tours, hiking, handicap access to restrooms/visitor center; bookstore by Theodore Roosevelt Nature and History Association. Accommodations at Williston and Sidney.

The trading post that stood here was the principal fur-trading depot in the Upper Missouri River region from 1829 to 1867. At the confluence of the Missouri and Yellowstone rivers, Fort Union served the Dakotas, Montana and the prairie provinces.

Right Prairie dogs live in the grasslands of Theodore Roosevelt National Park

Far right The curious rock formations, millions of years old, which are distinctive features of Theodore Roosevelt National Park

Knife River Indian Villages National Historic Site

RR 1, PO Box 168, Stanton, ND 58571
701/745-3309

3 miles north of Stanton. Visitor center, exhibits, guided tours, self-guiding tours, picnicking, backcountry permits, hiking, fishing, handicap access to restrooms/visitor center; bookstore. Accommodations in Stanton, Beulah and Washburn.

These are the remnants of historic and prehistoric Indian villages, last occupied in 1845 by the Hidatsa, containing an array of Plains Indian culture artifacts.

Theodore Roosevelt National Park

PO Box 7, Medora, ND 58645
701/623-4466

North Unit 15 miles south of Watford City on ND 85; South Unit Visitor Center is at Medora. Entrance fee; visitor centers; exhibits, guided tours, self-guiding trails, picnicking, camping, backcountry permits, hiking, horseback riding, boating, fishing, snowmobiling, handicap access to restrooms/visitor centers; bookstore by Theodore Roosevelt Nature and History Association. Accommodations at Medora and Watford City.

"I never would have been President if it had not been for my experiences in North Dakota," Theodore Roosevelt once remarked. Here many of his attitudes about and interest in nature and conservation were also sharpened and refined.

Roosevelt came to the badlands in September 1883 with big game hunting in mind. But when he arrived the last large herds of buffalo were gone, having been decimated by hide hunters and disease. And in the other years that he managed to spend some time in North Dakota, he became more and more alarmed by the damage that was being done to the land and its wildlife. He witnessed the virtual destruction of some big game species. Overgrazing destroyed the grasslands and with them the habitats for small mammals and songbirds.

When he became President in 1901 Roosevelt pursued the interest in conservation and natural history which he had developed by establishing the US Forest Service and signing the 1906 Antiquities Act under which he proclaimed 18 national monuments. He also obtained Congressional approval for establishing five national parks and 51 wildlife refuges and set aside land as national forests.

Theodore Roosevelt was a major figure in American conservation. And here in the North Dakota badlands he is remembered with a national park that bears his name.

About 60 million years ago streams carried eroded materials eastward from the young Rocky Mountains and deposited them on a vast lowland – today Great Plains. During the warm, rainy periods that followed dense vegetation grew, fell into swampy areas and was

later buried by new layers of sediment. Eventually this plant material turned to lignite coal. Some plantlife became petrified; today considerable amounts of petrified wood are exposed in the badlands. Betonite, the blue-gray layer of clay, may be traced to ash from ancient volcanoes far to the west. But even as sediments were being deposited, streams were starting to cut down through the soft strata and to sculpt the infinite variety of buttes, tablelands and valleys that make up the badlands we know today.

Though at first glance this landscape appears inhospitable and barren, it is home to a great variety of creatures and plants. Rainfall, scanty though it is, nourishes the grasses that cover the land. And when the wildflowers bloom in bright profusion, they add their vibrant colors to the reds, browns and greens of earth and grass. At home here, too, are more than 125 species of bird, many of which are songbirds. We can thrill to their songs today as much as Roosevelt did. "One of our sweetest, loudest songsters," he wrote, "is the meadowlark. The plains air seems to give it a voice and it will perch on top of a bush or tree and sing for hours in rich, bubbling tones."

Both mule deer and whitetail deer inhabit this park. The whitetails prefer the river woodlands and the mule deer like the more broken country and the uplands. Prairie dogs, historically a staple food source for many predators, live in "towns" in the grasslands. Through careful management some animals that nearly became extinct are once again living here. And, most special of all, through the efforts of Roosevelt and others, the great American bison was saved from

extinction and now live in this park. Today they graze in this very special place much as they once did before they were unmercifully hunted.

Top right *It is fitting that the American bison, which was saved from extinction partly through the efforts of Theodore Roosevelt, now thrive in the park which bears his name*

Bottom right *The forbidding badlands of Theodore Roosevelt National Park, where vegetation maintains a tenuous hold on the inhospitable rock*

Below *Horseback riding in the vast expanses of Theodore Roosevelt National Park*

OHIO

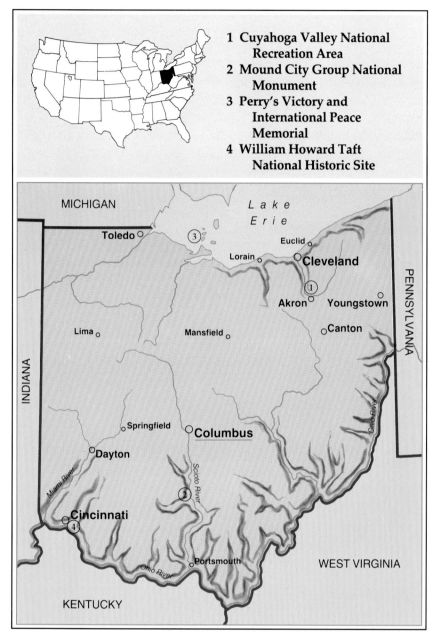

1 **Cuyahoga Valley National Recreation Area**
2 **Mound City Group National Monument**
3 **Perry's Victory and International Peace Memorial**
4 **William Howard Taft National Historic Site**

Cuyahoga Valley National Recreation Area

15610 Vaughn Road, Brecksville, OH 44141
216/650-4636

Happy Days Visitor Center on OH 303, 1 mile west of OH 8 and 2 miles east of Peninsula. Visitor centers, exhibits, guided tours, self-guiding trails, picnicking, hiking, fishing, bicycling, cross-country skiing, handicap access to restrooms/visitor centers; bookstore by Eastern National Park and Monument Association. Accommodations in Cleveland and Akron area.

The Cuyahoga Valley National Recreation Area preserves 32,000 acres of pastoral valley along 22 miles of the Cuyahoga river between Cleveland and Akron, Ohio. Rather than a distant and forbidding wilderness, this park is nearby, welcoming and comfortably familiar

to thousands of city dwellers. It is easily accessible, yet offers a sharp contrast to its urban surroundings.

Sculpted by glaciers, streams and the persistent forces of weather, the Cuyahoga river valley landscape is an enchanting diversity of river flood plain, steep and gentle valley walls forested by deciduous and evergreen woods, numerous tributaries and their ravines, and upland plateaus. It is home to a wide variety of wildlife and plants, amazingly numerous given their close proximity to major metropolitan and industrial areas. The Cuyahoga valley is a harmonious blend of human and natural history, managed today by the National Park Service in cooperation with others who own property within its boundaries.

Mound City Group National Monument

16062 State Route 104, Chillicothe, OH 45601
614/774-1125

3 miles north of Chillicothe via OH 104. Visitor center, exhibits, guided tours, self-guiding tours, picnicking, hiking, handicap access to restrooms/visitor center; bookstore by Eastern National Park and Monument Association. Accommodations in Chillicothe.

Twenty-three burial mounds of Hopewell Indians (200 BC-AD 500) yielded copper breastplates, tools, obsidian blades, shells, ornaments of grizzly bear teeth, and stone pipes carved as birds and animals. The mounds provide insights into the ceremonial customs of these prehistoric people.

Above *A platform pipe found in the Indian burial mounds of Mound City Group National Monument*

Left *The grass-covered burial mounds of Mound City Group blend naturally into the countryside*

The monument to the War of 1812 battle of Lake Erie

Perry's Victory and International Peace Memorial

PO Box 549, Put-in-Bay, OH 43456
419/285-2184

On South Bass Island in Lake Erie, about 4 miles from the mainland. Visitor center, exhibits, guided tours, fishing, handicap access to visitor center; bookstore by Eastern National Park and Monument Association. Accommodations on South Bass Island and on mainland.

Commodore Oliver H. Perry won the greatest naval battle of the War of 1812 on Lake Erie. The memorial – the world's most massive Doric column – was constructed in 1912-15 "to inculcate the lessons of international peace by arbitration and disarmament."

William Howard Taft National Historic Site

2038 Auburn Avenue, Cincinnati, OH 45219
513/684-3262

Near the intersection of Auburn and Dorchester Avenues. Exhibits, guided tours, handicap access to house; bookstore by Eastern National Park and Monument Association. Accommodations in Cincinnati.

This house was the birthplace and boyhood home of the only man to serve as both President and Chief Justice of the United States.

The William Howard Taft Home

OKLAHOMA

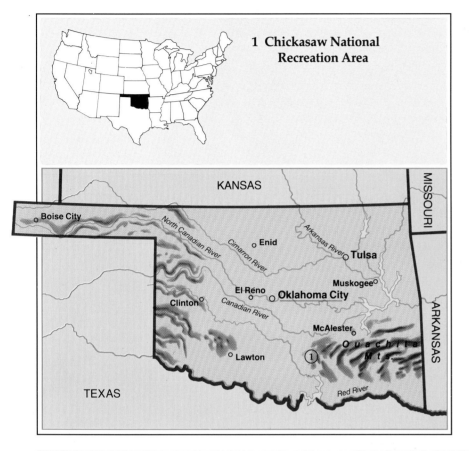

1 Chickasaw National Recreation Area

Chickasaw National Recreation Area
PO Box 201, Sulphur, OK 73086
405/622-3161

On US 177 and OK 7, near Sulphur. Visitor center, exhibits, guided tours, self-guiding tours, picnicking, camping, hiking, swimming, boating, fishing, hunting, handicap access to campgrounds/restrooms/visitor center. Accommodations at Sulphur.

The man-made Lake of the Arbuckles provides water recreation for an extensive midwest area, and numerous cold mineral and freshwater springs, including bromide waters, surface here. This relatively new park combines the former Platt National Park and Arbuckle National Recreation Area in what the US Congress called "a fitting memorialization of the Chickasaw Indian Nation."

Fort Smith, based in Arkansas, is listed under Oklahoma in recognition of "scenic easement" agreements with Oklahoma landowners whereby they maintain neighboring territory in keeping with the national historic site

OREGON

1 Crater Lake National Park
2 John Day Fossil Beds
   National Monument
3 Fort Clatsop National
   Memorial
4 Oregon Caves National
   Monument

Crater Lake National Park

PO Box 7, Crater Lake, OR 97604
503/594-2211

South and west entrances on OR 62. Entrance fee; visitor center, exhibits, guided tours, self-guiding trails, picnicking, camping, backcountry permits, hiking, mountain climbing, swimming, boating, fishing, snowmobiling, cross-country skiing, cabin rental, handicap access to campgrounds/restrooms/visitor center; bookstore by Crater Lake Natural History Association. Accommodations in park.

Crater Lake was once Mount Mazama, a 12,000-foot volcano that was part of the Cascades. Lassen to the south last erupted in 1915, St. Helens in 1980 and Mazama some 6,000 years before in what scientists believe was a most spectacular explosion.

The Klamath Indians' legend is that long ago the volcano Mazama was a passageway between the world above, ruled by the god Sahale Tyree, and the world below, ruled by Llao. One day the two gods quarreled and Llao caused a great eruption, spewing ash into the air and lava down the slopes. Great warriors, interpreting this as an omen, threw themselves into the crater in atonement. Sahale Tyree renewed his war and finally drove Llao into the earth, the mountain-top falling in on him. The crater filled with water and became a place of peace forever.

The scientific explanation of how Crater Lake was formed is more complicated than Indian legend, perhaps, but hardly less dramatic.

The plateau base of the Cascade range was built as the earth's crust

The flooded volcanic crater that is Crater Lake with a smaller volcanic core making an island in its deep blue waters

folded and uplifted, pushing seas westward. Molten rock pushed forcefully toward the surface, creating both violent eruptions and the welling up of lava through enormous cracks. Explosive eruptions built a string of volcanoes on this extensive plateau base, one of which, Mount Mazama, now holds Crater Lake. Satellite cones on Mazama's flanks created today's Mount Scott, Hillman Peak and The Watchman. Glaciers periodically covered Mount Mazama's flanks and carved out the U-shaped valleys such as Munson Valley and Kerr Notch. About 6,800 years ago the climactic eruptions occurred. The Mazama magma chamber emptied and the volcano collapsed, leaving a huge bowl-shaped caldera in its place. The once high mountain lies scattered over eight states and three Canadian provinces; some 5,000 square miles were covered with 6 inches or more of Mazama's ash. The explosions were 42 times greater than those of Mount St. Helens in 1980.

After the volcanic activity subsided, water began to collect. Springs, snow and rain filled the caldera. As the lake deepened and widened, evaporation and seepage balanced the incoming flow. The level now varies less than 3 feet annually in what is the nation's deepest lake.

John Day Fossil Beds National Monument

420 West Main, John Day, OR 97845
503/575-0721

Visitor center 40 miles west of John Day, near Dayville. Visitor center, self-guiding trails, picnicking, hiking, fishing, handicap access to restrooms/visitor center; bookstore by Pacific Northwest National Parks and Forests Association. Accommodations in nearby communities.

Plant and animal fossils here cover five epochs, from the Eocene to the end of the Pleistocene periods, the last 40 million years of the age of mammals.

Fort Clatsop National Memorial

Route 3, Box 604-FC, Astoria, OR 97103
503/861-2471

On US 101, 5 miles southwest of Astoria. Visitor center, exhibits, guided tours, self-guiding tours, picnicking, handicap access to restrooms/visitor center; bookstore by Fort Clatsop Historical Association. Accommodations in Astoria.

The Lewis and Clark Expedition camped here in the winter of 1805-06.

Oregon Caves National Monument

1900 Caves Highway, Cave Junction, OR 97523
503/592-2100

On OR 46, 20 miles east of Cave Junction. Self-guiding trails, picnicking, hiking, cabin rental, handicap access to restrooms; bookstore by Crater Lake Natural History Association. Accommodations in park and at Cave Junction.

Ground water dissolving marble bedrock formed these cave passages and intricate flowstone formations in what is called "The Marble Halls of Oregon."

Left *Mount Scott stands on the horizon above Crater Lake*

Below *Fort Clatsop, Astoria, where Lewis and Clark wintered in 1805-06*

PENNSYLVANIA

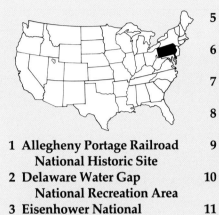

1 Allegheny Portage Railroad
   National Historic Site
2 Delaware Water Gap
   National Recreation Area
3 Eisenhower National
   Historic Site
4 Fort Necessity National
   Battlefield

5 Friendship Hill National
   Historic Site
6 Gettysburg National
   Military Park
7 Hopewell Furnace National
   Historic Site
8 Independence National
   Historical Park
9 Johnstown Flood National
   Memorial
10 Thaddeus Kosciuszko
   National Memorial
11 Edgar Allan Poe National
   Historic Site
12 Valley Forge National
   Historical Park

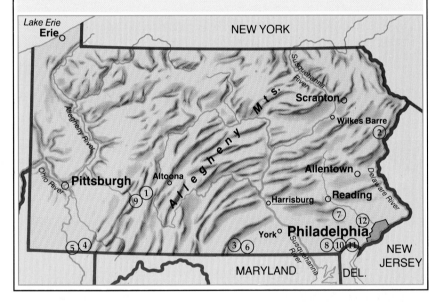

Allegheny Portage Railroad National Historic Site

PO Box 247, Cresson, PA 16630
814/886-8177

Visitor center on US 22, 2 miles east of Cresson. Visitor center, exhibits, guided tour, self-guiding tours, picnicking, hiking, handicap access to visitor center; bookstore by Eastern National Park and Monument Association. Accommodations in Cresson.

Traces of the first railroad crossing of the Allegheny Mountains can still be seen here. An inclined plane railroad, it enabled passengers and freight to be transported over the mountains, providing a critical link in the Pennsylvania Mainline Canal system and with the West. Built between 1831 and 1834, it was abandoned by 1857.

Delaware Water Gap National Recreation Area

(Pennsylvania, New Jersey)
Bushkill, PA 18324
717/588-6637

Kittatinny Point Information Station on I-80 in New Jersey. Visitor centers, exhibits, guided tours, self-guiding trails, picnicking, camping, hiking, mountain climbing, swimming, boating, fishing, hunting, snowmobiling, cross-country skiing, handicap access to restrooms/visitor centers; bookstore by Eastern National Park and Monument Association. Accommodations in nearby communities in Pennsylvania and New Jersey.

This scenic area preserves relatively unspoiled land on both the New Jersey and Pennsylvania sides of the middle Delaware river where it flows through the famous gap in the Appalachian Mountains.

Eisenhower National Historic Site

c/o Gettysburg National Military Park, Gettysburg, PA 17325
717/334-1124

Entrance fee; visitor center, exhibits, guided tours, self-guiding tours, handicap access to restrooms/house/visitor center; bookstore by Eastern National Park and Monument Association. Accommodations in Gettysburg area.

This was the only home ever owned by General Dwight D. Eisenhower and his wife Mamie. It served as a refuge when he was President and as a retirement home after he left office.

Left *Skew Arch bridge, about one mile east of the Lemon House, built to carry wagons and other traffic over the railroad at Alleghany Portage*

The Upper Falls at Van Campen's Glen, Delaware Water Gap National Recretion Area

Fort Necessity National Battlefield

RD 2, Box 528, The National Pike, Farmington, PA 15437
412/329-5512

On US 40, 11 miles east of Uniontown. Visitor center, exhibits, guided tours, self-guiding tours, picnicking, camping, hiking, handicap access to restrooms/visitor center; bookstore by Eastern National Park and Monument Association. Accommodations in Uniontown.

Colonial troops commanded by George Washington, then 22 years old, were defeated here in the opening battle of the French and Indian War on July 3, 1754. The park includes the nearby monument to Major General Edward Braddock and the early nineteenth-century Mount Washington Tavern, and Jumonville Glenn, the site of the first skirmishing of the war on May 28, 1754.

Colonial army "players" chat with visitors about army life in 18th century America at Fort Necessity National Battlefield

Friendship Hill National Historic Site

c/o Fort Necessity National Battlefield, RD 2, Box 528, The National Pike, Farmington, PA 15437
412/725-9190

On PA 166, 3 miles north of Point Marion. Exhibits, self-guiding tours, picnicking, hiking, handicap access to house. Accommodations in Point Marion and Masontown.

The young Swiss immigrant Albert Gallatin made his home here on the edge of the frontier in the 1780s. Gallatin, Secretary of the Treasury 1801-13 served his adopted country in business, politics, diplomacy and scholarship.

Gettysburg National Military Park

Gettysburg, PA 17325
717/334-1124

Visitor center at junction of PA 134 and US 15 in Gettysburg. Visitor center, exhibits, museum, guided tours, self-guiding tours, picnicking, camping, bicycling, handicap access to restrooms/ visitor center; bookstore and electric map by Eastern National Park and Monument Association. Accommodations in Gettysburg.

On July 1, 2 and 3, 1863, Confederate General Robert E. Lee battled unsuccessfully against the Army of the Potomac under General George G. Meade at Gettysburg, the "High Water Mark of the Confederacy," according to some. Physically exhausted and with spirits broken, the Confederacy never again tried such a monumental offensive action against the North.

Four months after the battle, President Abraham Lincoln traveled to Gettysburg to dedicate the national cemetery. It was here that he made a speech which has become famous as the Gettysburg address.

Hopewell Furnace National Historic Site

RD 1, Box 345, Elverson, PA 19520
215/528-8873

On PA 345, 5 miles south of Birdsboro. Visitor center, exhibits, self-guiding tours, handicap access to restrooms/visitor center; bookstore by Eastern National Park and Monument Association. Accommodations in Reading, Pottstown, and Morgantown.

This is the finest example of an early American iron plantation. Hopewell produced iron from 1773 until 1883. The restored charcoal-fueled iron furnace, waterwheel, cast house, ironmaster's mansion, workers' homes and other industrial and domestic buildings make up this unique park.

Visitors view the popular Cyclorama painting of the Civil War battle at Gettysburg National Military Park

Independence National Historical Park

313 Walnut Street, Philadelphia, PA 19106
215/627-1776

Visitor center at Third and Chestnut Streets. Visitor center, exhibits, guided tours, self-guiding tours, handicap access to restrooms/visitor center; bookstore by Eastern National Park and Monument Association. Accommodations in immediate area.

This has been called the "most historic square mile in America." It is the scene of the beginnings of the nation – where the Continental Congress met during the days of the American Revolution, where the Constitution was written and adopted, and where, beginning in 1790, the United States Congress and the Supreme Court met for ten years before moving to Washington DC. The park includes Independence Hall, Congress Hall, old City Hall, the First and Second Banks of the United States, Franklin Court, and other buildings associated with the founding and growth of the new nation.

Johnstown Flood National Memorial

PO Box 247, Cresson, PA 16630
814/886-8176

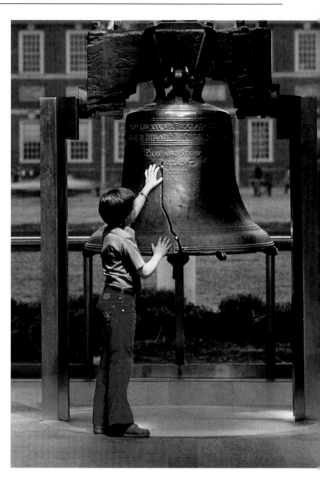

Above *A young visitor touches one of our most prized possessions, the Liberty Bell*

Left *Independence Hall and the Liberty Bell pavilion, the core of Independence National Historical Park*

Visitor center on dam site along US 219 and PA 869, 10 miles northeast of Johnstown, near St. Michael. Visitor center, exhibits, self-guiding tours, picnic area; bookstore by Eastern National Park and Monument Association. Accommodations in Johnstown.

The Johnstown Flood of 1889 caused by a break in the South Fork Dam is memorialized here.

Thaddeus Kosciuszko National Memorial

c/o Independence National Historical Park, 313 Walnut Street, Philadelphia 19106
215/597-8974

301 Pine Street. Exhibits, self-guiding tours. Accommodations in immediate area.

The life and work of this Polish-born patriot and hero of the American Revolution are commemorated at the house in which he lived while in this country.

Edgar Allan Poe National Historic Site

532 North Seventh Street, Philadelphia, PA 19123
215/597-8780

On 7th Street, 3 blocks north of Market Street. Exhibits, guided tours; bookstore by Eastern National Park and Monument Association. Accommodations in greater Philadelphia area.

The life and work of the gifted American author are portrayed in a three-building complex. Poe's six years in Philadelphia were his most productive.

Valley Forge National Historical Park

Valley Forge, PA 19481
215/783-7700

PA 363, off Exit 24 of Pennsylvania Turnpike, leads to visitor center about 20 miles west of Philadelphia. Visitor center, exhibits, self-guiding tours, picnicking, hiking, horseback riding, boating, fishing, bicycling, handicap access to restrooms/visitor center; bookstore by Valley Forge Interpretive Association. Food available in park; accommodations in immediate area.

This is the site of the Continental Army's winter encampment of 1777-78. The park contains General Washington's headquarters, original earthworks, a variety of monuments and markers and reconstructions of the log huts used by the colonial troops.

Above Edgar Allen Poe lived in this house for less than two years, but his life's work is commemorated by the National Park Service through splendid exhibits

Right A living history demonstration of the Continental Army's horrible winter of 1777-78 at Valley Forge, Pennsylvania

RHODE ISLAND

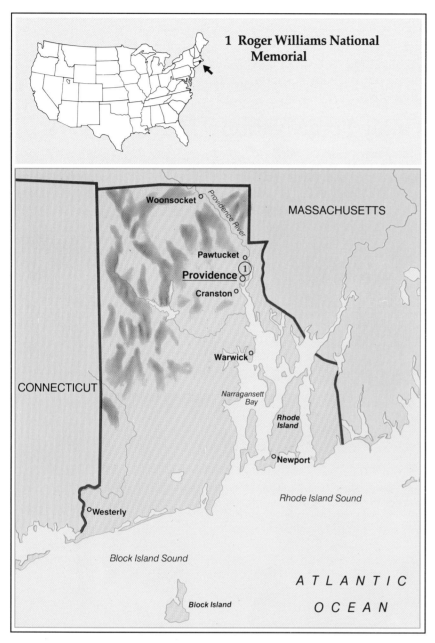

1 Roger Williams National Memorial

Roger Williams National Memorial

PO Box 367 Annex, Providence, RI 02901
401/528-5385

282 North Main Street, between Canal and North Main Streets, at corner of Smith Street. Exhibits. Accommodations in greater Providence area.

This memorial, at the site of the old town spring in Providence, honors the seventeenth century founder of the Rhode Island Colony and pioneer in religious and civil liberties.

Touro Synagogue, Newport, a magnificent example of colonial religious architecture which is still in use, is a national historic site. Not a unit of the National Park System, it is a related area which is assisted by the Service. Inset: *Scrolls of the Law*

SOUTH CAROLINA

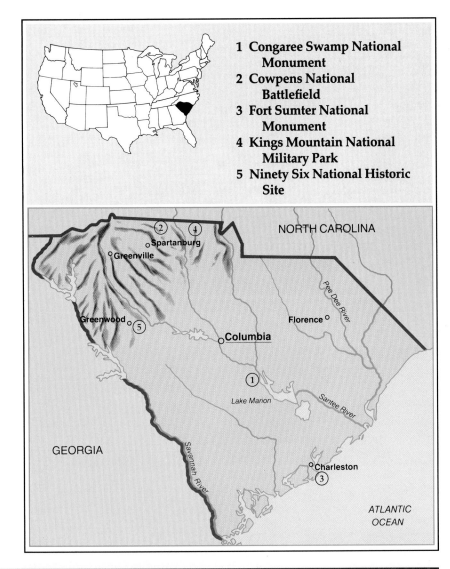

1 Congaree Swamp National Monument
2 Cowpens National Battlefield
3 Fort Sumter National Monument
4 Kings Mountain National Military Park
5 Ninety Six National Historic Site

Congaree Swamp National Monument

PO Box 11938, Columbia, SC 29211
803/765-5571

Off SC 48 (Bluff Road), 20 miles southeast of Columbia. Guided tours, hiking, boating, fishing. Accommodations at Columbia.

This new monument 20 miles southeast of Columbia contains the last significant tract of virgin southern bottomland hardwoods in the southeastern United States, including loblolly pines, bald cypress and tupelos, trees that have all but disappeared elsewhere in the country.

Cowpens National Battlefield

PO Box 308, Chesnee, SC 29323
803/461-2828

Intersection of SC11 and 110, 2 miles southeast of US 221 at Chesnee. Visitor center, exhibits, guided tours, self-guiding tours, picnicking, hiking, bicycle trail, handicap access to restrooms/visitor center; bookstore by Eastern National Park and Monument Association. Accommodations in Gaffney.

Daniel Morgan, fiesty brigadier general in the Continental Army, won a decisive Revolutionary War victory over British Lt. Col. Banastre Tarleton on January 17, 1781, at this place called "Hannah's Cowpens," a piece of high, rolling ground that was used for wintering cattle.

Fort Sumter National Monument

1214 Middle Street, Sullivan's Island, SC 29482
803/883-3123

Fort Sumter accessible by boat only; tour boats leave from Municipal Marina on Lockwood Drive, in Charleston. Fort Moultrie is on West Middle Street, Sullivan Island, 10 miles north of Charleston, off US 17 and SC 703. Visitor center, exhibits, guided tours, self-guiding tours, handicap access to restrooms/visitor center; bookstore by Eastern National Park and Monument Association. Accommodations in Charleston and surrounding area.

The opening shots of the Civil War were fired here on April 12, 1861, when South Carolina militia fired on Fort Sumter in Charleston Harbor. The park includes Fort Moultrie, the scene of the Patriot victory of June 28, 1776 – one of the early defeats of the British in the Revolutionary War. The fort has been restored to reflect nearly two centuries of seacoast defense.

Fort Sumter, defender of Charleston Harbor, defenseless against the opening shots of the Civil War

Kings Mountain National Military Park

PO Box 31, Kings Mountain, NC 28086
803/936-7921

On SC 216, just off I-85. Visitor center, exhibits, self-guiding trails, hiking, horseback riding, handicap access to restrooms; bookstore by Eastern National Park and Monument Association. Accommodations in Gaffney.

On October 7, 1780, during the most critical hours of the American Revolution in the southern colonies, a band of frontiersmen from Appalachia confronted loyalist forces here in the rolling hills just south of the North-South Carolina border. The victory for the Patriots was one of the most important of the war against the British.

Ninety Six National Historic Site

PO Box 496, Ninety Six, SC 29666
803/543-4068

On SC 248, 9 miles east of Greenwood and 2 miles south of Ninety Six. Visitor center, exhibits, guided tours, self-guiding trails; bookstore by Eastern National Park and Monument Association. Accommodations in Greenwood.

This important colonial backcountry trading village and government seat after 1769 was held briefly by the British during the Revolutionary War and is the scene of Nathanael Greene's month-long siege in 1781. The site contains earthworks of a 1781 fortification, the remains of two historic villages, a colonial plantation complex and prehistoric sites.

Ninety Six National Historic Site, the earthen remains of a backcountry trading village and Revolutionary War outpost

SOUTH DAKOTA

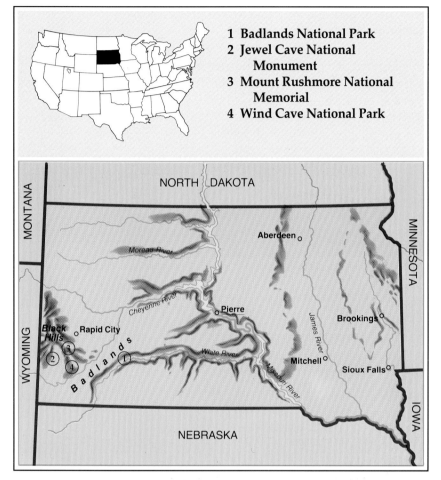

1 **Badlands National Park**
2 **Jewel Cave National Monument**
3 **Mount Rushmore National Memorial**
4 **Wind Cave National Park**

Badlands National Park

PO Box 6, Interior, SD 57750
605/433-5361

Cedar Pass visitor center on Route SD 240, 2½ miles northeast of Interior, 28 miles southwest of Kadoka and 29 miles southeast of Wall, both on I-90. Entrance fee; visitor center, exhibits, guided tours, self-guiding trails, picnicking, camping, hiking, cabin rental, handicap access to visitor center; bookstore by Badlands Natural History Association. Accommodations in park and in Wall, Kadoka, and Rapid City.

Out of the rolling Dakota prairie, known as the badlands, rain and wind and frost have carved steep canyons, sharp ridges, gullies, spires and knobs.

The water that today eats into the soft badlands formations falls mostly as rain during torrential spring and summer storms. Present annual precipitation, including the storms, is only 16 inches, just enough to sustain the grass.

Despite summer temperatures that may top 100° Fahrenheit, and frigid winter winds, many animals and plants still find the badlands a good place to live. White-throated swifts and cliff swallows nest on the faces of cliffs, and rock wrens build in the crevices. An occasional pair of golden eagles may rear their young on a high, inaccessible butte. Along the drainages and passes junipers patch the landscape with green and yuccas dot the broken slopes and valleys. Islands of life collect where water is found and cottonwoods, wild roses, skunkbush

Left and right *The dramatically desolate country of Badlands National Park*

The vast, uninhabited expanses of the South Dakota Badlands from the air

South Dakota

Right *Deer roam the rugged country of Badlands National Park*

Below *The monumental faces of some of America's most celebrated presidents gaze perpetually over the South Dakota landscape at Mount Rushmore National Memorial*

sumac and other trees and shrubs shelter birds. Wherever trees and shrubs grow, porcupines, chipmunks, mice and even bats are sure to live.

The great nineteenth-century migration of people from the Atlantic states doomed some of the large mammals of the plains – the gray wolf, the elk, the grizzly bear. Others, the mule deer and the pronghorn, decreased in number and then revived. Bison and bighorns were exterminated from the badlands, but the National Park Service, seeking to restore the vanished prairie scene, reintroduced them and they are doing well.

French-Canadian trappers were among early European visitors to the badlands. They called the region *les mauvaises terres à traverser* (bad lands to cross). Although relics thousands of years old have been found in the region, the Arikara are the earliest Indian tribe known to have lived on these plains. By the mid-eighteenth century, however, the Sioux dominated. During the next hundred years their culture, based on bison hunting, flourished. Then the US Army, miners and homesteaders moved in, changing the face of the prairie and the life of the native people forever. Forty years of struggle ended Sioux rule and put them on the reservation. Cattle replaced bison; wheat replaced prairie.

In a few more decades the badlands came to be regarded less as worthless wasteland than as a scenic and geologic wonder worthy of preservation. Authorized by Congress in 1929, Badlands National Monument was established by Presidential proclamation in 1939 to preserve the scenery, protect the fossils and wildlife and conserve the shortgrass prairie. The monument more than doubled in size in 1976 with the addition of 133,300 acres of the Pine Ridge Reservation, to be administered by the National Park Service in agreement with the Oglala Sioux Tribe. Called the South Unit, this stunning landscape of high grassy tableland and spectacular buttes is the scene of much Sioux history. The Ghost Dances at Stronghold Table in 1890 were a prelude to the bloodshed at Wounded Knee, 25 miles south of here. Congress elevated Badlands from national monument to national park in 1978, underscoring the value of the Badlands to present and future generations.

Jewel Cave National Monument

PO Box 351, Custer, SD 57730
605/673-2288

On US 16, 13 miles west of Custer. Visitor center, exhibits, guided tours, picnicking, handicap access to restrooms/visitor center; bookstore by Wind Cave/Jewel Cave Natural History Association. Accommodations in Custer and in Newcastle, WY.

This, the fourth largest explored cave in the world, is a wonderland of narrow passages and sparkling calcite crystals.

Mount Rushmore National Memorial

PO Box 268, Keystone, SD 57751
605/574-2523

On SD 244, 3 miles southwest of Keystone. Visitor center, exhibits, handicap access to restrooms/visitor center. Food available in park; accommodations in Keystone.

Gutzon Borglum's massive carved heads of George Washington, Abraham Lincoln, Thomas Jefferson and Theodore Roosevelt on 5,725-foot Mount Rushmore have become a national emblem of sorts. Work began on August 10, 1927, the same day President Calvin Coolidge officially dedicated Mount Rushmore as a national memorial. It took 14 years to complete because of delays caused by lack of funds and bad weather: only 6½ years were actually spent in carving.

Wind Cave National Park

Hot Springs, SD 57747
605/745-4600

On US 385, 11 miles from Hot Springs. Visitor center, exhibits, guided tours, self-guiding tours, picnicking, camping, hiking, handicap access to campgrounds/restrooms/visitor center; bookstore by Wind Cave/Jewel Cave Natural History Association. Food available in park; accommodations in Hot Springs.

The Wind Cave area has been protected since 1903 when it became the seventh national park. Although native Americans may have known of the cave, it was not discovered by white men until 1881 when two brothers, Jesse and Tom Bingham, were led by a loud whistling noise to a small hole in the ground, the cave's only natural opening. The wind causing the whistling, and which gave the cave its name, is created by different atmospheric pressures in the cave and outside and is still apparent at the cave entrance.

It was left to later adventurers such as Alvin McDonald to follow the wind and explore the cave's extensive network of passageways containing "boxwork," "popcorn" and "frostwork" formations, and other delicate irreplaceable features. Young Alvin and others who explored the cave before the turn of the century were fascinated by what they found – chocolate-colored crystals, formations resembling faces or animals and chambers that inspired names such as the "Garden of Eden" and the "Dungeon."

Reports of these discoveries drew a stream of curious tourists to the cave and local entrepreneurs, including the McDonald family, blasted open passages and guided tourists through for a fee. Cave specimens were removed and sold. Today the cave's fragile features are protected.

Wind Cave is one of the world's oldest caves, formed at least 60 million years ago when the same tremendous forces that uplifted the Black Hills cracked this area's limestone layers. Over millions of years water trickling through these fissures dissolved the rock and carved out the complex labyrinth of the cave.

After the cave formed colorful formations began to decorate its walls. One of the most prominent is "boxwork" – thin, honeycomb-shaped structures of calcite that protrude from the walls and ceilings. Nowhere else in the world is there such a large display of this formation although some of the better known cave formations such as stalactites and stalagmites are rare here.

There are more than a thousand passages yet to be explored in Wind Cave. In 1891 Alvin McDonald wrote: "Have given up the idea of finding the end of Wind Cave." The better-equipped spelunkers of today have not given up. They continue to push farther and farther into the cave's cool, black recesses of the already charted 37 miles of passageways.

TENNESSEE

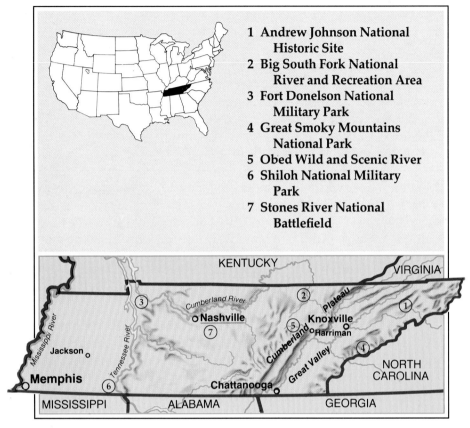

1 Andrew Johnson National
   Historic Site
2 Big South Fork National
   River and Recreation Area
3 Fort Donelson National
   Military Park
4 Great Smoky Mountains
   National Park
5 Obed Wild and Scenic River
6 Shiloh National Military
   Park
7 Stones River National
   Battlefield

Andrew Johnson National Historic Site

Depot Street, Greeneville, TN 37743
615/638-3551

In Greeneville, 70 miles northeast of Knoxville. Visitor center, exhibits, self-guiding tours, handicap access to restrooms/visitor center; bookstore by Eastern National Park and Monument Association. Accommodations in Greenville.

The site includes two homes and the tailor shop of the seventeenth President, who served from 1865 to 1869, and the Andrew Johnson National Cemetery, where the President, members of his family, and veterans of many wars are buried.

Big South Fork National River and Recreation Area

Drawer 630, Oneida, TN 37841
615/569-6389

On Kentucky-Tennessee border between US 27 and 127, 75 miles northwest of Knoxville; visitor center on Leatherwood Ford Road, 9 miles west of Oneida. Visitor center, hiking, swimming, boating, fishing, hunting; bookstore by Eastern National Park and Monument

Left *The kitchen of the home of our 17th President, Andrew Johnson*

Right *Sunrise over the Great Smoky Mountains National Park, North Carolina and Tennessee*

Association. Accommodations in Oneida and Jamestown, TN, and Whitney City, KY.

The free-flowing Big South Fork of the Cumberland river and its tributaries pass through scenic gorges and valleys containing a wide range of natural and historical features.

Fort Donelson National Military Park

PO Box F, Dover, TN 37058
615/232-5348

On US 79, west side of Dover. Visitor center, exhibits, guided tours, self-guiding tours, picnic area, handicap access to restrooms; bookstore by Eastern National Park and Monument Association. Accommodations in Dover.

Well-preserved earthen works, rifle pits and batteries near Dover, Tennessee mark the site of the first major Union victory in the Civil War, where, in February 1862 General Ulysses S. Grant and a force of 17,000 men encircled Fort Donelson. Grant's demand for "unconditional surrender" resulted in the capture of 14,000 Southern soldiers and opened a river route into the heart of the Confederacy.

Great Smoky Mountains National Park

(Tennessee, North Carolina)
Gatlinburg, TN 37738
615/436-5615

Sugarlands Visitor Center on US 441, 2 miles south of Gatlinburg. Visitor centers, exhibits, guided tours, self-guiding trails, picnicking, camping, backcountry permits, hiking, horseback riding, fishing, cabin rental, handicap access to campgrounds/restrooms/visitor centers; bookstores by Great Smoky Mountains Natural History Association. Accommodations in Gatlinburg.

The Great Smoky Mountains, the majestic climax of the Appalachian Highlands, are a wildlands sanctuary preserving the world's finest examples of temperate deciduous forest. The name comes from the

smoke-like haze enveloping the mountains, which stretch in sweeping troughs and mighty billows to the horizon. The park boasts unspoiled forests similar to those early pioneers found. Restored log cabins and barns stand as reminders of those who carved a living from this wilderness. Fertile soils and abundant rain have encouraged the development of a world-renowned variety of flora, including more than 1,400 kinds of flowering plants. In the coves, broadleaf trees predominate whereas along the crest – more than 6,000 feet elevation – conifer forests like those of central Canada thrive. Wildflowers and migrating birds abound in late April and early May. During June and July rhododendrons bloom in spectacular profusion. Autumn's pageantry of color usually peaks in mid-October. For many this is the finest time of the year, with cool, clear days ideal for hiking. In winter, an unpredictable season, a peace pervades the park. Fog rolling over the mountains may blanket the conifers in frost.

A scenic, high mountain road winds up through Newfound Gap, with a spur out to Clingmans Dome and its observation tower. There are superb views along the road and from the tower. But roads offer only an introduction to the Smokies. More than 800 miles of trails thread the whole of the Smokies' natural fabric – its waterfalls, coves, balds and rushing streams.

Obed Wild and Scenic River

PO Drawer 630, Oneida, TN 38376
615/569-6389

US 27 or TN 62 to Wartburg. Visitor center, swimming, boating, fishing, hunting; bookstore by Eastern National Park and Monument Association. Accommodations at Wartburg.

The Obed River and its two main tributaries, Clear Creek and Daddy's Creek, cut into the Cumberland Plateau of east Tennessee, providing some of the most rugged scenery in the southeast. Elevations range from 900 to 2,900 feet above sea level.

Shiloh National Military Park

Shiloh, TN 38376
901/689-5257

10 miles south of Savannah and Adamsville, via US 64 and TN 22. Visitor center, exhibits, guided tours, self-guiding tours, picnic area, handicap access to restrooms/visitor center; bookstore by Eastern National Park and Monument Association. Accommodations in Pickwick, Savannah and Adamsville.

Shiloh was the first major battle of the western campaign in the Civil War – two days of some of the war's most fierce fighting, April 6 and 7, 1862. With victory here, Grant began his campaign to control the Mississippi. More than 23,000 men on both sides were killed, wounded or missing at Shiloh, in what has been described as a "soldier's battle," devoid of much leadership. It has been known as "Bloody Shiloh" ever since.

Stones River National Battlefield

Route 10, Box 495, Old Nashville Highway, Murfreesboro, TN 37130
615/893-9501

On US 40, northwest corner of Murfreesboro. Visitor center, exhibits, guided tours, self-guiding tours, picnic area, hiking, bicycle trail, handicap access to restrooms/visitor center; bookstore by Eastern National Park and Monument Association. Accommodations in Murfreesboro.

On December 31, 1862, Confederate General Braxton Bragg and a force of 38,000 charged Union General William Rosecrans' 45,000 men near Murfreesboro, Tennessee. It was a tactical victory for the Confederates, but Bragg retreated after losing more than 11,000 men, leaving Rosecrans, who lost nearly 13,000, in command of Murfreesboro. In effect it was the first step toward splitting the Confederacy.

Left *The characteristic haziness and color of the Smoky Mountains which gave them their name*

Below *The wild turkey is quite common in Great Smoky Mountains National Park. Here it puts on its "threat" display*

TEXAS

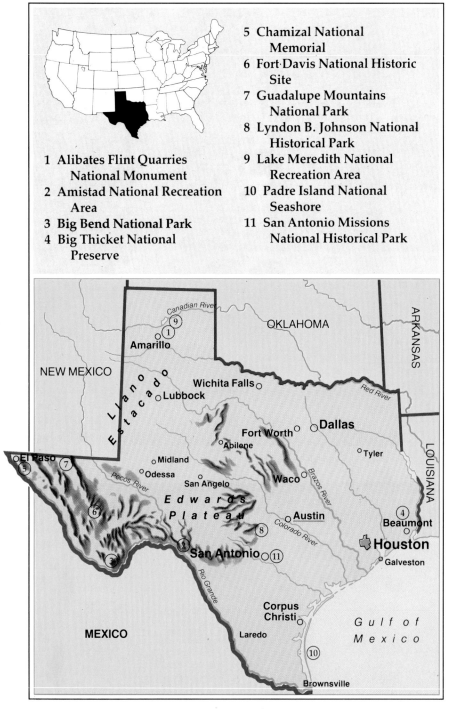

Alibates Flint Quarries National Monument

PO Box 1438, Fritch, TX 79036
806/857-3151

Adjoins Lake Meredith Recreation Area, 40 miles north of Amarillo.
Visitor center, exhibits, guided tours. Accommodations in Fritch
and Borger.

For more than 10,000 years pre-Columbian Indians dug agatized
dolomite from quarries here to make projectile points, knives,
scrapers and other tools.

Amistad National Recreation Area

Star Route 2, Box 5-P, Del Rio, TX 78840
512/775-7491

On US 90, in Del Rio. Self-guiding tours, picnic area, camping,
hiking, swimming, boating, fishing, hunting, handicap access to
campgrounds/restrooms/visitor center. Supplies in park;
commercial campsites near Diablo East, Rough Canyon, and Pecos.

Boating and watersports highlight activities in the US section of
Amistad Reservoir at the confluence of the Devil's, Rio Grande and
Pecos rivers.

Above *A leisurely waterborne outing in the tranquil waters of Amistad National
Recreation Area*

Right *Amistad National Recreation Area is administered in cooperation with
Mexico*

Big Bend National Park

Big Bend National Park, TX 79834
915/477-2251

323 miles from El Paso to visitor center at Panther Junction, via I-10 and US 90 to Alpine and TX 118. Visitor center, exhibits, guided tours, self-guiding trails, picnicking, camping, backcountry permits, hiking, horseback riding, boating, fishing, handicap access to restrooms/visitor center; bookstore by Big Bend Natural History Association. Accommodations in park and in Terlingua and Lajitas.

Indian legend has it that after making the earth, the Great Spirit simply dumped all the leftover rocks on the Big Bend. Spanish explorers called it "the uninhabited land." In this land of desert and mountains cut through by the Rio Grande you will find extraordinary creatures, including a desert amphibian, Couch's spadefoot toad; a mosquito fish which has its entire world range in a single pond in the park; a small mammal, the kangaroo rat, that metabolizes water; and a good-sized bird, the roadrunner, that would rather run than fly.

There are winged insects that live their entire lives in, on, and off one species of plant, and there are, by contrast, coyotes that may turn up anywhere and eat almost anything. The jackrabbits here have such large ears that they sometimes use them as radiators, transferring body heat to the environment. Motion can be almost imperceptible, or as fast as the peregrine falcon, clocked at more than 22 miles an hour in its dive.

Time can be measured . . . or you can leave it unmeasured. If you want the reaches of time, you can find them in the Fossil Bone Exhibit or, less apparently, in the deep rock strata of the three Big Bend canyons, Santa Elena, Mariscal and Boquillas. If you want fleeting glimpses of time, watch the jackrabbit sprint to elude its predators. If you are mildly patient, see how long it takes after the first good spring rainstorm for that "dead" desert to come alive with brightly colored flowers. The park can be thought of as having three natural divisions: the river, the desert and the mountains. River and mountains serve as counterpoints to the desert, the river as a linear oasis, and the mountains function, in relation to their arid desert surroundings, much like an island of temperate life.

Left *Beyond the mighty cleft it has carved in the Chisos Mountains the Rio Grande widens to a broad placid river*

Right The roadrunner is not completely flightless and is a favorite among the birdwatchers at Big Bend, an ornithologist's delight

Big Thicket National Preserve

PO Box 7408, Beaumont, TX 77706
713/839-2691

Information station on FM 420, 2½ miles east of US 69, 7 miles north of Kountze. Visitor center, exhibits, self-guiding tours, backcountry permits, hiking, boating, fishing, hunting, handicap access to restrooms; bookstore by Southwest Parks and Monuments Association. Accommodations in Beaumont.

Big Thicket has been called "an American ark," "the biological crossroads of North America," and "North America's best-equipped ecological laboratory." The preserve was established to protect the remnants of this complex biological diversity. What is extraordinary is not the rarity or abundance of life forms, but how many species coexist in this shrinking remnant of a once vast combination of virgin pine and cypress forest, hardwood forest, meadow and blackwater swamp. This unique ecosystem is a mingling of diverse plant associations resulting in a large variety of plant species found in close proximity.

Chamizal National Memorial

PO Box 722, El Paso, TX 79944
915/543-7780

In south central El Paso on the Mexican border. Visitor center, exhibits, guided tours, picnicking, handicap access to restrooms/visitor center; bookstore by Southwest Parks and Monuments Association. Accommodations in El Paso and in Juarez, Mexico, adjacent to park.

The peaceful settlement of a 99-year boundary dispute between the United States and Mexico is memorialized here. The Chamizal Treaty, ending the dispute, was signed in 1963. An amphitheater and 500-seat auditorium are used by theatrical groups from both nations.

Fort Davis National Historic Site

PO Box 1456, Fort Davis, TX 79734
915/426-3225

In Fort Davis, TX, from I-10 via TX 17 and 118, or from US 90 via 505 and 166 to TX 17. Entrance fee; visitor center, exhibits, self-guiding tours, picnicking, hiking, handicap access to restrooms/visitor center; bookstore by Southwest Parks and Monuments Association. Accommodations in Fort Davis.

A key post in the West Texas defensive system, the fort guarded emigrants on the San Antonio-El Paso road from 1854 to 1891. Troops from Fort Davis campaigned against Comanche and Apache Indians.

Guadalupe Mountains National Park

3225 National Parks Highway, Carlsbad, NM 88220
915/828-3385

Access via US 62 and US 180, 55 miles southwest of Carlsbad. Visitor center, exhibits, guided tours, self-guiding trails, picnicking, camping, backcountry permits, hiking; bookstore by Carlsbad Caverns Natural History Association. Accommodations at Carlsbad.

The Guadalupe mountains stand like an island in the desert, silent sentinels watching over the most extensive fossil reef complex known to man. Trace the trails of human history here or gaze on vast dimensions of geologic time in the spectacular exposure of Capitan Reef.

The mountain range resembles a massive wedge – rising in Texas, its arms reach northward into New Mexico. At its apex stands El Capitan, a 2,000-foot sheer cliff. The mountains and canyons shelter a unique remnant of forest plants and animals which have struggled for survival since the end of the ice ages about 10,000 years ago. The 76,000-acre park lies astride these mountains' most scenic, rugged portions. Here, the highest point in Texas, 8,749-foot Guadalupe Peak stands in sharp contrast with the park's lowest elevation, 3,650 feet at the base of the western escarpment.

In the park you can explore desert lowlands, superb canyons and forested mountains. You can study geology, visit historic sites and see plants and animals uncommon to the surrounding semiarid lowlands. Those who climb into the high country can enjoy outstanding views across the Salt Basin to the west, the Delaware Basin to the south and east and into the deeply cut canyons to the north.

Below Brilliantly colored flowers in Guadalupe Mountains National Park in stark contrast to the barren forbidding hills behind

Right A rare sign of human habitation in the unspoiled vastness of the Guadalupe Mountains

Lyndon B. Johnson National Historical Park

PO Box 329, Johnson City, TX 78636
512/868-7128

One unit of park in Johnson City, the other in Stonewall; both on US 290. Visitor center, exhibits, guided tours, handicap access to restrooms/visitor center; bookstore by Southwest Parks and Monuments Association. Accommodations in Johnson City, Stonewall, Blanco, and Fredericksburg.

The birthplace, boyhood home, and ranch of the thirty-sixth President, 1963-69, and his grandparent's old ranch make up this park.

Lake Meredith National Recreation Area

PO Box 1438, Fritch, TX 79036
806/857-3151

Headquarters at Fritch on US 136. Visitor center, exhibits, picnicking, camping, swimming, boating, fishing, hunting; bookstore by Southwest Parks and Monuments Association. Food available in park; accommodations at Fritch.

Lake Meredith lies on the dry, windswept High Plains of the Texas Panhandle, part of a larger region covering 24,000 square miles known as the Llano Estacado. This is the land of cowboys and natural gas refineries. But cowboys of yesterday never dreamed of anything like this sparkling oasis of recreation called Lake Meredith. Manmade Lake Meredith on the Canadian river is one of the most popular water-activity centers in the southwest.

Padre Island National Seashore

9405 South Padre Island Drive, Corpus Christi, TX 78418
512/937-2621

Only auto access over causeway from Corpus Christi to Mieces County Park, and from Port Aransas down Mustang Island via Park Road 53. Visitor center, exhibits, self-guiding tours, picnicking, camping, hiking, horseback riding, swimming, boating, fishing, hunting, handicap access to restrooms/visitor center; bookstore by Southwest Parks and Monuments Association. Food available in park; accommodations in Port Isabel, Corpus Christi and South Padre Island.

Stretching for 113 miles along the Texas gulf coast from Corpus Christi on the north almost to Mexico on the south, the island ranges in width from about a few hundred yards to about three miles. It is separated from the mainland by Laguna Madre, a shallow body of water with a maximum width of 10 miles. At each end of the island, some development has been completed by the counties and individuals. The park boundaries encompass the undeveloped part of the island, 80½ miles long.

From gulf to lagoon the island consists of a wide, clean beach of sand that in places gives way to small shells; next an alignment of dunes paralleling the shore; then grassy flats, broken here and there by smaller dunes; and last a vaguely defined area of sand dunes and mudflats that merges with the waters of the lagoon.

Left *Most of the shoreline of Padre Island is a National Seashore – a paradise for the beachcomber and the birdwatcher*

Right *Pelicans on Padre Island*

San Antonio Missions National Historical Park

727 East Durango, Room A612, San Antonio, TX 78206
512/229-6000

Signed driving trail to all missions begins at Mission San Antonio Valero, also known as the Alamo, in south San Antonio. Exhibits, guided tours, self-guiding tours, bicycling, handicap access to restrooms. Accommodations in greater San Antonio area.

Four Catholic frontier missions, part of a system that stretched across the Spanish southwest in the eighteenth century, are commemorated here.

UTAH

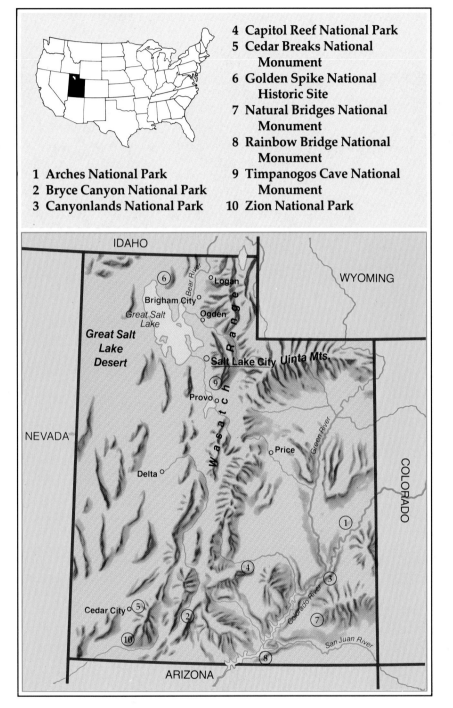

4 Capitol Reef National Park
5 Cedar Breaks National Monument
6 Golden Spike National Historic Site
7 Natural Bridges National Monument
8 Rainbow Bridge National Monument
9 Timpanogos Cave National Monument
10 Zion National Park

1 Arches National Park
2 Bryce Canyon National Park
3 Canyonlands National Park

Arches National Park

125 West Second, South, Moab, UT 84532
801/259-8161

Visitor center on US 191, 5 miles northwest of Moab. Entrance fee; visitor center, exhibits, guided tours, self-guiding trails, picnicking, camping, backcountry permits, hiking, handicap access to campground/restrooms/visitor center; bookstore by Canyonlands Natural History Association. Accommodations in Moab.

Wind and water, extreme temperatures and underground salt movement are responsible for the sculptured rock scenery of Arches

National Park. On blue-sky days, it is hard to imagine such violent forces – or 100 million years of erosion of sandstone – creating this land that boasts the greatest density of natural arches in the world. The more than 200 catalogued arches range in size from a 3-foot opening, the minimum considered an arch, to Landscape Arch. This 105-foot-high ribbon of rock measures 291 feet from base to base. All stages of arch formation and decay are found here. Delicate Arch, an isolated remnant of a bygone fin, stands on the brink of a canyon, with the white-capped La Sal mountains for a backdrop. Spires and pinnacles and balanced rocks perched atop seemingly inadequate bases vie with the arches as scenic spectacles. Early explorers thought the huge arches and monoliths in the Windows Section were, like Stonehenge in England, works of some lost culture.

Arches National Park lies in southeastern Utah's red rock country. For a short stretch the Colorado river borders the park. A bridge on US Highway 191 connects the park with Moab, Utah. Near this bridge users of the Old Spanish Trail swam mules across in the 1830s. A remnant of the trail adds historical intrigue to Arches. So does Wolfe Ranch, the remains of a typical early-West cattle operation.

The national park lies atop an underground salt bed which is responsible for the arches and spires, balanced rocks, sandstone fins and eroded monoliths that make the area a sightseer's mecca. Thousands of feet thick in places, this salt bed was deposited over the Colorado plateau some 300 million years ago when a sea flowed into

the region and eventually evaporated. Over millions of years the salt bed was covered with residue from floods and winds and the oceans that came in intervals. Much of this covering debris was compressed into rock. The earth covering over Arches may have been a mile thick. The unstable salt bed below Arches was no match for the weight of this thick cover of rock. Under such pressure it shifted, buckled, liquefied and repositioned itself, thrusting the earth layers upward into domes. Whole sections dropped into cavities; one such 2,500-foot displacement, the Moab Fault, is visible from the visitor center.

As this subsurface movement of salt shaped the earth, surface erosion stripped away the younger rock layers. Except for isolated remnants the major formations visible in Arches today are the salmon-colored entrada sandstone, in which most of the arches form, and the buff-colored Navajo sandstone. These are placed in layer-cake fashion throughout most of the park. Over time the superficial cracks, joints, and folds of these layers were saturated with water. Ice formed in the fissures, melted under extreme desert heat, and winds cleaned out the loose particles. A series of free-standing fins remained. Wind and water attacked these fins until, in some, the cementing material gave way and chunks of rock tumbled out. Many damaged fins collapsed. Others, with the right degree of hardness and balance, survived despite their missing middles. These became the famous arches. This is the probable geologic story of Arches: the evidence is largely circumstantial.

Far left *The startling formation known as Balanced Rock in Arches National Park*

Left *The unlikely but beautiful Delicate Arch in Arches National Park*

Bryce Canyon National Park

Bryce Canyon, UT 84717
801/834-5332

On UT 12, 17 miles from US 89. Entrance fee; visitor center, exhibits, guided tours, self-guiding trails, picnicking, camping, backcountry permits, hiking, horseback riding, cabin rental, handicap access to campgrounds/restrooms/visitor center; bookstore by Bryce Canyon Natural History Association. Accommodations in park.

Mormon settler Ebenezer Bryce lived here for five years and tried to make a go of it. He left only his name and his description: "A hell of a place to lose a cow!" Paiute Indians did not find easy living here either. Their name for Bryce Canyon was simply a description which translates: "Red rocks standing like men in a bowl-shaped canyon." It would be hard to gauge the Paiutes' attitude from such a straightforward description if we knew nothing else about them. But we know that they attached spiritual values to Bryce Canyon, just as many people today who witness this landscape experience a sense of the awesome or supernatural.

It was nearly 40 years after Bryce lived here that word began to trickle out about the beauty of this wilderness. In 1916 an article appeared in a railroad magazine, and it was not long before tourists began to arrive. By 1923 the boundaries of Bryce Canyon National Monument had been set; it was doubled in 1928 and established as a national park.

Bryce Canyon is not really a canyon at all. Unlike nearby Zion, which is the canyon of the Virgin river, Bryce is the side of a plateau of varying kinds of stone that simply melted or washed away. Water has been almost the sole erosive agent at Bryce, in the form of heavy rains and snow and ice. It is more a washing process than cutting or carving as in the Grand Canyon.

There seems to have been some uplifting and tilting going on here in Utah millions of years ago, leaving great plateaus that form a natural staircase, so to speak, from Bryce southwest to the Grand Canyon. These plateaus, separated by the mighty forces of rivers, are all different in composition, and it is that composition, layer upon layer of sediment deposited when this land was all part of a great inland sea, that not only gave them their colors and names, but determined the erosion aftermath. There are the Chocolate Cliffs of Arizona at the Grand Canyon; working north are Vermilion Cliffs, then the White Cliffs, the Gray Cliffs, and at Bryce, the Pink Cliffs. The brilliant Pink

Far left *Paiute Indians described Bryce Canyon as "red rocks standing like men in a bowl shaped canyon."*

Left *Highly colored fantastically shaped rock formations typical of Queen's Garden, Bryce Canyon National Park*

Cliffs are about 54 million years old and some 9,000 feet above sea level. The Kaibab limestone of the Grand Canyon is 225 million years old and about 2,500 feet above sea level.

The rock formations in all these great chasms are initially dependent on the kind of sediment laid down. Freshwater lakes covered the Bryce area leaving a very fine-grained and soft siltstone and a slightly harder limestone, sprinkled throughout with thin layers of shale, all of which erode at a different rate, resulting in a variety of shapes and sizes of formations.

What entices the eye most at Bryce Canyon is, of course, the color.

Iron, in the form of iron oxides, mixed with varying concentrations of manganese and copper, is responsible. The more iron, the more pink and red; the more manganese and copper, the more lavender and green. The white formations have simply had the iron leached from them.

Someday the spires and arches will fall and the colors will change, but new ones will appear as the eroding waters seek their way to the seas; new domes and temples, some as delicate as needles, others as colossal as mountains, all molded by nature and untouched by human hands.

Left *A prairie dog, one of the many creatures which make their home at Bryce Canyon*

*Pinnacles of the imagination soar into the blue skies
of Bryce Canyon*

*Bryce Canyon is misleadingly named: it has been
eroded out of the plateau into a vast amphitheater*

Canyonlands National Park

125 West Second, South, Moab, UT 84532
801/259-7164

Park is 35 miles southwest of Moab; Needles area is on US 211, 35 miles west of US 193; Island in the Sky is on UT 313, 30 miles southwest of US 191; Maze area is 45 miles east of UT 24 via dirt road. Visitor center, self-guiding trails, picnicking, camping, backcountry permits, hiking, horseback riding, boating, handicap access to campgrounds; bookstore by Canyonlands Natural History Association. Accommodations in Moab.

This is a land that took 200 million years to build; sandstone from oceans, winds, floods, and eroded mountains, each with its own effect, each in its own time. But time passes slowly here; change is imperceptible. Canyonlands – or the national park called Canyonlands, for all this is the land of canyons – is a rough rectangle approximately 35 miles long and 20 miles wide at the heart of the Colorado plateau. With the exception of the Grand Canyon farther on down the Colorado river, it is one of the most breath-taking and geologically important areas of the nation. It is made up of four main sections: the Island in the Sky, a 6,000-foot mesa dominating the region between the Colorado and Green rivers; the two rivers and their canyons; the Maze District to the west and the Needles area to the south. In and around these is a blazing mass of deep canyons, valleys and basins, extraordinary buttes, mesas, towers, domes, knobs, fins, arches and caves and hundreds of red-rock and sandstone formations at once frightening and beautiful.

The Colorado and its major tributary the Green river are responsible for this sweeping landscape, cutting through the rock and stripping away, bit by bit for millions of years, the plateau and walls. Grandview Point, a finger in the Island in the Sky pointing south toward the confluence of the two rivers, is aptly named, but from here the rivers are mere streams, twisting and turning through gorges, disappearing at times, shining in the bright sunlight around this bend and that. To the west of Grandview lies the Green river flowing placidly south from Wyoming; across it can be seen the Land of the Standing Rocks and the Maze; to the south the Colorado and the confluence with the Green and farther on the Needles; the grand, snow-capped La Sal mountains rise off to the east; and immediately below, terraced toward the rivers, the White Rim, some 1,000 feet down, with still another 1,000-foot drop to the basin. The vastness of the place is staggering; the feeling of openness – the broad, clear skies, the sound of wind and the occasional cry of a bird – is magnificent.

Canyonlands National Park from Dead Horse Point is a blazing mass of deep canyons, valleys, extraordinary buttes as well as hundreds of red-rock and sandstone formations

Capitol Reef National Park

Torrey, UT 84775
801/425-3871

Visitor center on UT 24, 11 miles east of Torrey. Visitor center, exhibits, guided tours, self-guiding trails, picnicking, camping, backcountry permits, hiking, mountain climbing, horseback riding, handicap access to campground/visitor center; bookstore by Capitol Reef Natural History Association. Accommodations in Torrey.

Capitol Reef National Park lies in the slickrock country of southern Utah, an area where water has cut monoliths, arches and mazes of canyons out of a sandstone-and-shale desert. The term reef as applied to land formations means a ridge of rock that is a barrier. This reef was named for one of its high points, Capitol Dome, that resembles the dome of the US Capitol. Penetrated and explored only in the last 100 years, much of the park remains a rugged wilderness.

The rock you see today in the park was laid down, layer upon layer, in past ages. At times this area was a tidal flat whose ripple marks are now hardened into stone. At other times sand dunes drifted across the land, and they eventually were consolidated into crisscrossing beds of sandstone.

You can see present-day counterparts of Capitol Reef's former landforms at the Great Salt Lake in northern Utah, in Everglades National Park, Florida, and in Great Sand Dunes National Monument, Colorado. The rock of Capitol Reef, like that of many other parks in the southwest, reveals the earth's history millions of years ago, when dinosaurs were the dominant land animals.

Capitol Reef is on the Colorado plateau. It and the Rocky mountains began rising to their present heights toward the end of the age of dinosaurs. Pressures on the rock increased as the plateau rose, and resulted in the folding of the rock into a 100-mile-long formation called the Waterpocket Fold, considered unique by geologists because of its great size and a primary reason for the establishment of the park. As the rock was folding, it was also eroding, creating the cliff faces, arches, monoliths and canyons that we see today.

Cedar Breaks National Monument

PO Box 749, Cedar City, UT 84720
801/586-9451

23 miles from Cedar City, off I-15. Visitor center, guided tours, self-guiding tours, picnic area, camping, hiking, fishing, handicap access to restrooms/visitor center; bookstore by Zion Natural History Association. Accommodations in Cedar City.

A huge natural amphitheater has eroded into the variegated Pink Cliffs (Wasatch Formation), which are 2,000 feet thick at this point.

Golden Spike National Historic Site

PO Box W, Brigham City, UT 84302
801/471-2209

Off US 83, 30 miles west of Brigham City. Visitor center, exhibits, self-guiding tours, handicap access to visitor center; bookstore by Southwest Parks and Monuments Association. Accommodations in Brigham City and Tremonton.

Completion of the first transcontinental railroad in the United States was celebrated here when the Central Pacific and Union Pacific railroads met in 1869.

Natural Bridges National Monument

Star Route, Blanding, UT 84511
801/259-7164

40 miles west of Blanding, via UT 95. Entrance fee; visitor center, exhibits, self-guiding trails, picnicking, camping, hiking, handicap access to visitor center; bookstore by Canyonlands Natural History Association. Accommodations in Blanding.

Three natural bridges – Sipapu, Kachina, Owachomo – each eroded by streams from sandstone and measuring from 180 to 268 feet in span and 9 to 93 feet thick, are protected in this small park.

Rainbow Bridge National Monument

c/o Glen Canyon National Recreation Area, PO Box 1507, Page, AZ 86040
602/645-2471

Reached by trail from base of Navajo Mountain (15 miles); also by water from Lake Powell in Glen Canyon National Recreation Area. Accommodations in Page; camping in Glen Canyon NRA.

The greatest known natural bridge anywhere, this symmetrical arch of salmon-pink sandstone rises 290 feet above the floor of Bridge Canyon.

Far left *A storm brews over the rugged cliffs of Capitol Reef National Park*

Left *The multicolored rocks of Cedar Breaks National Monument*

Inset *Rock carvings dating to about 1700 found in Capitol Reef National Park*

Timpanogos Cave National Monument

Rural Route 3, Box 200, American Fork, UT 84003
801/756-5238

Access via UT 92 and UT 146. Visitor center, exhibits, guided tours, self-guiding trail, picnicking, handicap access to restrooms/visitor center; bookstore by Southwest Parks and Monuments Association. Accommodations at American Fork, Highland, and Pleasant Grove.

The colorful limestone cavern on the side of Mount Timpanogos is noted for helictites – water-created formations that grow in all directions and shapes, regardless of gravity.

Zion National Park

Springdale, UT 84767-1099
801/772-3256

On UT 9, off I-15 and US 89. Entrance fee; visitor center, exhibits, guided tours, self-guiding trails, picnicking, camping, backcountry permits, hiking, horseback riding, cabin rental, handicap access to campgrounds/restrooms/visitor center; bookstore by Zion Natural History Association. Accommodations in park and at Springdale.

Zion Canyon was cut by the Virgin river in southwestern Utah, and like other areas of the plateau, the erosional effects of rain, wind and frost have continued the process of forming another extraordinary pocket of beauty just 90 miles from Bryce Canyon. The Virgin rages on, and carries on toward the Colorado – for it is the largest tributary in southern Utah – hundreds of thousands of tons of rock each year.

Placid at times, the Virgin river can rage during replenishing torrential rains, and when it does its force against rock is astounding; three million tons a year are moved out of Zion and on to Lake Mead, where the Virgin joins the Colorado. The Virgin river "seethes like a thing alive, a serpent devouring red watery tons of mud and sand from countless tributaries," wrote a park ranger. "We stand awe-struck as enormous boulders crash and split asunder. Uprooted cottonwoods tumble and upend like jackstraws."

Zion's architecture is Navajo sandstone: sand dunes built on a desert plain for millions of years, slowly cemented in layers, and then washed and crumbled away. The brilliantly colored monoliths left standing were named by the Mormons: Great White Throne, Angel's Landing, The Sentinel, Towers of the Virgin. Zion itself means "The Heavenly City of God." It is a land of "peace and comfort," as they said, but to the geological eye this is a less than harmonious landscape. The thrones and towers and sentinels stand as mute testimony to millions of years of erosion typical of southern Utah and the Colorado plateau.

Far left *The North American otter is a large aquatic weasel with a thick neck, short legs and a long, heavy tail*

Left *The Weeping Rock Trail in Zion National Park in glorious fall foliage*

VIRGINIA

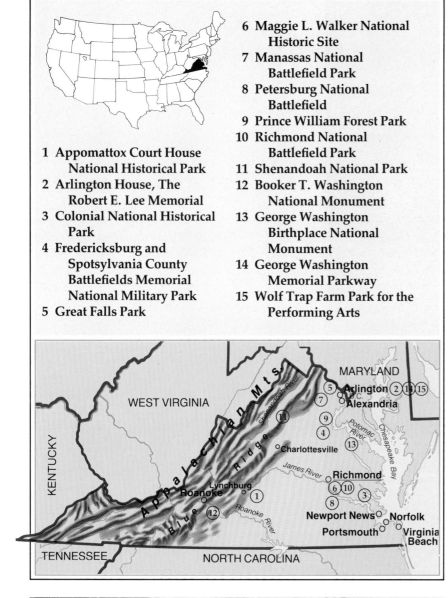

1 Appomattox Court House
  National Historical Park
2 Arlington House, The
  Robert E. Lee Memorial
3 Colonial National Historical
  Park
4 Fredericksburg and
  Spotsylvania County
  Battlefields Memorial
  National Military Park
5 Great Falls Park
6 Maggie L. Walker National
  Historic Site
7 Manassas National
  Battlefield Park
8 Petersburg National
  Battlefield
9 Prince William Forest Park
10 Richmond National
  Battlefield Park
11 Shenandoah National Park
12 Booker T. Washington
  National Monument
13 George Washington
  Birthplace National
  Monument
14 George Washington
  Memorial Parkway
15 Wolf Trap Farm Park for the
  Performing Arts

Appomattox Court House National Historical Park

PO Box 218, Appomattox, VA 24522
804/352-8987

On VA 24, 3 miles northeast of town of Appomattox; 75 miles from Roanoke. Entrance fee; visitor center, exhibits, guided tours, self-guiding tours, picnicking, hiking, handicap access to restrooms/visitor center; bookstore by Eastern National Park and Monument Association. Accommodations in Appomattox.

The McLean house in Appomattox Court House was the scene of the surrender of the Confederate Army of Northern Virginia at the end of the Civil War in the United States when, on April 9, 1865 General Robert E. Lee presented his sword to Lieutenant General Ulysses S. Grant. Appomattox Court House has been restored; some 27 buildings now depict the village as it was more than a century ago.

Arlington House, The Robert E. Lee Memorial

c/o George Washington Memorial Parkway, Turkey Run Park, McLean, VA 22101
703/557-0613

Access from Washington via Memorial Bridge; parking available at Arlington Cemetery Visitor Center. Exhibits, handicap access to restrooms/house; bookstore by Parks and History Association. Accommodations in greater Washington area.

George Washington Parke Custis, grandson of Martha Washington by her first marriage to Daniel Parke Custis and the adopted son of George Washington, began this house in 1802; it was finished in 1817 and has become a treasury of Washington family heirlooms. Custis married Mary Lee Fitzhugh in 1804 and their only child to survive infancy was Mary Anna Randolph Custis, who married West Point graduate Lieutenant Robert E. Lee here on June 30, 1831. It was while on leave from the army to oversee improvements to this estate that Lee decided to support the state of Virginia in the forthcoming civil war. Lee departed from here on April 22, 1861 to command Virginia's military forces.

In 1864 the federal government confiscated the Arlington property when Mrs. Lee failed to appear in person to pay her taxes. A 200-acre section of the estate was set aside as a military cemetery, the beginning of today's Arlington National Cemetery.

Left *Appomattox Court House National Historical Park vividly recreates a crucial moment in American history*

Right *Arlington House, the home of Robert E. Lee, sits majestically on a hill overlooking Washington and the Potomac River*

Colonial National Historical Park

PO Box 210, Yorktown, VA 23690
804/898-3400

Jamestown and Yorktown off US 17 and I-64; both accessible via the Colonial Parkway. Entrance fee; visitor centers, museums, exhibits, guided tours, self-guiding trails, picnicking, hiking, bicycling, handicap access to restrooms/visitor centers; glass house and bookstores by Eastern National Park and Monument Association. Accommodations in Yorktown and Williamsburg.

Three important sites make up this park, all linked by the Colonial Parkway – Jamestown, Yorktown and Williamsburg. Yorktown is administered by the National Park Service, Jamestown jointly by the Service and the Association for the Preservation of Virginia Antiquities and Williamsburg is managed by Colonial Williamsburg, Inc. Yorktown, where Lord Cornwallis surrendered the British Army to George Washington on October 17, 1781 has been remarkably preserved. The redoubts, with cannon in place, the Moore House, where the terms of surrender were drafted and the site of Washington's headquarters can all be seen along a self-guided tour route. The foundations of the first permanent Virginia colony in the New World, established in 1607, are preserved at Jamestown. The "working" glass house is one of the most popular areas of the site. Here costumed artisans demonstrate seventeenth-century glass-blowing and make objects for sale.

Fredericksburg and Spotsylvania County Battlefields Memorial National Military Park

PO Box 679, Fredericksburg, VA 22404
703/373-4461

Parts of 4 battlefields and 3 related sites within 60 miles of Washington via US 1 and I-95. Main visitor center on US 1 at Lafayette Boulevard in Fredericksburg; another is at Chancellorsville, 10 miles west of Fredericksburg on VA 3. Visitor centers, museums, exhibits, guided tours, self-guiding trails, picnicking, hiking, bicycling, handicap access to restrooms/visitor centers; museum displays at Chatham Manor; outdoor displays at Salem Church and Jackson Shrine; bookstores by Eastern National Park and Monument Association. Accommodations in Fredericksburg.

Four major Civil War battles within a 17-mile radius – Fredericksburg, Chancellorsville, the Wilderness and Spotsylvania Court House – resulted in more than 100,000 casualties. No other area of comparable size in the country witnessed such a concentration of continuous and heavy fighting.

The Union army, commanded by Ambrose E. Burnside, arrived on Stafford Heights overlooking Fredericksburg in mid-November 1862 and on December 13 was beaten by Lee in one of the most one-sided victories of the war.

Following the Fredericksburg debacle, Lincoln replaced Burnside with Joseph Hooker. At Chancellorsville on May 2 Stonewall Jackson destroyed the Federal right wing in a spectacular surprise attack and Lee eventually drove Hooker back. Unfortunately, on the night of May 2, Jackson was mortally wounded.

The first of the classic encounters between Lee and Grant took place in the dense thickets and tangled over-growth of the Wilderness on May 5-6, 1864. Tactically the battle was a draw, but Grant broke the stalemate by marching his army south to Spotsylvania Court House.

On the morning of May 12, 1864 both armies engaged in the most intense hand-to-hand combat of the Civil War at Spotsylvania Court House. The desperate fighting at the "Bloody Angle" gave Lee time to build new earthworks which he defended until Grant abandoned the field on May 21.

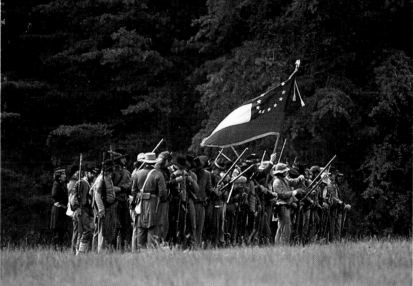

Far left *Yorktown Battlefield, one of the historic sites within the Colonial National Historical Park*

Above *A reenactivated Confederate military regiment prepares to attack in mock battle at Fredericksburg*

Left *A Civil War cannon on the battlefield at Fredericksburg is serenaded by an admiring visitor*

Great Falls Park

9200 Old Dominion Drive, Great Falls, VA 22066
703/759-2915

15 miles from Washington, at junction of VA 193 (Old Georgetown Pike) and VA 738 (Old Dominion Drive), in Great Falls. Visitor center, exhibits, guided tours, self-guiding trail, picnicking, horseback riding; bookstore by Parks and History Association. Food available in park; accommodations in Washington and surrounding Virginia communities.

This is a nature park providing a fine view of the impressive great falls of the Potomac river from the Virginia side.

Jamestown National Historic Site

(see Colonial National Historical Park)

Maggie L. Walker National Historic Site

c/o Richmond National Battlefield Park, 3215 East Broad Street, Richmond, VA 23223
804/226-1981

Downtown Richmond at 110 ½ East Leigh Street, in Jackson Ward National Historic Landmark District. Visitors must call in advance. Exhibits, guided tours. Accommodations in Richmond.

This site preserves the restored home of a prominent black community leader who was the first woman president of a US financial institution.

Manassas National Battlefield Park

PO Box 1830, Manassas, VA 22110
703/754-7107

26 miles southwest of Washington via I-66 and VA 234. Visitor center, exhibits, guided tours, self-guiding trails, picnicking, hiking, camping, handicap access to restrooms/visitor center; bookstore by Eastern National Park and Monument Association. Accommodations at Manassas.

Two great battles took place on these fields – First Manassas (First Bull Run), July 21, 1861, and Second Manassas (Second Bull Run), August 28-30, 1862.

Early on July 21, 1861, the armies of the Union and the Confederacy engaged across Bull Run near the village of Manassas, Virginia – 35,000 men in blue under General Irvin McDowell against 32,000 men in gray under Generals P.G.T. Beauregard and Joseph E. Johnston. It ended in a devastating defeat for Mr. Lincoln's new army and an inspiration for the South.

By August 1862 commands, even armies, had changed. The Army of Northern Virginia came under the command of Robert E. Lee. Pieces of Union armies were pulled together quickly under John Pope, who marched out of Washington toward Manassas where after savage, brutal fighting unlike any yet seen in the war the Union army withdrew once again to the defenses of Washington.

This startling Confederate victory opened the way for Lee's first invasion of the North, the Maryland campaign of September 1862.

Shenandoah National Park is one of the best for sighting the chipmunk

Petersburg National Battlefield

PO Box 549, Petersburg, VA 23834
804/732-3531

On VA 36, 2½ miles east of center of Petersburg. Visitor center, exhibits, guided tours, self-guiding trail, picnicking, hiking, horseback riding, bicycling, handicap access to visitor center; bookstore by Eastern National Park and Monument Association. Accommodations in Petersburg.

In a grim ten-month (June 1864-April 1865) struggle, Ulysses S. Grant's Union army gradually but relentlessly encircled Petersburg and cut Robert E. Lee's railroad supply lines from the south.

The battlefield's visitor center is the beginning of a one-way, 4-mile auto tour of the most interesting points, not the least of which is "The Crater." Here Union troops from Pennsylvania, mostly coal miners, dug a tunnel under Confederate lines and exploded four tons of gunpowder on July 30, 1864, leaving a crater 170 feet long, 60 feet wide, and 30 feet deep. The ensuing battle cost the Union more than 4,000 casualties, and the Confederacy, 1,500.

Prince William Forest Park

PO Box 208, Triangle, VA 22172
703/221-7181

Main entrance on VA 619, just off I-95 near the Quantico Marine Base, 32 miles south of Washington, DC. Visitor center, exhibits, guided tours, self-guiding trails, picnicking, camping, backcountry permits, hiking, fishing, bicycling, cabin rental, handicap access to restrooms/visitor center; bookstore by Parks and History Association. Accommodations at Triangle and Dumfries.

This is a splendid forested parkland for camping trips to the nation's capital. Some 35 miles of trails and fire roads lead through the lush countryside of northern Virginia.

Richmond National Battlefield Park

3215 East Broad Street, Richmond VA 23223
804/226-1981

Chimborazo Visitor Center at 3215 East Broad Street, Richmond, overlooking James river. Visitor center, exhibits, self-guiding tours and trails, picnicking; bookstore by Eastern National Park and Monument Association. Accommodations in Richmond.

Federal forces made seven attempts to take Richmond, the Confederate capital, virtually from the very beginning of the Civil War. None was successful; not until the final days of the war and Grant's siege of Petersburg did the Confederacy abandon the city. Richmond National Battlefield Park links that series of battles and defensive positions, from the 1862 Seven Days Battles of the Peninsula Campaign to Grant's 1864 campaign, nine units in a 100-mile drive around the city.

1862: Chickahominy Bluff, Beaver Dam Creek, Gaines' Mill Battlefield, Malvern Hill, and Drewry's Bluff.

1864: Cold Harbor, Garthright House, Fort Harrison and vicinity, Parker's Battery.

Shenandoah National Park

Luray, VA 22835
703/999-2243

Headquarters on US 211, 4 miles west of Thornton Gap and 4 miles east of Luray; visitor centers along Skyline Drive at Dickey Ridge and Big Meadows. Entrance fee; visitor centers, museums, exhibits, guided tours, self-guiding trails, picnicking, camping, backcountry permits, hiking, mountain climbing, horseback riding, fishing, cross-country skiing, cabin rental, handicap access to campgrounds/restrooms/visitor centers; bookstore by Shenandoah Natural History Association. Accommodations and supplies available in park.

Shenandoah National Park lies astride a beautiful section of the Blue Ridge, which forms the eastern rampart of the Appalachian Mountains between Pennsylvania and Georgia. In the valley to the west is

A National Parks ranger demonstrates archery to a young visitor at Richmond National Battlefield Park

the Shenandoah river, from which the park gets its name, and between the north and south forks of the river is Massanutten, a 40-mile-long mountain. To the east is the rolling Piedmont country. Providing vistas of the spectacular landscape is Skyline Drive, a winding road that runs along the Blue Ridge through the length of the park.

Most of the rocks that form the Blue Ridge are ancient granitic and metamorphosed volcanic formations, some exceeding one billion years in age. By comparison, humans have been associated with this land only about 9,000 years. Primitive food gatherers and later Indian hunters used the land for centuries but left little evidence of their presence. Settlement of the Shenandoah Valley began soon after the first expedition crossed the Blue Ridge in 1716. By 1800 the lowlands had been settled by farmers, while the rugged mountains were still relatively untouched. Later, as valley farmland became scarce, settlement spread into the mountains. By the twentieth century, these people had developed a culture of their own, born from the harshness and isolation of mountain living. However, the forests were shrinking, game animals were disappearing, the thin mountain soil was wearing out, and people were beginning to leave.

Top left *As the snows depart, blossom whitens Shenandoah hillsides*

Bottom left *A magnificent view from a high trail in Shenandoah National Park*

Right *Part of the plentiful wildlife of the Shenandoah Valley the elk was imported from Wyoming. A member of the deer family, second only in size to the moose, it is one of North America's largest herbivores*

Right below *Of the six species of fox in North America, the red fox is the one most commonly found in national parks, including Shenandoah. Because it is nocturnal, however, it is rarely seen*

In 1926 Congress authorized the establishment of Shenandoah National Park. The Commonwealth of Virginia then purchased nearly 280 square miles of land to be donated to the federal government. More than half the population had left the mountain area, and the remaining residents sold their land or were relocated with government assistance. In dedicating the park in 1936 President Franklin D. Roosevelt initiated a novel experiment in returning an overused area to its original natural beauty. Recreational facilities were built by the Civilian Conservation Corps, and in 1939 Skyline Drive was completed. Croplands and pastures soon became overgrown with shrubs, locusts and pine; these in turn were replaced by oak, hickory and other trees that make up a mature deciduous forest. Now more than 95 percent of the park is covered by forests with about 100 species of trees. The vegetation regeneration has been so complete that in 1976 Congress designated two-fifths of the park as wilderness. The largest remaining open area is Big Meadows, which is kept in its historically open condition by management fires. Here the abundance of wildflowers, strawberries and blueberries attract both wildlife and humans.

Left *A reconstructed slave's home at the Booker T. Washington National Monument*

Booker T. Washington National Monument

Route 1, Box 195, Hardy, VA 24101
703/721-2094

16 miles northeast of Rocky Mount, VA, via VA 122N, and 20 miles southeast of Roanoke, VA, via VA 116S and 122N. Visitor center, exhibits, guided tours, self-guiding trail, picnicking, camping, hiking, handicap access to visitor center; bookstore by Eastern National Park and Monument Association. Accommodations in Roanoke and Rocky Mount.

This is the site of the birthplace and childhood home of black leader and educator Booker T. Washington, comprising most of the original plantation and replicas of buildings Washington could have known as a boy. It is the only site in the national park system that interprets America's slavery years. Farm animals and period crops cultivated with nineteenth-century implements by people in costumes make this a superb example of the "Living Farm" concept in our parks.

George Washington Birthplace National Monument

Washington's Birthplace, VA 22575
804/224-0196

On Potomac River, 38 miles east of Fredericksburg, accessible via VA 3 and 204. Visitor center, exhibits, guided tours, self-guiding trail, picnicking, hiking, fishing, handicap access to restrooms/visitor center; bookstore by George Washington Birthplace National Memorial Association. Accommodations at Montross and Colonial Beach.

Wakefield, the ancestral plantation where George Washington was born and spent his earliest days, is on lovely Pope Creek amidst a pastoral scene typical of seventeenth- and eighteenth-century colonial Virginia. The original house burned, but the carefully reproduced brick home is furnished in the period of Washington's youth.

Washington lived the first three and a half years of his life here, and later as a teenager spent several years with his brother who had inherited the property. His father, grandfather and greatgrandfather are buried here in the family cemetery. A "living farm" has been created around the house, with costumed people working the fields and kitchen.

George Washington Memorial Parkway

(Virginia, Maryland)
Turkey Run Park, McLean, VA 22101
703/285-2598

Access from all Washington bridges and numerous side streets from Virginia. Areas assigned to the Parkway's administration such as Arlington House, Great Falls Park, Clara Barton National Historic Site, and Theodore Roosevelt Island offer opportunities for picnicking, climbing, hiking, biking and fishing.

The Parkway is a landscaped scenic road parallel with the Potomac river from the Capital Beltway (I-495), past Washington, Arlington National Cemetery, National Airport and Alexandria, to Mount Vernon.

Wolf Trap Farm Park for the Performing Arts

1551 Trap Road, Vienna, VA 22180
703/255-1800

From downtown Washington, take George Washington Memorial Parkway to Capital Beltway (I-495) south to Virginia; exit at 11-S (VA 123) and follow US 7 to Towlston Road; turn left at Wolf Trap sign. Guided tours, self-guiding trails, handicap access to restrooms.

The only park for the performing arts in the national park system has become a popular center for opera, ballet, jazz, pop and symphony concerts, and Broadway shows.

Far left *The kitchen in the log cabin that represents the birthplace of Booker T. Washington*

WASHINGTON

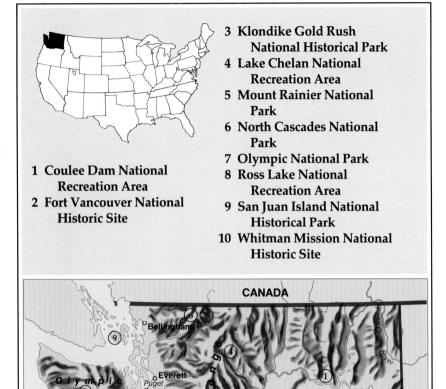

1 Coulee Dam National
   Recreation Area
2 Fort Vancouver National
   Historic Site

3 Klondike Gold Rush
   National Historical Park
4 Lake Chelan National
   Recreation Area
5 Mount Rainier National
   Park
6 North Cascades National
   Park
7 Olympic National Park
8 Ross Lake National
   Recreation Area
9 San Juan Island National
   Historical Park
10 Whitman Mission National
   Historic Site

Coulee Dam National Recreation Area

PO Box 37, Coulee Dam, WA 99116
509/633-0881

Headquarters on Columbia River; US 2 to Wilbur, WA, WA 174 to Coulee Dam. Visitor centers, exhibits, guided tours, self-guiding trails, picnicking, camping, swimming, boating, water skiing, fishing, hunting, handicap access to campgrounds/restrooms/visitor center; bookstore by Pacific Northwest National Parks and Forests Association. Accommodations at Coulee Dam and Kettle Falls.

Coulee Dam is the largest dam on the Columbia River. Behind it Franklin D. Roosevelt Lake stretches 150 miles, nearly to Canada. Park includes Fort Spokane, an 1880 frontier military outpost.

The snowshoe hare, found in Mount Rainier National Park, is brown in summer but white in winter

Fort Vancouver National Historic Site

Vancouver, WA 98661
206/696-7655

On East Evergreen Boulevard, Vancouver; turn east off I-5 at Mill Plain Boulevard interchange and follow signs. Visitor center, exhibits, guided tours, self-guiding tours, handicap access to restrooms/visitor center; bookstore by Pacific Northwest National Parks and Forests Association. Accommodations in greater Vancouver area; private campground nearby.

Established by the Hudson's Bay Company in 1825 and moved to this site in 1829, Fort Vancouver became the political and trading hub of the Pacific northwest. Six major buildings of the old fortification have recently been reconstructed based on archeological finds.

Klondike Gold Rush National Historical Park

117 South Main Street, Seattle, WA 98104
206/442-7220

117 S. Main Street in Seattle's Pioneer Square area. Visitor center, exhibits, handicap access to restrooms; bookstore by Pacific Northwest National Parks and Monuments Association. Accommodations in immediate area.

This small unit of the national park system interprets Seattle's role as the main supply center for the Alaska and Klondike gold fields, 1897-98, complementing the Klondike Gold Rush National Historical Park in Skagway, Alaska.

Lake Chelan National Recreation Area

North Cascades Complex, 800 State Street, Sedro Woolley, WA 98284
206/855-1331

Here the beautiful Stehekin Valley, with a portion of the fjord-like Lake Chelan, adjoins the southern unit of North Cascades National Park. See North Cascades for guide information.

Mount Rainier National Park

Tahoma Woods, Star Route, Ashford, WA 98304
206/569-2211

Longmire Visitor Center on WA 706, off WA 7, 70 miles southeast of Tacoma. Entrance fee; visitor center, exhibits, guided tours, self-guiding trails, picnicking, camping, backcountry permits, hiking, mountain climbing, fishing, snowmobiling, cross-country skiing, handicap access to restrooms/visitor center; bookstore by Pacific Northwest National Parks and Forests Association. Accommodations in park.

There are several mountains in the United States higher than Mount Rainier, but none quite so captures the eye for its sheer bulk and beauty. Its gleaming summit – acres of ice and snow that blanket all but the most jagged peaks – is 14,410 feet high, and with its foothills it covers nearly 400 square miles.

Bottom *Dramatic shadows intensify the alpine beauty of Mount Rainier*

Below *The solid and reassuring guide service center in Mount Rainier National Park*

Mount Rainier is in fact a dormant volcano. Although there was minor activity in the mid-1800s, there has not been an eruption in more than 2,000 years. There is still activity beneath its snows, however, and one day it may erupt again.

There are four life-zones on Rainier: below 3,000 feet is the humid transition zone with a dense forest of Douglas-fir, western hemlock, big-leaf maple and red cedars that reach 250 feet; such plants as blackberry, trillium, and sasal are all along the roads and trails. The Canadian zone, between 3,000 and 5,000 feet, is where the Pacific silver fir dominates. There are plenty of wild flowers – beargrass, twinflower, Oregon grape – but not as spectacular as above in the Hudsonian zone, 5,000 to 6,000 feet, where broad meadows of red heather, glacier lily, blue gentian and monkey flower girdle the mountain. At about 6,000 feet, the highest one can drive, and from there to the summit, the mountain is mostly barren rock and snow and ice. But near this point is where the Alaska spirea, painted cups, lupine, alpine Jacob's ladder and a variety of other brilliantly colored plants cling precariously to the tundra just below the snow line. This

earth is soft volcanic soil and plants lead a fragile life. A footprint off the trail can cause a chasm as big as the Grand Canyon to these flowers, and their lives can be snuffed quickly by a tiny rain channel caused by a thoughtless "big foot." Wildlife is abundant here too – the mule deer, marmot and mountain goat are well protected.

Rainier's glaciers are one of the park's main features. The Emmons Glacier is the largest – five miles long and a mile wide. There are 27 named rivers of ice on the mountain covering about 40 square miles. Nearly half of them originate on or near the summit, and each slowly works its way down the slopes, pushing before it and dragging beneath it tons of rocky debris that continues to shape and form the Mount Rainier of the future.

The unspoilt mountainous landscape of Mount Rainier National Park extends to the horizon

North Cascades National Park

800 State Street, Sedro Woolley, WA 98284
206/855-1331

Access via WA 20, off I-5 at Burlington; headquarters at Sedro Woolley on WA 20. Camping, backcountry permits, hiking, mountain climbing, horseback riding, fishing; bookstore by Pacific Northwest National Parks and Forests Association. Accommodations in Sedro Wooley and Burlington.

The Cascades rank among the world's great mountain ranges. Extending from Canada's Fraser river south beyond Oregon, they contribute greatly to shaping the Pacific northwest's climate and vegetation. The North Cascades National Park complex sits deep in the wild, nearly impenetrable northernmost reaches of the Cascades Range in northwestern Washington. Few people were familiar with the wonders of this area until the establishment in 1968 of the North Cascades National Park complex, composed of North Cascades National Park and Ross Lake and Lake Chelan National Recreation Areas. Today, these three adjoining areas complement each other as park and recreation lands.

Recent exploration began in 1814 when Alexander Ross crossed the present national park's southern unit. The handful of explorers who followed Ross commented on the region's rugged, isolated nature. Miners prospected for gold, lead, zinc, and platinum here from 1880 to 1910. They recorded moderate strikes, but transportation proved arduous and profits so limited that mining was abandoned. Some logging and homesteading occurred around 1900. The electricity generating potential of the Skagit river was recognized early. Between 1924 and 1949 Seattle City Light built three dams on the river.

The park complex is flanked on the south, east and west by national forest lands and on the north by provincial lands of British Columbia, Canada. Only an invisible boundary separates the two national park units from the two national recreation areas and the adjoining national forest lands.

Even though early Indians and their ancestors left some imprints on the land, history has touched little of the park complex. Readily reached areas are heavily visited, but some remote locations have yet to feel the boots of today's backcountry traveler. Forest giants of western red cedar and Douglas-fir dot the deep valleys. Off the trail tangled growths of vine maple, stinging nettles and devil's club still defy cross-country hikers. Glaciers scored by crevasses; permanent snowfields; and sheer-walled cliffs, spires, and pinnacles challenge the mountaineer. From the North Cascades Highway, on clear days, you may get glimpses of alpine wonders that lie just beyond.

Olympic National Park

600 East Park Avenue, Port Angeles, WA 98362
206/452-4501, ext. 230

Main visitor center just south of Port Angeles, off US 101. Visitor centers, exhibits, guided tours, self-guiding trails, camping, backcountry permits, hiking, mountain climbing, horseback riding, swimming, boating, fishing, cross-country skiing, cabin rental, handicap access to campgrounds/restrooms/visitor centers; bookstore by Pacific Northwest National Parks and Forests Association. Accommodations in park and at Port Angeles.

Olympic National Park is a rain forest; it is a lofty mountain, millions of years old; it is a stretch of nearly virgin Pacific coastline; it is a classic wilderness with wild rivers and streams, alpine lakes and meadows, a host of animal life, 1,000 species of plants, and tall trees... Olympic National Park is all of these.

It begins along a 50-mile section of rugged coast where trees grow on the very edge of the Pacific Ocean and where the life-giving water cycle that is Olympic has its start and end. This islanded and rocky strip of beach along Washington's Pacific shore is one of the most primitive sections of seacoast remaining in the United States. Here is the great Olympic rain forest, a luxuriously green woodland that rivals any tropical jungle for beauty and wildlife – an environment where trees a thousand years old survey the world from 3,000 feet and shield a carpet of dense moss and ferns.

Forty miles to the east stands Mount Olympus, the highest of the Olympic mountains at 7,965 feet. The Olympics of the Coast Range are among the youngest mountains in the world – perhaps 2 million years old. They rise from lush, green lowlands to gleaming snow-capped peaks and ridges on the Olympic Peninsula, an area of 5,000 square miles, of which 4,000 are mountainous.

Right The lush rain forest of Olympic National Park

Below The rugged coastal section of Olympic National Park, one of its many diverse elements

Right below *Strange looking "sea stacks", the remains of eons of wear and tear by wind and ocean along the Pacific coast at Olympic National Park*

Far right inset *Worn by the ceaseless action of waves, seastacks like this one at Cape Alava in Olympic National Park stand as the remnants of some ancient headland*

Right *The dense rain forest in Olympic National Park*

Below *Mountainous scenery and wildlife (a marmot), yet more of the astonishing diversity of Olympic National Park*

Ross Lake National Recreation Area

North Cascades Complex, 800 State Street, Sedro Woolley, WA 98284
206/855-1331

Ringed by mountains, this reservoir in the Skagit river drainage separates the north and south units of North Cascades National Park. See North Cascades for guide information.

San Juan Island National Historical Park

PO Box 429, Friday Harbor, WA 98250
206/378-2240

Access by autoferry from Anacortes, WA, about 88 miles north of Seattle. Visitor center, exhibits, self-guiding tours, picnicking, hiking, handicap access to restrooms/visitor center; bookstore by Pacific Northwest National Parks and Forests Association. Limited accommodations at Friday Harbor and Roche Harbor.

This park commemorates the events on the island from 1853 to 1871 in connection with the final settlement of the Oregon Territory's northern boundary, including the so-called Pig War of 1859.

Whitman Mission National Historic Site

Route 2, Box 247, Walla Walla, WA 99362
509/522-6360

7 miles west of Walla Walla, off US 12. Visitor center, exhibits, self-guiding tours, picnicking, handicap access to restrooms/visitor center; bookstore by Pacific Northwest National Parks and Forests Association. Accommodations in Walla Walla.

This park commemorates Marcus and Narcissa Whitman's courage and labor among Native Americans in Old Oregon when American immigrants began coming down the Oregon Trail. A clash between Indian and American cultures led to their deaths in 1847.

WEST VIRGINIA

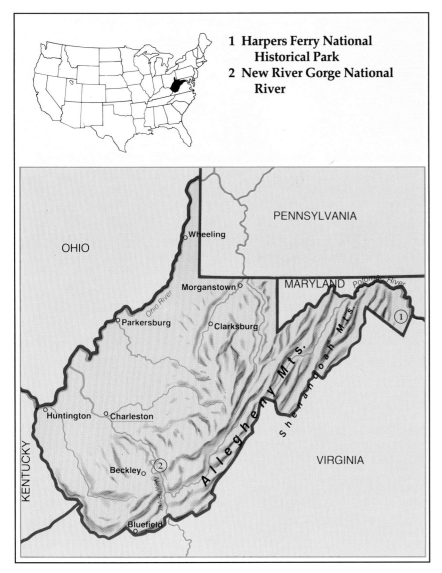

1 Harpers Ferry National
  Historical Park
2 New River Gorge National
  River

Harpers Ferry National Historical Park

(West Virginia, Maryland, Virginia)
PO Box 65, Harpers Ferry, WV 25425
304/535-6371, ext. 6222

20 miles northwest of Frederick, MD, via US 340; 6 miles south of Charles Town via US 340. Visitor center, museum, exhibits, guided tours, self-guiding trails, hiking, mountain climbing, horseback riding, fishing, bicycle trail, handicap access to restrooms/visitor center; bookstore by Harpers Ferry Historical Association. Accommodations in Harpers Ferry and Bolivar.

Harpers Ferry, on a point of land at the confluence of the Shenandoah and Potomac rivers and dominated by the Blue Ridge mountains, was a beckoning wilderness in the early 1700s. By the mid-nineteenth century it was a town of some 3,000 inhabitants, an important arms-producing center, and a transportation link between east and west. John Brown's raid in 1859 and the Civil War thrust the town into national prominence. The destruction wrought by the war and repeated flooding was responsible for the town's eventual decline and

demise. Today the historic part of the town continues to undergo extensive restoration to a Civil War-period appearance by the National Park Service.

New River Gorge National River

Drawer V, Oak Hill, WV 25901
304/465-0508

Visitor center 2 miles north of Fayetteville, on east side of New River on US 19; seasonal visitor center at Hinton on WV 3 bypass. Visitor center, handicap access to visitor center; bookstore by Eastern National Park and Monument Association. Accommodations in nearby communities.

This new park includes 50 miles of one of North America's oldest rivers, with spectacular scenery, and including historical themes such as railroading, coal mining, and lumbering.

WISCONSIN

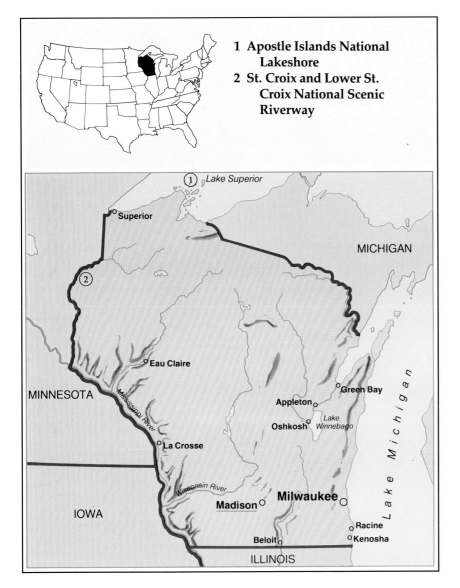

1. **Apostle Islands National Lakeshore**
2. **St. Croix and Lower St. Croix National Scenic Riverway**

Apostle Islands National Lakeshore

Route 1, Box 4, Bayfield, WI 54814
715/779-3397

Visitor center at Bayfield on WI 13, off US 2. Visitor center, museum, exhibits, guided tours, self-guiding trails, picnicking, camping, hiking, swimming, boating, fishing, hunting, handicap access to restrooms/visitor center; bookstore by Eastern National Park and Monument Association. Accommodations at Bayfield, Cornucopia, Ashland, Washburn, and Madeline Island.

Lying off the tip of the northern Wisconsin mainland in the sparkling blue waters of Lake Superior are the 22 Apostle Islands, ranging in size from tiny three-acre Gull Island to 14,000-acre Madeline. The islands and surrounding waters provide a variety of recreational opportunities in an everchanging panorama of scenic beauty. Twenty of the 22 islands and a 12-mile section of mainland shoreline have been set aside as the Apostle Island National Lakeshore.

Left *Fall splendor at Harpers Ferry at the confluence of the Potomac and Shenandoah rivers*

Right *The rugged, rocky shore so typical of Apostle Islands National Lakeshore*

Devil's Island, one of the twenty islands which make up Apostle Islands National Lakeshore

St. Croix and Lower St. Croix National Scenic Riverway

(Wisconsin, Minnesota)
PO Box 708, St. Croix Falls, WI 54024
715/483-3287

Park headquarters at Hamilton and Massachusetts Streets in St. Croix Falls. Exhibits, self-guiding trails, picnicking, camping, hiking, swimming, boating, fishing, hunting, cross-country skiing, cabin rental, handicap access to campground/restrooms/visitor center; bookstores by Eastern National Park and Monument Association.

Food available in park; accommodations at Hayward, Hudson, Trego, St. Croix Falls, Stillwater and other villages along the river.

About 200 miles of the beautiful St. Croix river and its Namekagon tributary make up this area, an initial component of the National Wild and Scenic Rivers System.

St. Croix National Scenic Riverway, exceptionally beautiful when bordered with fall foliage

WYOMING

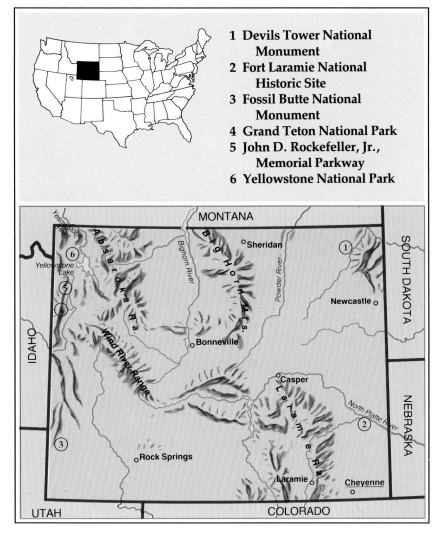

1 **Devils Tower National Monument**
2 **Fort Laramie National Historic Site**
3 **Fossil Butte National Monument**
4 **Grand Teton National Park**
5 **John D. Rockefeller, Jr., Memorial Parkway**
6 **Yellowstone National Park**

Devils Tower National Monument

Devils Tower, WY 82714
307/467-5370

Off WY 24, 7 miles north of US 14; 29 miles northwest of Sundance, WY; 33 miles northeast of Moorecroft, WY. Entrance fee; visitor center, exhibits, self-guiding trails, picnicking, camping, hiking, climbing, swimming, fishing, handicap access to campground; bookstore by Devils Tower Natural History Association. Accommodations in Sundance and Hulett.

Our first national monument, established on September 24, 1906, Devils Tower is an 865-foot tower of columnar rock, the remains of a volanic intrusion. This national park site is probably most familiar for its feature role in a 1981 motion picture.

Fort Laramie National Historic Site

Fort Laramie, WY 82212
307/837-2221

On US 26, 3 miles southwest of town of Fort Laramie. Visitor center, exhibits, self-guiding trail, picnicking, handicap access to restrooms/visitor center; bookstore by Fort Laramie Historical Association. Accommodations in town of Fort Laramie.

A fur-trading post once stood here, but the surviving buildings are those of a major military post that guarded covered-wagon trails to the West, 1849-90.

Fossil Butte National Monument

PO Box 527, Kemmerer, WY 83101
307/877-3450

On US 30, 10 miles north of Kemmerer. Entrance fee; visitor center, exhibits, self-guiding trails, picnicking, hiking, horseback riding; bookstore by Dinosaur Nature Association. Accommodations in Kemmerer.

An abundance of rare fish fossils, 40-65 million years old, is evidence of former habitation of this now semiarid region.

Grand Teton National Park

PO Drawer 170, Moose, WY 83012
307/733-2880

Visitor center at Moose, 13 miles north of Jackson on US 26, 89 and 187. Entrance fee; visitor center, exhibits, guided tours, self-guiding trails, picnicking, camping, backcountry permits, hiking, mountain climbing, horseback riding, swimming, boating, fishing, snowmobiling, cross-country skiing, cabin rental, handicap access to campground/restrooms/visitor center; bookstore by Grand Teton Natural History Association. Accommodations in park and in Jackson.

An early French-speaking trapper dubbed these mountains *Les Trois Tetons*, The Three Breasts, the Grand, Middle and South peaks, measuring 13,770, 12,798 and 12,505 feet respectively. The mountains played little part in Indian life: there is some evidence of temporary camps in the park, no doubt hunting parties, but the winter is so harsh here that it seems certain the Shoshone, Crow, Bannock, Nez Perce and Gros Ventre tribes, all of whom passed through, simply followed wildlife to warmer climates. It was left then to a hunter-trapper by the name of John Colter to "discover." Colter left nothing but his name and the date 1808 inscribed on a rock that was plowed up in a field near Tetonia, Idaho, in 1931. Colter seemed more impressed with the cauldrons and geysers of Yellowstone, so his many tales revealed, but Colter Bay on Jackson Lake honors his visit here.

The fur trapping business began to boom in the early 1800s and hundreds of intrepid hunters followed Colter into Wyoming; rather

Left *This bull moose in Yellowstone National Park is the largest member of the deer family and probably weighs up to 1,400 pounds, stands 7½ feet at the shoulder, and may have an antler spread of up to five feet*

Below *The unmistakable fossil of an ancient bat at Fossil Butte National Monument*

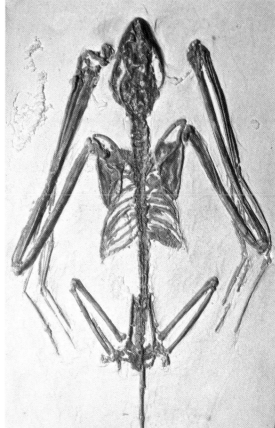

they followed the beaver, for it was this animal that was mainly responsible for the first surge of civilization into the Teton country. But even then there was no settlement. One man, Davey Jackson, preferred a single spot for his traps and the place took on his name – Jackson's Hole – but for many years the Tetons area was more a crossroads than a development.

Then suddenly the whims of fashion in the East and in Europe brought an end to trapping and for the next 20 or so years Jackson's Hole was virtually deserted.

In about 1870 the US Geological Survey began its work in the West and for a while there were teams here and there in the mountains. A few years later there was a gold rush of sorts, but that fizzled out. In 1900 there were only four buildings in Jackson, but scattered about the countryside there were homesteaders raising sheep and cattle, and hay to feed the elk herd in which everyone had taken great pride.

It was this herd of elk that began the process of protection of the Teton wilderness. First in 1913 came the National Elk Refuge, just north of Jackson. There was interest in extending preservation efforts from the boundaries of Yellowstone National Park to the north as far as Jackson to the south, but this met with opposition from ranchers. Then in 1926 John D. Rockefeller, Jr, visited Jackson Hole and was so impressed with what he saw that he vowed to do all the could to create a national park here. Rockefeller founded the Snake River Land Company and began buying property. By 1930 the Land Company owned much of the valley. In 1950 Grand Teton National Park was established. Today only two percent of this land is privately owned. Grand Teton National Park is one of our most precious.

John D. Rockefeller, Jr, Memorial Parkway

c/o Grand Teton National Park, PO Drawer 170, Moose, WY 83012
307/733-2880

Parkway Ranger Station ¼ mile north of Flagg Ranch Villages on US 89, 287.

Linking West Thumb in Yellowstone with Grand Teton National Park, this scenic 82-mile corridor commemorates Rockefeller's aid in the establishment of many parks, including Grand Teton.

Yellowstone National Park

(Wyoming, Idaho, Montana)
PO Box 168, Yellowstone National Park, WY 82190
307/344-7381

Entrances on US 89 on north at Gardiner; US 212 on northeast at Silver Gate; US 14, 16, 20 at East Entrance; US 20, 191 at West Yellowstone. Entrance fee; visitor centers, museums, exhibits, picnicking, guided tours, self-guiding trails, camping, backcountry permits, hiking, horseback riding, boating, fishing, bicycling, snowshoeing, cross-country skiing, handicap access to campground/restrooms/visitor centers; bookstores by Yellowstone Library and Museum

Far left *The magnificent Grand Teton range, showing clearly the decline of vegetation with altitude*

Left *Dawn over Yellowstone with Canada geese wading in the foreground*

Association. Accommodations and supplies available in park; meals and accommodations in West Yellowstone, Gardiner, Cooke City, Silver Gate, Livingstone, Boseman, MT; Cody and Jackson, WY.

The sheer wonder, the mystery and the beauty of this high mountain plateau challenged the early explorers. Here in Yellowstone were features of such significance that men were inspired to evolve a new philosophy for the land; a new land-use ethic based on preserving a part of our natural scene for the future.

This is where the national park system really began. There are those who will argue for Yosemite, but Yellowstone was the first national park established by the US Congress in 1872. To many Yellowstone is a fleeting glimpse of a geyser or an elk or a canyon, but certainly it is more than this. Yellowstone is an idea, a philosophy, and a monument to farsighted conservationists who more than a century ago foresaw the need to preserve a bit of primitive America; a symbol of America's reverence for the great untouched North American wilderness.

In Yellowstone is a land born in the fires of thundering volcanoes and sculpted by glacial ice and running water into a fascinating landscape. The present-day thermal features bear testimony to the fact that, at a comparatively shallow depth, the fiery hearts of volcanoes still beat. Literally thousands of hot springs dot the thermal basins; gigantic columns of boiling water are hurled hundreds of feet into the air causing the ground to shake; hissing steam vents punctuate the valley floors; and stumps of redwood forests buried by volcanic ash and petrified upright stand out starkly.

More recently glaciers have reworked the land's surface by smoothing canyons and leaving myriad sparkling blue ponds and lakes across the landscape. And now mountain streams carve beautiful canyons and leap over resistant rock ledges in breathtaking cascades and waterfalls.

Geologically Yellowstone is young, with the last lava flows burning their way across the surface less than 100,000 years ago. Soil development is shallow and pioneer plants are common. Even today fire and water, in the form of thermal heat, snow and rain, dominate the landscape and determine which plants and animals will make up Yellowstone's natural communities.

No one believed the stories from the early explorations of the Yellowstone country. "Thank you, but we do not print fiction," wrote the editor of *Lippincott's Magazine* to an aspiring author who had been

Left *Elk tracks on the Grand Prismatic Spring in Yellowstone*

Below *Morning Glory spring in Yellowstone, one of the surface exhibitions of the thermal activity below ground*

Left *Dwarfing spectators, the lower falls of the Yellowstone River plunge hundreds of feet into the river basin*

Below *The bison at Yellowstone are some of the few totally wild and free-ranging herds, once so plentiful, remaining in North America*

there. One reviewer of an article on Yellowstone wrote that the author "must be the champion liar of the Northwest." And so Yellowstone remained a mystery until 1870, when Lieutenant Gustavus Doane, a young cavalry officer on the Henry Washburn military surveying expedition in 1870, wrote in his official report: "A single glance at the interior slopes of the ranges shows that...the great basin has been formerly one vast crater of a now extinct volcano. The nature of the rocks, the steepness and outline of the interior walls, together with other peculiarities, render this conclusion a certainty."

Doane's report came at a time when Henry David Thoreau and Ralph Waldo Emerson were writing essays on conservation. "Why should not we...have our national preserve," wrote Thoreau, "in which the bear and panther and even some of the hunter race may still exist and not be 'civilized off the face of the earth'...for inspiration and our true re-creation? Or should we, like villains, grub them all up for poaching on our own national domains?"

Washburn, whose expedition had included some prominent people, led the march on Congress. Yellowstone, as yet untouched by those who would exploit the land, had to be saved, he said. The idea had been discussed in the wilderness. "It was at the first camp after leaving the Lower Geyser Basin," wrote Cornelius Hedges, a lawyer and correspondent, "when all were speculating which point in the region we had been through would become most notable, when I first suggested uniting all our efforts to get it made a national park, little dreaming such a thing possible."

It was the worst possible timing. The country, still reeling under the strains of the Civil War, economic instability and the throes of westward expansion, faced the harsher realities of life. Words like aesthetics, natural beauty and inspiration were viewed with great suspicion. It was all quite natural. The unnatural thing was that such idealism ultimately prevailed.

Left *Old Faithful Geyser, Yellowstone's best known feature*

Right The Yellowstone River braids and spreads across the floor of Hayden Valley in Yellowstone National Park flanked by dense coniferous forests

Hayden Valley, Yellowstone National Park, where wildlife of all kinds can be seen on almost any day, in any season

GUAM

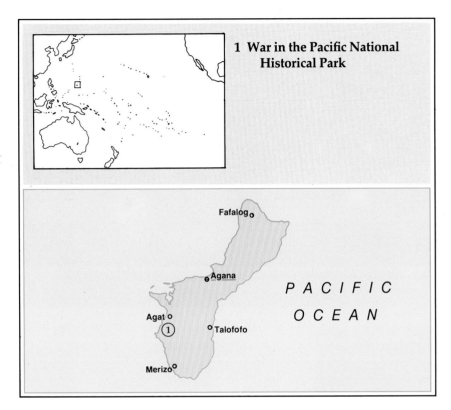

1 War in the Pacific National Historical Park

War in the Pacific National Historical Park

PO Box FA, Agana, Guam 96910
671/477-8528

Agana Harbor area. Visitor center, exhibits. Resort hotels within 5 miles.

Dozens of national historic sites commemorate the American Revolution, the Civil War and the Indian wars of the west; only two cover World War II. This is one, and it honors the people of nine nations involved in the war's Pacific Theater, including Japan. The park includes the major sites associated with the 1944 battle for Guam, exemplifying America's island-hopping military campaign against the Japanese.

This tranquil tropical scenery seems a world away from the World War II battleground that Guam became

NORTHERN MARIANA ISLANDS

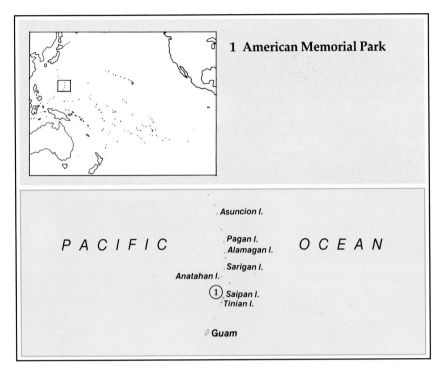

1 American Memorial Park

American Memorial Park

PO Box 198 CHRB, Saipan, CM 96950

North of Garapan Village. Museum, exhibits, picnic area. Meals and lodging within ½ mile of park.

These 133 scenic areas along the shoreline of Tanapag Harbor outside Garapan on the island of Saipan were authorized by the Congress in 1978 as a memorial to Americans who died in World War II.

The Saipan beach and shoreline of American Memorial Park, a recreational park and memorial honoring those who died in the Marianas Campaign of World War II

PUERTO RICO

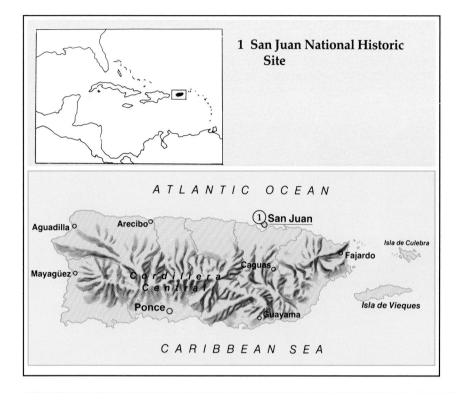

1 San Juan National Historic Site

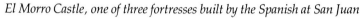

ATLANTIC OCEAN

Aguadilla ○
Arecibo ○
① San Juan
Mayagüez ○
Isla de Culebra
Caguas ○
Fajardo
Cordillera Central
Ponce ○
Guayama
Isla de Vieques

CARIBBEAN SEA

San Juan National Historic Site

PO Box 712, Old San Juan, Puerto Rico 00902
809/724-1974

Information center on entry plaza level of forts El Morro and San Cristobal. Visitor center, exhibits, handicap access to visitor center; bookstore by Eastern National Park and Monument Association. Accommodations in San Juan.

These massive masonry fortifications, the oldest in the territorial limits of the United States, were begun by the Spanish in the sixteenth century to protect a strategic harbor guarding the sea lanes to the New World.

El Morro Castle, one of three fortresses built by the Spanish at San Juan

VIRGIN ISLANDS

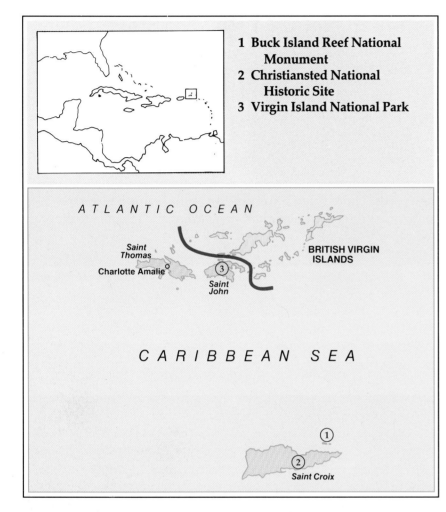

1 Buck Island Reef National
   Monument
2 Christiansted National
   Historic Site
3 Virgin Island National Park

Buck Island Reef National Monument

PO Box 160, Christiansted, St. Croix, Virgin Islands 00820
809/773-1460

Private or charter boat from Christiansted Wharf; 5½-mile sail. Self-guiding underwater trail, picnicking, hiking, swimming, boating, fishing. Meals and accommodations at St. Croix.

Coral grottoes, sea fans, gorgonias and tropical fish – along an underwater trail – make this one of the finest marine gardens in the Caribbean, and one of the unique national park sites. The island is a rookery for frigate birds and pelicans and the habitat of green turtles.

Christiansted National Historic Site

PO Box 160, Christiansted, Virgin Islands 00820
809/773-1460

Headquarters in Old Customs House in downtown Christiansted. Visitor center, exhibits, self-guiding tours; bookstore by Eastern National Park and Monument Association. Accommodations at Christiansted.

Three city blocks on the Christiansted waterfront preserve the colonial period Danish plantation society in the New World. The architecture is reflected in the Customhouse, Steeple Building and Government House.

Bottom left *The captivating beauty of Buck Island Reef National Monument, the only national monument almost entirely under water*

Above *Ancient fortifications now put to a more peaceful use in Christiansted*

Left *A fine colonial style building, and lush tropical vegetation in Christiansted, the capital of St Croix in the Virgin Islands*

275

Virgin Island National Park

PO Box 7789, Charlotte Amalie, St. Thomas, Virgin Islands 00801
809/776-6201 or 775-2050

Headquarters and visitor center in Red Hook at National Park Service Dock on St. Thomas; another visitor center at Cruz Bay on St. John. Fly directly to Charlotte Amalie, or by ship. A ferry runs across Pillsbury Sound from Red Hook to Cruz Bay. Visitor centers, exhibits, guided tours, self-guiding trails, picnicking, camping, hiking, swimming, boating, fishing, cabin rental, handicap access to restrooms/visitor centers; bookstore by Eastern National Park and Monument Association. Food available in park; accommodations at St. Thomas.

In 1917, fearing that Germany had its eye on the Danish-owned Virgin Islands in the Caribbean as a naval base, the United States bought the three largest islands, St. Thomas, St. Croix and St. John, and approximately 50 small islets and cays for $25 million. Whether or not this altered the war in the Atlantic is questionable, but, following hostilities, the purchase of a group of seemingly useless islands 900 miles off shore caused considerable debate. It was hailed as another "Seward's folly," referring to the purchase of Alaska from Russia for $7.2 million in 1867. But, as with the Alaska investment, time vindicated.

Columbus discovered these tropical islands on his second voyage in 1493, but he was not the first; South American Indians had been there since AD 300. Their village remains and petroglyphs have been found scattered about St. John.

Although there were various claims on the islands during the next 200 years, St. Thomas and St. John were not formally settled until the early eighteenth century and then by private, chartered companies that established sugar and cotton plantations. The Danes were the first on St. John in 1718. Within a short time they had built mills and roads and imported slaves from West Africa, but neither sugar nor

cotton were suited to the islands and the industries were never really successful. The slaves rebelled in 1733. Production dropped significantly and prosperity waned until, in 1848, emancipation was proclaimed by the Danish governor, to prevent what was believed to be a major revolt. The plantation era soon ended, but the island had been virtually stripped of its native growth and wildlife.

By the time the United States took possession in 1917 some attempts were being made to reintroduce native plants and animals. Of course, by now nature has reclaimed much of the land. Evidence of the previous occupation is most noticeable in the ruins of the Danish industries. More than 80 separate estates operated at one time or another. The remains of the Annaberg, Cinnamon Bay and Reef Bay plantations are particularly significant and while subject to the whims of the jungle, they remain as vivid and picturesque reminders of the island's past.

The Virgin Islands are the tips of ancient sedimentary deposits and volcanic activity and were formed much the same as other areas in the national parks. Even here the theories of plate tectonics and the moving of the earth's crust over explosive funnels in the core beneath explains much of the land construction. What all of this has left us is a priceless tropical island of sparkling bays, brilliant beaches, and forested mountains and valleys.

Interest in setting aside the entire island of St. John as a national park began in the early 1950s with the rapid growth of tourism and commercial development on nearby St. Thomas. Word has spread about this little, out-of-the-way place called St. John – white beaches, mountains rising 1,200 feet, and a year-round average temperature of 78° Fahrenheit. Only a few miles from St. Thomas, and 40 miles from St. Croix, it was virtually inaccessible, so few got here to vacation. One who did, however, was Laurence Rockefeller, who contributed 5,000 acres of privately owned land to the federal government. Additional land was acquired, and, on August 2, 1956, Virgin Islands National Park was established.

Luxuriant vegetation goes down to the brilliant Caribbean waters which lap St. Thomas

277

Index

Index

Picture Credits

Arizona Office of Tourism 25 top, 34; **Bruce Coleman** half title, 7, 12, 19, 21, 26, 29 right, 33, 35, 36, 40, 44-45, 46, 47, 52-53, 55, 57, 62, 63, 64, 70-71, 73, 78, 82-83, 85, 93 inset, 97, 98-99, 144, 155, 159, 160 top, 166, 168-169, 186, 195, 196, 199, 212 bottom, 227, 229, 232-3, 238, 242, 244, 250, 255, 256 right, 257 bottom, 263, 264, 266 right, 267 right, 273, 276-7; **Everglades National Park** 86; **Robert C. Gildart** endpaper, 9 top, 68-69, 118, 154, 186, 187, 188, 189 bottom, 221, 230; **Image Bank** 30-31, 48-9, 51, 59 right, 100-101, 101, 102, 103, 105, 106, 107 inset, 125 left, 126, 132, 133, 146-147, 153, 165, 167, 172, 181, 182, 208, 210-211, 212 top, 215, 236, 251, 252-253; **B. Langrish** 65; **Andrew Johnson Hist. Home** 214; **Maryland Office of Tourism** 127 left; **P. Morris** 59 left, 60-61, 166 inset, 184-5, 256 inset, 280; **Photosource** 75 top; **Spectrum** contents page; **Tennessee Tourist Authority** 119; All other images courtsey of the National Park Service, US Department of the Interior.

Map artwork by Creative Cartography Ltd

Multimedia Publications have endeavoured to observe the legal requirements with regard to the rights of suppliers of photographic material.